Conquerors of the Roman Empire

To my children Katharina and Alexander –
modern descendants of the Alamanni.

Conquerors of the Roman Empire

The Franks

Simon MacDowall

Pen & Sword
MILITARY

First published in Great Britain in 2018 by
Pen & Sword Military
An imprint of
Pen & Sword Books Ltd

ISBN 978 1 47383 742 3

A CIP catalogue record for this book is
available from the British Library

Typeset in Ehrhardt
by Mac Style

Printed and bound in the UK
by TJ International Ltd, Padstow, Cornwall

Pen & Sword Books Limited incorporates the imprints of Atlas,
Archaeology, Aviation, Discovery, Family History, Fiction, History,
Maritime, Military, Military Classics, Politics, Select, Transport,
True Crime, Air World, Frontline Publishing, Leo Cooper,
Remember When, Seaforth Publishing, The Praetorian Press, Wharncliffe
Local History, Wharncliffe Transport,
Wharncliffe True Crime and White Owl.

For a complete list of Pen & Sword titles please contact

PEN & SWORD BOOKS LTD
47 Church Street, Barnsley, South Yorkshire, S70 2AS, England
E-mail: enquiries@pen-and-sword.co.uk
Website: www.pen-and-sword.co.uk

Contents

List of Illustrations

1. Barbarian captives taken by the Romans on the Middle Rhine.
2. King Childeric's signet ring.
3. Gold and garnet bees from Childeric's grave.
4. The tombstone of Lepontius, a fourth century Roman soldier stationed on the Upper Rhine.
5. A silver disc from the horse harness of an Alamannic noble of the late sixth-early seventh century.
6. The head of a dragon standard which the Romans adopted from the Sarmatians for their cavalry units.
7. A depiction of a Frankish warrior on a gravestone from the Rhine.
8. Combs found in an Alamannic grave near Strasbourg.
9. Alamannic weapons.
10. Modern reconstructions of Frankish shields.
11. Iron boss covering the central hand grip of Frankish shields.
12. A prominent shield boss, which would have been a very effective offensive weapon when thrust against an opponent.
13. A reconstruction of a Roman patrol ship of the *Classis Germanica* based on wrecks found at Mainz.
14. A Frankish horse burial.
15. Modern recreation of an alliance being formed between two Frankish war leaders.
16. A sixth century silvered Frankish belt buckle proclaiming the owner's Christian faith.
17. A recreation of fourth century negotiations between a Roman frontier commander and a Frankish chieftain seeking land in exchange for providing troops for the Roman army.
18. Re-enactors equipped as fourth-fifth century Roman soldiers.
19. Reconstruction of the arms and armour of a fully equipped sixth-seventh century Frankish warrior.

Maps

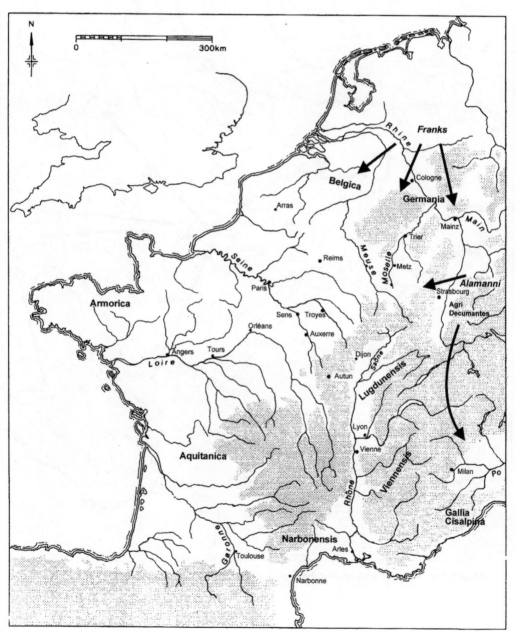

Map 1: Third century Gaul.

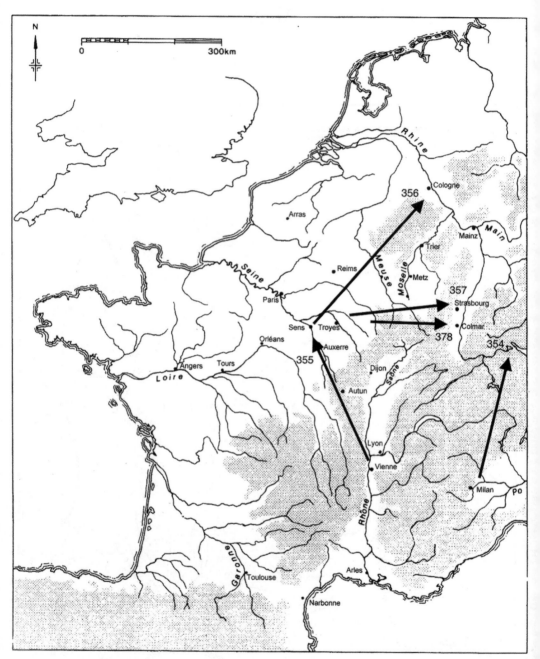

Map 2: Roman campaigns against the Franks and Alamanni, AD 355–378.

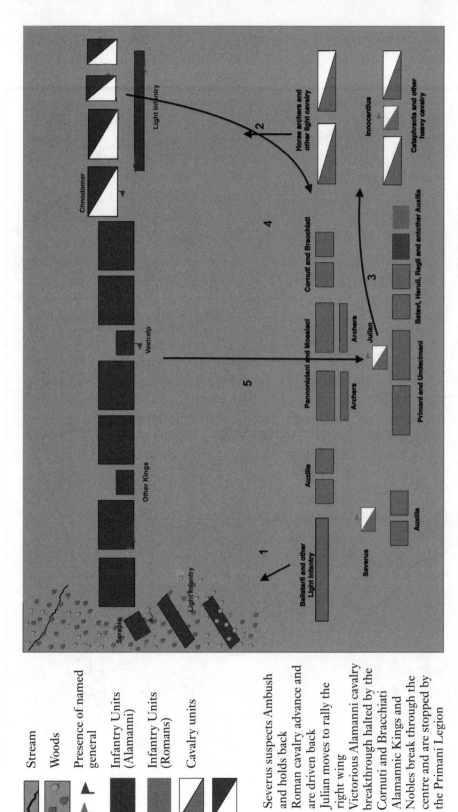

Map 3: The disposition of troops and opening moves of the battle fought near Strasbourg in AD 357 between the Romans, commanded by Caesar Julian, and the Alamanni, led by Chnodomar and Vestralp.

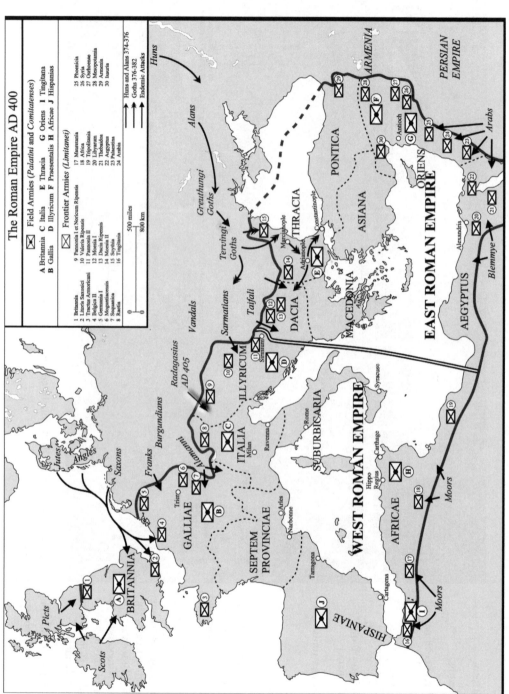

The Roman Empire AD 400

Field Armies (*Palatini and Comitatenses*)

A Britannia C Italia E Thracia G Oriens I Tingitana
B Gallia D Illyricum F Praesentalis H Africae J Hispanias

Frontier Armies (*Limitanei*)

9 Pannonia I et Noricum Ripensis
10 Valeria Ripensis
11 Pannonia II
12 Moesia I
13 Dacia Ripensis
14 Moesia II
15 Scythia
16 Tingitania

1 Britannia
2 Litoris Saxonici
3 Tractus Armoricani
4 Belgica II
5 Germania I
6 Mogantiacensis
7 Sequanica
8 Raetia

17 Mauretania
18 Africa
19 Tripolitania
20 Libyarum
21 Thebaidos
22 Aegyptus
23 Palaestina
24 Arabia

25 Phoenicia
26 Syria
27 Osrhoene
28 Mesopotamia
29 Armenia
30 Isauria

Hums and Alans 374–376
Goths 376–382
Endemic Attacks

0   500 miles
0   800 km

Map 4: The disposition of Roman armies and the main barbarian movements at the start of the fifth century.

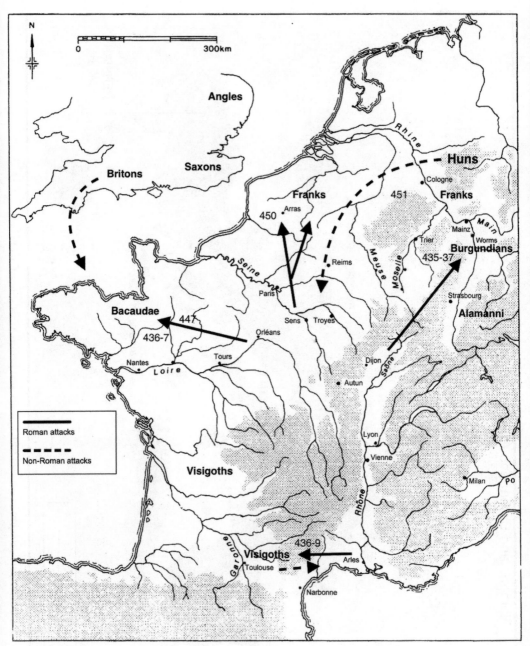

Map 5: Aetius' campaigns in Gaul, AD 430–451.

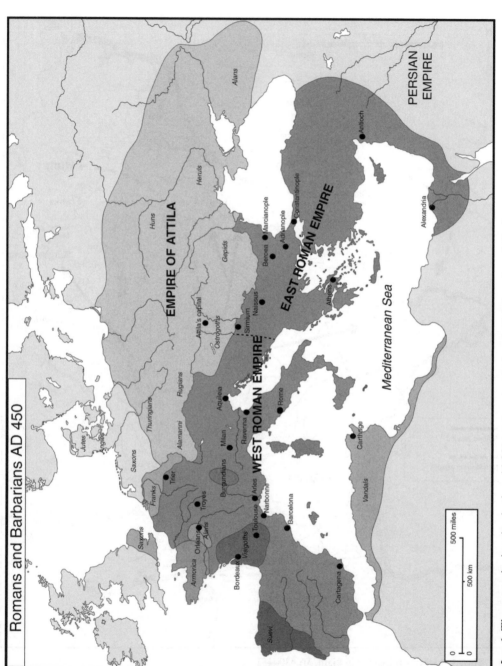

Map 6. The strategic situation in the mid fifth century just before Attila's invasion of Gaul.

Romans and Barbarians AD 450

EMPIRE OF ATTILA

WEST ROMAN EMPIRE

EAST ROMAN EMPIRE

PERSIAN EMPIRE

Mediterranean Sea

Persian Empire

Huns

Alans

Heruls

Gepids

Ostrogoths

Attila's capital

Sirmium

Naissus

Beroea

Marcianople

Adrianople

Constantinople

Athens

Antioch

Alexandria

Rugians

Thuringians

Alamanni

Saxons

Jutes

Angles

Franks

Trier

Burgundians

Milan

Aquileia

Ravenna

Rome

Carthage

Vandals

Armorica

Orléans

Troyes

Alans

Visigoths

Bordeaux

Toulouse

Arles

Narbonne

Barcelona

Cartagena

Suevi

Saxons

500 miles

500 km

0

0

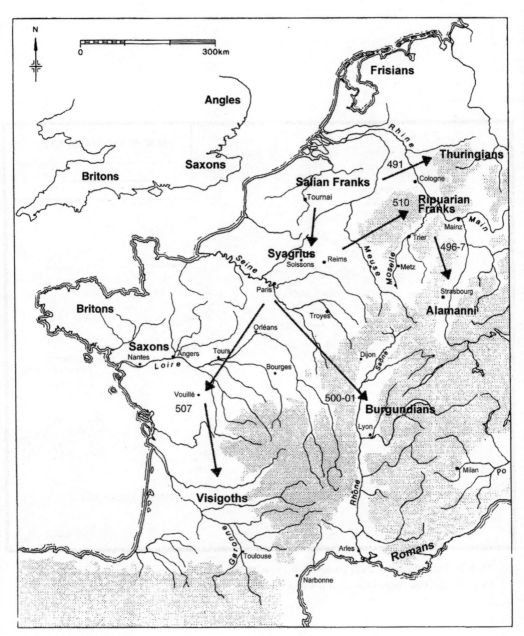

Map 7: Clovis' campaigns.

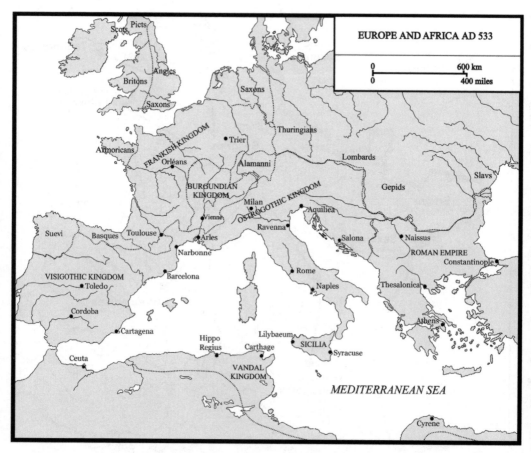

Map 8: The kingdoms and peoples of Europe and North Africa just before the East Roman Emperor Justinian began his reconquest of the West.

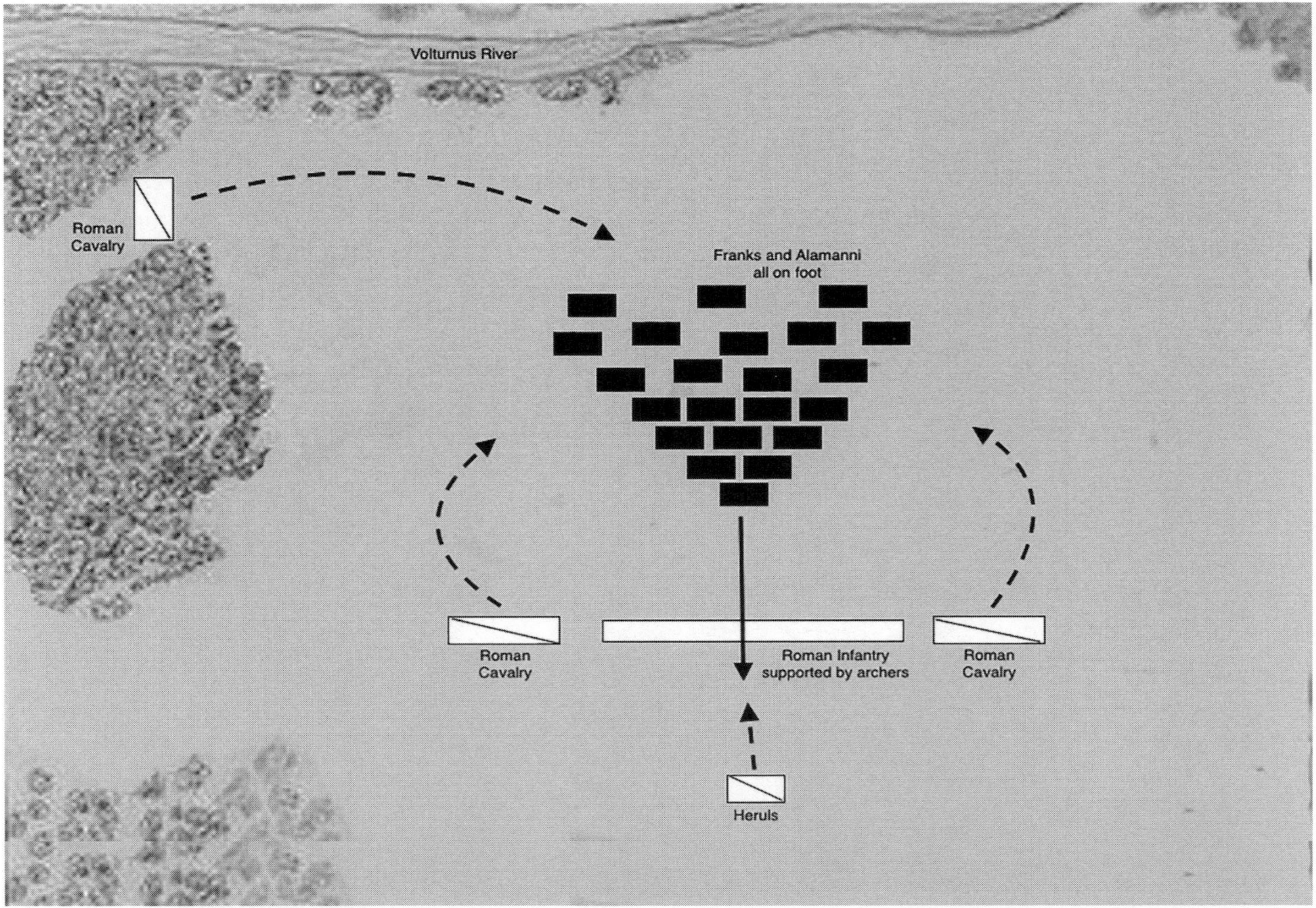

Map 9: The Battle of Casilinum, AD 554.

Chapter 1

The Rhine Tribes

Theodomer, king of the Franks, son of Richimer, and Ascyla his mother, were once upon a time slain by the sword. They say also that Chlogio, a man of ability and high rank among his people, was king of the Franks then, and he dwelt at the stronghold of Dispargum which is within the borders of the Thuringians. And these parts, that is, towards the south, the Romans dwelt as far as the Loire. But beyond the Loire the Goths were in control; the Burgundians also, who belonged to the sect of the Arians, dwelt across the Rhône in the district which is adjacent to the city of Lyons.

This passage, from Gregory, Bishop of Tours, is a sixth century take on the situation several decades earlier as the Franks were poised to take over most of the country we now call France – taking its name from this Germanic people who came to rule it.

Scope and Sources

The previous two books in this series told the stories of the Vandals and Goths – two East Germanic tribes that migrated thousands of miles to carve kingdoms for themselves out of the carcass of the West Roman Empire in the fifth century AD. In the process of their long migrations both peoples sacked Rome – the Goths in 410 and the Vandals in 455.

The Franks too were a Germanic people but their story is quite different. Unlike the Vandals or Goths, the Franks expanded gradually from their homes on the east bank of the Rhine to take over Roman Gaul and give their name to modern France.

Technically the Franks were not actually conquerors of Rome. They did not sack the city and, although they did invade Italy, theirs is a story of gradual expansion and absorption rather than long migration or the outright conquest of swathes of Roman territory. Indeed, their greatest conquests were against the other Germanic peoples who had previously moved into the Roman provinces of Gaul.

This book will tell the story of how the Franks emerged from the banks of the Rhine to become the rulers of France as the West Roman Empire collapsed. In doing so the tale of the other peoples absorbed by the Franks will also be told, including the Burgundians, Armorican Britons, and the Alamanni. Many of these peoples had much in common with the early Franks, rising to prominence at the same time and in similar circumstances. While the Franks gave their name to modern France, the Alamanni (also Alemanni, Alamans or Alemannen) gave theirs to the modern Germany which in French is called *Allemagne*. The Burgundians gave their name to modern Burgundy and the Britons to Brittany.

This is primarily a military history, examining how the Franks fought both for and against the Romans and how they managed to achieve supremacy in late Roman Gaul (roughly modern France, Belgium and that part of modern Germany to the west of the Rhine). All of this will be placed in the political, economic and social context of the times. The story of the Franks does not end when they first established their rule over France. As this series is concerned with the Germanic conquests of the Roman Empire, however, I have chosen to end their story in the mid sixth century after the last conflict between the Franks and Romans in Italy. This book does not cover the later years of the Frankish Merovingian dynasty beyond the mid sixth century.

The narrative is aimed at the general reader with an interest in the military aspects of the barbarian conquests of Rome rather than the academic specialist. In recent years there have been a number of excellent books about the end of the Roman Empire in the West and the barbarian invasions which helped to bring it about. Many of these I have found very useful in placing the story of the Franks in a wider context. I have listed the most helpful ones in the Bibliography.

Gregory, the Bishop of Tours (538–594), tells the story of the Franks from his point of view. His *History of the Franks* was written when Frankish kings had established their hegemony over Roman Gaul after having defeated the Alamanni, Burgundians and Visigoths. He is, however, more interested in political and ecclesiastical matters than military or social developments. As he himself says in his introduction he was interested in: 'The struggles of kings with the heathen enemy, of martyrs with pagans, of churches with heretics.' He does describe some military actions but these tend to be relatively small encounters focusing on the deeds of notable individuals. The larger engagements, such as the critical victory of the Franks over the Visigoths in 507, are only given a few lines with an unfortunate paucity of informative detail. The lives of the ordinary Franks and Romans are ignored.

All other contemporary accounts come from Roman sources. Of these, the writings of Ammianus Marcellinus, Procopius and Agathias are the most interesting and complete. The first was a Roman military officer turned historian who wrote a history of the Roman Empire at the end of the fourth century. He describes in detail the campaigns of the Emperor Julian against Franks and Alamanni in the 350s. As a soldier himself, he had first-hand knowledge of what ancient battle was like and he lived through the events he described. Procopius, secretary to the East Roman general, Belisarius, gives similar near first-hand information at the other end of our story. Writing in the mid sixth century he tells of the first Frankish invasions of Italy in the 550s and gives some background of their earlier years. His account is supplemented by Agathias who deals with the later Frankish involvement in Italy and also describes the fighting methods of the Franks in the sixth century from a Greco-Roman perspective.

We have very little information about the Franks before the fourth century apart from tantalizing snippets in various panegyrics to Roman Emperors and a few lines in other Roman histories. Tacitus, who wrote a detailed description of the German peoples in the first century AD, does not mention the Franks – probably because they were a later coalition of some of the tribes he described under different names. Tacitus does, however, provide quite a lot of detail about the fighting methods of the earlier Germans. He would have heard much of this from Roman officers who fought them, other aspects he probably made up to make a moral point. How much of this would still have been applicable to the Franks remains a matter of conjecture.

Naturally we know more about the Romans at the time of the initial Frankish expansion. One source which gives great detail about the structure and organization of later Roman armies is the *Notitia Dignitatum*. This a list of offices and army units from the end of the fourth century in the east and early fifth century in the west. This tells us the official orders of battle of the Roman army at the time the Franks were beginning to flex their muscles in Gaul. While the *Notitia* needs to be treated with a fair degree of caution it is invaluable in building a picture of the Roman army and political structures in the late fourth-early fifth centuries. Appendices I and II replicate the list of Roman army units in Gaul and Italy in the early fifth century. At this time the Empire was divided in two. The Western Empire was ruled from Ravenna. Rome was still the most important city in the West but it had ceased to be the seat of power during the third century. The Eastern Empire was ruled from Constantinople and it continued to survive for another millennium after the fall of the West.

Helpfully the Franks and other western Germans buried their dead with weapons and accoutrements from the fourth century onwards. This has left us with good archeological evidence to supplement the literary sources.

The Ancestors of the Franks

The Franks (or *Franci*) are first mentioned in late third century Roman sources. It is likely that at this time a number of smaller Germanic tribes living on the north-eastern banks of the Lower Rhine began to coalesce into a larger, loose federation. They were not the only ones. At the same time other Germanic tribes to the south moved into the Agri Decumates (the Upper Rhine Valley of modern Baden in Germany) which had been abandoned by the Romans. This triangle, bound by the Rhine, Danube, Black Forest and the Alps, was never really properly Romanized. In the first century AD Tacitus described it as a place where 'all the most despicable characters in Gaul, all the penniless adventurers, seized on a territory that was a kind of no-man's-land'. The southern Germanic tribes which moved into the Agri Decumates became known as the Alamanni or Alemannen (literally 'all men').

Those first century tribes mentioned by Tacitus which coalesced into the Franks probably included the Chatti, Chamavi, Chauci, Bructeri,

Chasuari, Angrivarii, Tubantes, Tencteri and Frisii. The Frisii (Frisians) retained a separate identity into modern times so their association with the other Frankish tribes may have been more tenuous. Tacitus assessed some of the customs and military capabilities of many of these early ancestors of the Franks in some detail:

> The Chatti are distinguished by hardy bodies, well-knit limbs, fierce countenances and unusual mental vigour. They have plenty of discernment measured by German standards. They appoint picked men to lead them and then obey them. They know how to keep rank and how to recognise an opportunity or else postpone their attack. They can map out the duties of the day and make sure the defences of the night... All their strength lies in their infantry, which in addition to their arms, are burdened with entrenching tools and provisions. Other tribes may be seen going forth into battle – the Chatti come out for a campaign. They seldom engage in swift rushes or in casual fighting – tactics which properly belong to cavalry with their quick successes and quick retreats.

He adds that young Chatti men were not allowed to shave their beards until they had shown bravery in battle. Our traditional view of Germanic barbarians is that they were bearded while Romans were clean-shaven. In the latter years of the West Roman Empire the opposite was true. Most Romans sported short, trimmed beards with short hair while Germans tended to wear their hair long and shaved their beards, sometimes leaving a moustache. More detail of the appearance of the Franks is given in Chapter 5.

Tacitus says that the Tencteri, who occupied the east bank of the Middle Rhine in his day, 'excelled in horsemanship'. The degree to which the later Franks took to mounted warfare will be discussed more fully later on. Germanic tribes did not have clear delineations between cavalry or infantry as the Romans did, nor as we now understand the terms. To own a horse was a mark of wealth and prestige. If a man had a horse he would ride it for strategic mobility or to chase down scattered bands of enemies and then might dismount to fight on foot in a formal battle line. A warrior was a warrior not a cavalryman or an infantryman. He would fight on foot or on horseback according to his means and the tactical situation. Tacitus tells us that amongst the Tencteri: 'Horses pass by inheritance along with slaves, homestead and rights of succession. The horses go to a son not necessarily, like the rest of the property to the eldest, but to the one who is the keenest and ablest soldier.'

It is quite probable that the Chamavi (also Hamavi) was the core tribe around which others coalesced to form the Franks in the third century. An inscription on a first century Roman map (the *Tabula Peutingeriana*) located the Chamavi on the north bank of the Rhine in the modern Netherlands with the inscription *Hamavi qui et Franci* – Hamavi (or Chamavi) who are called Franks.

Tacitus says that the Chamavi and Angrivarii moved into the territory of the Bructeri and nearly wiped them out. 'We were even permitted to witness the battle. More than 60,000 were killed – not by Roman swords or javelins but (more splendid still) as a spectacle before our delighted eyes. Long, I pray, may foreign nations persist if not in loving us then at least in hating one another.'

Of some of the other tribes which may eventually have become Franks, Tacitus has only this to say: 'The Angrivarii and Chamavi have a common frontier with the Dulgubinii, Chasuarii and other tribes of no special fame. To the northwest they are succeeded by the Frisii… They have the Rhine as their common frontier right down to the ocean. Their settlements extend around vast lagoons which have been sailed by Roman fleets.'

The Alamanni

To the south of those tribes who eventually made up the Franks, the Suebi held sway. They have given their name to modern Swabia in Baden-Württemberg (south-west Germany). Tacitus seems to lump together all the Germanic tribes as Suebi, except for those on the Lower Rhine.

They (the Suebi) occupy more than half Germany and are divided into a number of separate tribes under different names, though all are called by the generic title of 'Suebi'. It is a special characteristic of this nation to comb their hair sideways and tie it in a knot. This distinguishes the Suebi from the rest of the Germans... Their elaborate coiffure is intended to give them greater height as to look more terrifying to their foes when they are about to go into battle.

Given that he includes the east Germanic tribes (such as the Lombards and Goths) amongst the Suebi, we can only assume that Tacitus really did not really know much about them. Those eastern tribes had little in common with those of the Upper Rhine and Danube. He claimed that the Semnones were the most powerful of the Suebic tribes but does not say where they lived. Modern historians tend to think that they may have occupied the Middle Rhine in Tacitus' day, eventually moving further south to become part of the Alamannic confederacy. A third century Roman inscription from Augsburg equates the Semnones with the later Juthungi who lived to the east of the Alamannic heartland and who appear to have maintained a separate identity from the Alamanni.

The Hermunduri were another notable first century tribe who lived along the Upper Danube. They were broken up in the tribal movements which sparked off the Marcomannic War (see Chapter 2). Some may have been absorbed into the later Thuringians and others helped to found the Alamanni. Tacitus has this to say of them:

Nearer to us... are our faithful allies the Hermunduri. Because they are so loyal they are the only Germans who trade with us, not merely on the banks of the river, but far within our borders, and in the most flourishing colony of the province of Raetia (roughly modern Switzerland). Everywhere they are allowed to pass without a guard. While to the other tribes we display only our arms and our camps, to them we have thrown open our houses and country-seats, which they do not covet.

The Alamannic confederacy is first mentioned by the Roman author Cassius Dio describing a campaign by the Emperor Caracalla (Severus Antoninus) in the early years of the third century. 'Antoninus made a campaign against the Alamanni and whenever he saw a spot suitable for habitation, he would order a fort to be erected or a city to be built. He gave these places names relating to himself.'

By the mid third century the Alamanni were a force to be reckoned with. Made up from fragments of earlier tribes, who then disappeared from history, they moved into the Agri Decumates which had been abandoned by the Romans. Some of them were from the Suebic tribes mentioned by Tacitus but other Suebi maintained a separate identity. In 406 some Suebi joined the Vandals and Alans when they crossed the Rhine, eventually ending up in Spain. Others remained behind in Germany to the east of the Alamanni.

Even today there is some confusion between the present-day descendants of the Alamanni and Suebi. The German-speaking inhabitants of Alsace tend to refer disparagingly to their compatriots on the German side of the Rhine as 'Swabians'. To the Germans of the Upper Rhine, the Swabians are those who live beyond the Black Forest in modern Württemberg. This more or less equates to the fifth century locations of the ancient Alamanni and Suebi. The Alamanni occupied the Upper Rhine Valley while those Suebi who did not go on to Spain remained further east. The modern descendants of the Alamanni are the peoples of Baden in Germany, Alsace in France and the German-speaking Swiss in the Canton of Basel.

Early German Society

Tacitus paints a picture of a fairly egalitarian society amongst the early Germans with all freemen bearing arms. It was a warrior society with warfare at its heart and the only manly occupation.

> A German is not so easily prevailed on to plough the land and wait patiently for the harvests to challenge a foe and earn wounds for his reward. He thinks it spiritless to accumulate slowly by the sweat of his brow what can be got quickly by the loss of a little blood. When not engaged in warfare they spend a certain amount of time hunting but much more in idleness, thinking of nothing else but sleeping and eating. For the boldest and most warlike men have no regular employment. The care of house, home and fields are left to the women, old men and weaklings of the family.

The Romans tended to deal with leaders, not whole tribes. Invariably they called tribal leaders 'kings' even if in the early days such men may only have had a few hundred followers. They rewarded those leaders who behaved themselves (from a Roman point of view) and punished those who did not. Increasingly wealth became concentrated in the hands of a few powerful men who benefited from trade, alliance or military service with Rome. These men used their new-found prosperity to increase their followings, maintain larger bands of full-time retainers and consolidate their control over an increasingly wider area.

Acknowledging the leadership of a such a powerful man gave the followers a cut of his wealth and prestige. Ambitious young men would join the warband of a leader who would be able to reward him with gifts of weapons, precious metals and luxury goods. In this way the smaller tribal groupings described by Tacitus coalesced into the larger federations of the Franks and Alamanni. These were not single political entities but rather people with similar culture and dialect whose newly enriched leaders were able to hold sway over an increasingly large number of followers. There was no single acknowledged leader of either the Franks or the Alamanni as these federations began to emerge on the Rhine. A particularly rich, charismatic or successful 'king' would have a larger warband than others and lesser 'kings' might be induced to follow him. There was, however, no overarching political structure.

Thus it was that two kings who led the Alamanni in the mid fourth century were followed by 'five other kings who were but little inferior in power to themselves, by ten petty princes and a vast number of nobles' (Ammianus Marcellinus). Early Frankish and Alamannic kings held power not through some kind of divine right, as in later medieval times, but rather through their reputation and their ability to reward their followers. It was not until much later that a hereditary dynasty emerged amongst the Franks. This was accomplished through force of arms and killing off all potential rivals, including siblings.

Despite the image of an egalitarian Germanic society that Tacitus paints, he points out that hierarchy based on military prowess already existed in the first century AD.

There are grades of rank even in the retinues determined at the discretion of the chief whom they follow. There is great rivalry amongst the followers to obtain the highest place in their leader's estimation. Also amongst the chiefs there is rivalry for the honour of having the biggest and most salient retine. Both power and prestige depend on being continually attended by a large train of picked young warriors which is a distinction in peace and a protection in war.

The retinue, or *comitatus*, of retainers became increasingly important to the emerging leaders of the Franks and Alamanni. They found that they could accomplish much more with a strong band of well-equipped full-time warriors than by mobilizing every able-bodied man of the tribe. This was particularly true for raids into Roman territory where a few hundred first-rate fighters could accomplish much more than a large horde which would consume far too many supplies and add little additional fighting strength.

These retinues were not just drawn from local tribesmen. The warriors who filled the ranks of a Frankish or Alamannic leader's *comitatus* were recruited from across tribal lines. 'Many noble youths, if the land of their birth is stagnating in a long period of peace and inactivity, deliberately seek out other tribes which have some war in hand' (Tacitus).

Heroic poetry gives examples of this. The *Nibelungenlied* – a medieval retelling of a fifth century legend – tells of Siegfried arriving from Frankish lands to seek service at the Burgundian court. The concept of nationality is a very modern construct. At the time the Germanic tribes on the Rhine were beginning to call themselves Franks or Alamanni, their identity was not based on the birthplace or ethnicity of their members. Just as a 'British' bank based in London today will recruit the people it wants from around the world and even be led by a non-British chief executive, so a Frankish warband would have been made up of the best men drawn from all over without regard to ancient tribal origins. Some would even have been Romans.

Maintaining a full-time *comitatus* of young energetic men looking to enhance their reputation and wealth led to a cycle of never-ending warfare. If there was no action to enrich them, or if their leader proved weak, the men would seek other leaders to follow. 'A large body of retainers cannot be kept together except by means of violence and war. They are always making demands on the generosity of their chief, asking for a coveted war-horse or a spear stained with the blood of a defeated enemy. Their meals, for which plentiful if homely fare is provided, count in lieu of pay. The wherewithal for this open-handedness comes from war and plunder' (Tacitus).

Fighting methods

Early Germanic warfare, like that of most warrior societies, was almost a ritual part of life. Struggles between families and clans had the aims of accumulating wealth, women, livestock and prestige, or to exact revenge for a previous wrong. They were rarely aimed at the total annihilation and destruction of an enemy people.

Tacitus gives some detail about the fighting methods of several of the tribes who later formed the Franks and Alamanni, as well as generic descriptions of the early Germans as a whole. In his generic description of the first century Germans Tacitus says:

> Generally speaking, their strength lies in infantry rather than cavalry. So foot soldiers accompany the cavalry into action... The best men are chosen from the whole body of young warriors and placed with the cavalry in front of the main battle line... The battle line is made up of wedged-shaped formations.

I will have more to say of the wedge-shaped formation later. Ammianus Marcellinus tells us that the tactic of mixing light infantry with cavalry still existed in the mid fourth century amongst the Alamanni. It is reasonable to assume that it also did amongst the Franks, even if there is no hard evidence to prove or disprove it.

Tacitus makes much of the lack of armour and primitive weaponry of the early Germans.

> Iron is not plentiful... Only a few of them use swords or lances. They carry spears – called *frameae* – with short narrow blades, but so sharp and easy to handle that they can be used as required either at close quarters or in long-range fighting. Their horsemen are content with a shield and a spear, the foot soldiers also rain javelins on their foes, each of them being naked or lightly clad in short cloaks. There

is nothing ostentatious about their equipment, only their shields are picked out in the colours of their choice. Few have breastplates, and only one here and there has a helmet of metal or hide.

In describing their cavalry Tacitus goes on to say,

Their horses are not remarkable for either beauty or speed and are not trained to execute various evolutions as ours are. They ride them straight ahead or with just a single wheel to the right, keeping their line so well that not a man falls behind the rest.

We cannot know how much of these descriptions is correct or what was invented to make a moral point. Like eighteenth century Europeans writing about the 'noble savage', Tacitus was at pains to contrast the primitive, virile Germans with the decadence of early Imperial Rome. By the time the Rhine tribes coalesced into the Frankish and Alamannic confederacies their weapons and accoutrements were as good as what the Romans had even if they did not have the same capability for mass production or logistics. Trade and booty from Rome, combined with the skills of local smiths, produced a wide array of spears, swords, axes, helmets and body armour. This is confirmed by the goods found in later Frankish and Alamannic graves.

Writing several centuries after Tacitus, Agathias perpetuated the image of the Franks as naked savages: 'They do not know the use of the coat of mail or greaves (leg armour). The majority leave their heads uncovered, only a few wear a helmet. They have their chests bare and backs naked to the loins. They cover their loins with either leather or linen.' This was written at the time that the Franks had taken over all of Roman Gaul, absorbed rival kingdoms and had access to former Roman armouries along with all the skilled Gallo-Roman artisans. That a sixth century Frank would have gone to war in the state of undress Agathias described is beyond belief. Contrasting the naked barbarian to the civilized Roman was a literary construct designed to tap into the prejudices of their readers – just as many modern newspapers still do today.

Most contemporary evidence, confirmed by archaeology, suggests that the Rhenish tribes continued to find their strength in infantry rather than cavalry. We have little detail of any third century battles but in 357, when the Alamanni fought against Julian's Romans, the mounted nobles dismounted to fight on foot alongside the lesser men who did not have horses. Graves from the fourth century onwards reveal throwing axes and prominent shield bosses suitable for men who tended to fight dismounted even if they might have owned horses.

Sixth century descriptions of the Franks by Procopius and Agathias tend to confirm a preference for fighting on foot. At that time virtually every East Roman soldier of note fought on horseback, as did his Persian, Vandal and Gothic opponents. In the East, infantry was used mainly to hold ground, provide missile support or to garrison towns. That many sixth century Franks still fought on foot aggressively must have been a surprise to the sixth century Romans who encountered them. Therefore it would be natural that they would have made much of it. A more detailed analysis of Frankish fighting methods is given in Chapter 10.

Eventually Frankish armies evolved into those of feudal France who were noted for their mounted knights. Tacitus mentions that the Tencteri, who were amongst the ancestors of the Franks, were renowned horsemen. Gregory of Tours also describes several Frankish mounted actions and horse furniture has been found in a number of Frankish and Alamannic graves. It is reasonable to assume, therefore, that the Franks and Alamanni fought mounted if they had horses and if the circumstances were suitable for mounted action but fought on foot in other circumstances. Quite probably, in their early years, only a few men had horses but the number of well-mounted warriors increased over the fourth and fifth centuries in concert with their increased power, lands and wealth.

Close contact with Rome had many effects on Germanic society over the second and third centuries. Warfare became deadlier, weapons and equipment improved and those tribes living along the Rhine frontier often found themselves having to fight for survival, either against Romans or against other tribes which Rome had equipped and encouraged.

The tribes which came to make up the Frankish and Alamannic confederacies benefited from their close contact with Rome. Trade and service in the Roman army brought material wealth which far exceeded that of their ancestors and of the other German tribes living further from Roman territory.

Chapter 2

Gaul on the Brink

The Roman Crisis

W hen Tacitus wrote his *Germania* in the first century AD, Rome
was at the height of her power. The destruction of a Roman
legion by the Germans in the Teutoburger Wald in AD 9
shocked the imperial establishment and ended any ideas of expanding
beyond the Rhine-Danube frontiers. The risk was simply not worth
it, especially as the lands of Germania had little to offer in the way of
portable wealth.

Rome's policy towards the German tribes then became one of
maintaining a balance of power beyond the frontier. She rewarded
friendly leaders and punished those who were hostile, often playing
various factions against each other so, to paraphrase Tacitus' words, if
the German tribes did not love Rome then at least they would hate each
other more.

German recruits were welcomed into the Roman army. Prisoners of
war were settled on Imperial territory as *laeti* – military colonists who
were given marginal land to farm in return for military service. Some
Germans were recruited individually into the ranks of the army while
others were hired en masse as temporary allies.

The Imperial frontiers were relatively porous with trade and interaction
benefiting Germans and Romans alike. As a result, those tribes living
close to the frontier became increasingly wealthy in comparison to those
of the interior. Powerful men could afford to maintain larger warbands of
permanent retainers, their power derived from trade with Rome or from
service in her armies rather than subsistence farming. So it was that the
small tribes of Tacitus' first century descriptions evolved into the larger
groupings of the Franks and Alamanni with far more material wealth and
greater hierarchy than that of their ancestral tribes.

For many years this interaction between Romans and Germans resulted in a relatively peaceful equilibrium, apart from the odd raid or two. Both benefited from the status quo so neither sought to break it. Germans began to fill out the ranks of the Roman army while Roman material goods and skills transformed the economies of those Germans living close to the frontier. If some ambitious war leader was tempted to overstep the mark he could expect swift and terrible retribution from a powerful Roman army, a coalition of other warbands paid by Rome, or a combination of both.

The first major break in this equilibrium happened in the mid second century AD, probably sparked off by internal displacements deep in the forests of Germania. The Marcomanni, Quadi and Sarmatians on the Middle Danube were losing territory to the Goths and Vandals who had started to move down from their homelands further north. We do not know what caused this movement of Goths and Vandals from modern Poland and the Baltic coast towards the Black Sea and the Danube. The result was a knock-on effect and a major incursion into Imperial territory by the tribes of the Danube frontier who were feeling the pressure.

The Marcomannic War (166–180) was hard fought but ended in a typical Roman victory. The frontiers were restored and punitive raids cowed the hostile tribes. New alliances were made, new leaders installed and the traditional balance was restored. The Rhine frontier remained relatively stable at this time. The tribes of the Rhine were not entirely untroubled by the southern movement of other Germans towards the Danube. Some of them joined the Marcomanni and Quadi to invade Roman territory and the ancient tribes fragmented with their remnants coalescing into larger confederations which would become the Franks and Alamanni.

The end of Marcus Aurelius' reign (121–180) is seen by many as the end of Roman greatness. As Sir Edward Gibbon put it:

In the second century of the Christian Era, the Empire of Rome comprehended the fairest part of the earth and the most civilised portion of mankind... During a happy period [AD 98–180] of more than fourscore years, the public administration was conducted by the virtue and abilities of Nerva, Trajan, Hadrian and the two Antonines.

> It is the design [of the first three chapters of his monumental work]
> to describe the prosperous condition of their empire; and afterwards,
> from the death of Marcus Aurelius, to deduce the most important
> circumstances of its decline and fall.

From the death of Marcus Aurelius onwards the Empire was plagued
by civil war as the army made and broke emperors with frightening
frequency. The mid third century saw an almost complete collapse of
Roman order as the Empire was wracked with endless coups and counter-
coups. Between 235 and 284, twenty-six emperors reigned and many
more vied for the title.

Much of Rome's wealth had come from her earlier conquests. By the
end of the second century there were no more conquests to be had which
would increase wealth by more than the effort needed to take it. The
forests of Germany and Scotland, or the deserts of North Africa, offered
little prospect of loot. Meanwhile the rising power of the Sassanid Persian
dynasty protected the richer east and proved more than a match for the
best armies Rome could send against it. In 360 the Emperor Valerian was
captured by the Persians after a disastrous campaign. Goths and other
eastern Germanic tribes took advantage of the situation to raid deeply into
Greece and Asia Minor by land and sea. The Roman economy collapsed as
the succession of emperors emptied the treasury and devalued the coinage
to pay for armies to fight off rivals for the throne and to stem the invasions.
Barter again became a way of doing business and even taxes were gathered
in kind as this was a more reliable alternative to using baseless coinage.

While the Persians and the Danubian tribes took advantage of the chaos
to raid Roman territory or take bits of it for themselves, the Rhenish tribes
were consolidating into the confederations of the Franks and Alamanni.
They were poised to expand their territories over the Rhine and to act
as power brokers for various Roman usurpers as they made their bids for
the throne.

According to the fifth century Roman historian Zosimus, when Valerian
became emperor in 253 he shared power with his son Gallienus.

> Valerian went himself into the east to oppose the Persians. He
> entrusted to his son the care of the forces in Europe, thus leaving

him to resist the Barbarians who poured in upon him in every direction. As the Germans were the most troublesome enemies, and harassed the Gauls in the vicinity of the Rhine, Gallienus marched against them in person, leaving his officers to repel, with the forces under their command, any others that should enter Italy, Greece or Illyricum [former Yugoslavia of modern times]. With these designs, he possessed himself of and defended the passages of the Rhine, at one time preventing their crossing, and at another engaging them as soon as they had crossed it. But having only a small force to resist an immense number, he was at a loss how to act, and thought to secure himself by a league with one of the German princes. He thus not only prevented the other Barbarians from so frequently passing the Rhine, but denied them access to other auxiliaries.

Gregory of Tours tells of Gaul being overrun by the Alamanni at this time:

> Valerian and Gallienus received the Roman imperial power… At that time Chrocus, the famous king of the Alamanni, raised an army and overran the Gauls. This Chrocus is said to have been very arrogant. And when he had committed a great many crimes he gathered the tribe of the Alamanni by the advice, it is said, of his wicked mother. They overran the whole of the Gauls, and destroyed from their foundations all the temples which had been built in ancient times. And coming to Clermont he set on fire, overthrew and destroyed that shrine which they call *Vasso Galatæ* in the Gallic tongue.

After Valerian's capture by the Persians in 260, Gallienus became sole emperor and immediately had to deal with a series of revolts in addition to the rising power of Persia and Gothic raids throughout Asia Minor, Greece and the Balkans. This gave the Rhenish tribes new opportunities to flex their muscles. As Gallienus was forced to withdraw troops to deal with other threats, the Alamanni pushed in to occupy the Agri Decumates on the east bank of the Rhine which Gallienus abandoned. Then they advanced further into Roman territory, crossing the Rhine and forcing the Alpine passes. One tribe, the Juthungi, invaded Italy and even reached the outskirts of Rome. Returning home, ladened with loot, the invaders were later destroyed by a Roman army near Milan.

It is around the mid third century that Roman sources start to mention the Franks for the first time. Like the Alamanni, they too took advantage of the chaos in the Roman Empire to cross the Lower Rhine and raid deep into Gaul. One band is said to have reached Spain, sacked Tarragona and some of them may even have gone on to cross over to Africa in a foreshadowing of the later Vandal migration. Others are said to have taken to the sea to raid the coasts of Gaul and Britain.

Archeology reveals that the mid third century was a time of upheaval in Roman Gaul. Large numbers of coin hordes, buried by their owners and never recovered until found by modern archeologists, tell a story of collapsing order, fear and the displacement of people. Walls were built around towns in the interior far from the frontier – places which for more than two and a half centuries had no fear of attack.

Not for the last time, the Gallo-Romans felt abandoned by the Imperial authorities who not only failed to protect them but drew off troops to fight usurpers or to defend Italy and the East. In 260, the Roman army in Gaul proclaimed Marcus Postumus as emperor. He was a Gallo-Roman who may have had Germanic ancestry, and was supported by the men who had defeated the Alamanni at Milan. He had a record of success in defending the frontiers and was a capable administrator. The *Historia Augusta* (a fourth century collection of Imperial biographies) has this to say about Postumus:

This man, most valiant in war and most steadfast in peace, was so highly respected for his whole manner of life that he was even entrusted by Gallienus with the care of his son … The Gauls themselves, hating Gallienus most bitterly… hailed [Postumus] as their ruler… Postumus was gladly accepted by the entire army and by all the Gauls, and for seven years he performed such exploits that he completely restored the provinces of Gaul, while Gallienus spent his time in debauchery and taverns and grew weak in loving a barbarian woman. Great, indeed, was the love felt for Postumus in the hearts of all the people of Gaul because he had thrust back all the German tribes and had restored the Roman Empire to its former security… If anyone, indeed, desires to know the merits of Postumus, he may learn Valerian's opinion concerning him from the following letter which he wrote to the Gauls: 'As general in charge of the Rhine frontier and governor of Gaul we have named Postumus, a man most worthy of the stern discipline of the Gauls. He by his presence will safeguard the soldiers in the camp, civil rights in the forum, law-suits at the bar of judgement, and the dignity of the council-chamber, and he will preserve for each one his own personal possessions. He is a man at whom I marvel above all others and well deserving of the office of prince, and for him, I hope, you will render me thanks.'

For nearly ten years Postumus ruled over what modern historians have called *The Gallic Empire* which came to include Britain and Spain as well as Gaul. Possibly Postumus had ideas of confronting Gallienus to extend his power and he certainly knew that at some point Gallienus would be able to turn his attention from the threats to the Roman East to confront him. This happened in 265 but Postumus was able to fend off the attack. He did not follow up to take over all of the Roman Empire for himself. Instead he consolidated his power in Gaul and maintained order there.

As far as we can tell Postumus not only defeated the Franks and Alamanni but he incorporated many of them into his army to fight against their compatriots. Neither of these two confederations of Rhine Germans had any sort of cohesive political structure. Individual bands operated independently, vying for power which came from Roman wealth and could be secured either by raids or alliances. Some bands tried to expand their position by attacking Roman territory while others found it more profitable to side with Rome, perfectly happy to engage their rival compatriots.

Postumus was killed when the garrison of Mainz revolted and set up one of their men in his place. The so-called Gallic Empire collapsed rapidly. Several other men took on Postumus' mantle but none were able to do much more than hang on to a declining position. By 274 Aurelian had brought the western provinces back under Imperial authority. The later reigns of Diocletian (284–305) and Constantine (306–337) restored order, transformed the Roman Empire and brought a semblance of stability that would last until the end of the fourth century.

Renewed political stability towards the end of the third century gave Rome the ability to restore order but it did not happen quickly nor did the Franks and Alamanni lose the strength or ambition they had acquired over the preceding decades. Diocletian appointed Maximian as co-ruler in the West. Maximian established his capital at Trier on the middle-Rhine frontier and throughout his reign (285–305) he had to campaign vigorously against both the Germanic tribes and Gallo-Roman rebels known as Bacaudae.

A panegyric of Maximian tells of how he fought in the front rank amongst his men and even crossed the Rhine into the Alamannic homelands to 'tame those wild and untamed nations by ravaging, battles and massacres with fire and sword. Let the Rhine dry up, and with its gentle current scarcely move the smooth pebbles in its transparent shallows – there is no fear from that quarter. All that I see beyond the Rhine is Roman'.

Maximian built a fleet and used it to clear the English Channel of pirates and to patrol the Rhine. By the latter part of the 280s he and his men had re-established ascendancy over the Alamanni and restored the Rhine frontier. It is at this time that we learn the name of one of the earliest Frankish leaders, a man called Gennobaudes, who submitted to Maximian probably to avoid the fate which had befallen the Alamanni when Maximian crossed the Rhine bringing death and destruction. Other Frankish leaders seem to have followed Gennobaudes' example.

As the fourth century dawned the relatively easy opportunities offered by Rome's earlier internal convulsions had passed. A raid across the Rhine to secure wealth and reputation would now invariably end in defeat and might also bring on horrific reprisals. The old equilibrium seemed to have been re-established although occasional incursions by small bands of Franks and Alamanni continued.

The New Roman Army

In the half-century dominated by Diocletian and Constantine (284 to 337) the Romans restructured their armies and evolved a new defensive strategy. Realizing that it was impossible to hold every stretch of frontier against determined enemies, they downgraded the frontier forces and built up centrally located field armies of high-quality troops. These field armies had no fixed bases and could be deployed relatively quickly and easily to deal with whatever threat emerged from wherever it came.

The old legions of nearly 5,000 men with additional supporting auxiliaries, based close to the frontiers, were too large and slow moving to deal with relatively small bands of barbarians which could bypass them. Increasingly throughout the third century, detachments (known as vexillations) were drawn off from the legions to deal with an incursion or to become part of an ad-hoc force operating far from their home base and sometimes never returning to it. In need of fast-moving troops able to rush to deal with a sudden threat, Gallienus created a central cavalry reserve in the mid third century. Diocletian and Constantine built on this. Constantine raised many new small units of mobile auxiliaries (*Auxilia Palatina*) that came to have higher status than many of the ancient legions.

The remnants of the old legions and auxiliaries, deployed along the frontiers, became known as *limitanei* – guarding the *limes* (border defences); or *riparenses* – guarding the river frontiers. Despite their ancient lineage, these units became static garrison troops. They were no longer expected to fight the enemy in open battle far away from their bases. The soldiers were often given patches of frontier land where they could supplement their income and raise families without the risk of being drawn off to some other far-flung part of the Empire.

Although it is tempting to disparagingly think of the *limitanei* as second-rate troops, they were immensely useful. Along the Rhine frontier there were many forts which did not need elite troops to defend them. Local men with local knowledge and a stake in protecting what was theirs could hold a strongpoint against a barbarian incursion. Their patrols would gather intelligence and provide early warning.

In most cases, barbarian invaders would initially bypass these strongpoints to seek easier pickings. When they did, the regional field armies (*comitatenses*) would move from their central locations to deal with them. Many of the units in these field armies were newly raised without links to the legions of previous centuries. They had a high proportion of German recruits and included strong cavalry contingents. Elite troops (*palatini*) were originally those under the emperor's personal command. Later, the field armies contained both *palatini* and *comitatenses*. Constantine disbanded the Praetorian Guard and replaced them with a new corps of guard cavalry known as the *Schola*. Fast-moving mounted reserves had proved their worth to the Romans in the third century. Many more such units were created and cavalry increased in importance and status in the early years of the fourth century although infantry still formed the backbone of all Roman armies.

This new Roman defensive strategy was criticized by historians from its inception. Zosimus has this to say of it:

Constantine adopted a measure which gave the barbarians free access into the Roman dominions. For the Roman Empire [in the third century] was protected on its remote frontiers by towns and fortresses in which soldiers were placed. It was consequently impossible for the barbarians to pass them, there being always a sufficient force to oppose their inroads. But Constantine destroyed that security by removing the greater part of the soldiers from those barriers of the frontiers, and placing them in towns that had no need of defenders; thus depriving those who were exposed to the barbarians of all defence, and oppressing the towns that were quiet with so great a multitude of soldiers, that many of them were totally forsaken by the inhabitants. He likewise rendered his soldiers effeminate by accustoming them to public spectacles and pleasures. To speak in plain terms, he was the first cause of the affairs of the Empire declining to their present miserable state.

The reality was that the immense borders of the Roman Empire could never be defended strongly enough to create an impenetrable fortress. The many incursions of the third century demonstrated pretty clearly that Zosimus was wrong in claiming that the former frontier strategy stopped all barbarian invasions. Just as the European Union today finds it impossible to seal off all access to migrants, the Romans had to accept that their borders could always be penetrated. It was better to keep concentrations of high-quality forces in central locations that could deal with serious problems rather than try in vain to turn all of Europe, the Middle East and North Africa into a sealed fortress. This is not to say that the frontier was only lightly defended – far from it. In the late third and early fourth centuries, Roman emperors were very active on the

Rhine and Danube and it would be a mistake to think of the field armies as passively waiting deep in the interior until they had to deal with an incursion which had bypassed or overwhelmed the *limitanei*. Very often they took offensive action against their enemies.

The new order imposed by Diocletian and Constantine transformed Roman society. The plague of civil war was not ended, the bitter rivalry with Persia continued and so did barbarian raids but Roman strength had returned and was now better organized and deployed to defend the Empire. As a result the German tribes had to adopt different policies. A young aspiring war leader might gather his *comitatus* and a few other ambitious followers to try his luck in a quick raid across the Rhine. This, however, became increasingly dangerous and was most likely to end up in defeat followed by brutal reprisals. A better route to wealth and reputation was to take payments for keeping the peace, trade with the Empire and to serve in the Roman army.

Gaul at the end of the third century had not returned to the *Pax Romana* of previous centuries. The Franks and Alamanni may have been cowed for a time but they were still far stronger militarily, economically and politically than any of their ancestral tribes. Meanwhile Gallo-Roman society had changed. Just as it is today in many modern western countries, large numbers of people felt that the benefits of Imperial Rome had left them behind. The rich grew richer while those in other echelons of society, even the middle classes, found their lives becoming evermore difficult. The authorities had been unable to provide security for the bulk of the population. Increasing tax burdens fell on those least able to pay while rich landowners were powerful enough to avoid their obligations. The assumed contract was that in exchange for paying taxes to maintain the army, the emperor would provide protection and security. This had been shown up to be no longer true. Taxes were still demanded but the army, which was funded by those taxes, increasingly served to prop up emperors or usurpers rather than to maintain the peace or protect the provincials.

The Bacaudae

Before returning to the story of the Franks it is worth understanding more about the plight of the Gallo-Romans in the waning years of the

Empire. Their story is inextricably bound up with the Franks who later became their overlords, quite possibly with their collusion.

Out of the chaos of civil war and economic collapse that characterized the third century AD, came a prolonged series of local revolts that threatened the very fabric of Roman society. These revolts were most prevalent in Gaul and Spain. Here, escaped slaves, oppressed peasants and even disillusioned municipal officials, artisans and landowners banded together with military deserters to defy Imperial authority. These rebels were called Bacaudae (or sometimes Bagaudae). By the fifth century AD, some of them had become so powerful that they were minting their own coins and were strong enough to require the Imperial authorities to call in barbarian armies to suppress them.

The Spartacus revolt is well known yet the Bacaudae, who were more successful and who survived for more than two centuries, are virtually unknown today. The increased reliance on barbarian troops to fill the ranks of the Roman army in Gaul was in part a response to the impact of the Bacaudae. Alans, for example, were settled around the city of Orléans in the early fifth century to keep the Bacaudae of Armorica (modern Brittany and parts of Normandy) in check.

Early revolts

Although the Bacaudae are most notable for their activities towards the end of the Roman Empire in the West, revolts were recorded as early as the second century. The Marcomannic War, followed by plague, currency devaluation and corruption led to a great revolt in AD 186 led by a former soldier by the name of Maternus. According to the Roman historian Herodian:

> Maternus gathered together a numerous band of rascals, and at first he overran villages and estates, and plundered them; but when he was master of great wealth he collected a more numerous throng of rascals with promises of large gifts and a share of what was taken, so that they no longer had the status of brigands but of enemies. For they now proceeded to attack the largest cities, and forcing open the prisons they set free those who had been confined in them, no

matter what they had been charged with, promised them impunity, and by good treatment won them over to join them. They overran the whole land of the Gauls and the Spaniards attacking the largest cities, burning parts of them and plundering the rest before retiring.

Many of Maternus' followers were initially army deserters like himself but as the revolt gained momentum he was joined by many others. In a relatively short time the rebels had near complete control of much of Gaul and Spain. It took several campaigns to regain Imperial authority. Two legions were brought over from Britain to restore order and a military campaign led by Pescennius Niger had some success. Despite the military action against him, however, Maternus was still strong enough a year later to contemplate an invasion of Italy. His intent was to assassinate the Emperor Commodus and set himself up in his place. This did not go down well with his followers who had no desire to move from their homeland. So they betrayed him.

The execution of Maternus did not end revolts against the central authority of the Roman Empire. Although the term Bacaudae did not come into use until the third century, the coming together of brigands, deserters, escaped slaves and impoverished provincials to set up some sort of Robin Hood-like alternative society carried on for centuries. The weakening of central authority in the civil wars that followed the death of Commodus was probably a contributing factor as was the currency devaluation and economic decline of the third century. Twenty years after the death of Maternus, four legions were required to conduct a campaign against rebels in Gaul.

In the second century, these revolts were led by army deserters. Other deserters went over to join the various barbarian tribes on the other side of the Rhine and Danube. Marcus Aurelius' peace settlement with the Marcomanni included the demand to return thousands of deserters. It is not unlikely that such large numbers of former Roman soldiers going over to the barbarians had an impact on improving the military capabilities of the Franks and Alamanni.

The underlying discontent amongst the local population no doubt made it easier for Postumus to establish his 'Gallic Empire' a few decades later. When Diocletian appointed Maximian as co-ruler in the West

(286) he gave him the specific task of crushing the Bacaudae. Maximian achieved some temporary success, although part of his army mutinied on one occasion when it was ordered to fight the rebels. Although military success might destroy a particular group of Bacaudae, as the underlying causes of discontent were never dealt with, the Bacaudae were never suppressed. In the early fifth century, the authorities had to call in the Visigoths to deal with Bacaudae in Spain as well as Huns and Alans to contain them in Gaul. In Britain, the Saxons were brought in to deal with Irish raiders and it is quite possible that Romano-British warlords who fought the Saxons – such as the legendary Arthur – may well have had origins that were similar to the Gallic Bacaudae.

> The misery of these times was further increased by the insatiable covetousness of [the Emperor's] tax-collectors, who brought him more odium than money; and to many persons this seemed the more intolerable, because he never listened to any excuse, never took any measures for relief of the provinces when oppressed by the multiplicity of taxes and imposts; and in addition to all this he was very apt to take back any exemptions which he had granted. (Ammianus Marcellinus)

Who were the Bacaudae?

The term Bacaudae came into common usage at the end of the third century when Maximian campaigned against them. While second century sources frequently mention army deserters as the core rebels, writers from the third century onwards rarely speak of military men amongst them. More often the Bacaudae are referred to disparagingly as 'rustics' or 'slaves'. The name they took for themselves appears to have a Celtic root which may derive from *baga*, meaning 'warrior'.

The economic and social reforms of the Emperor Diocletian (284–305) bound people to their professions. A soldier's son become a soldier, a peasant's son would be a peasant and was tied by life to a patch of land probably owned by an aristocratic magnate. Service as a magistrate was also hereditary and unavoidable. Such men were responsible for collecting taxes from an increasingly impoverished population. If they were unable to raise their quota, they had to make up any shortfall from their own pockets. As a result, it was not only slaves who might think about 'taking to the greenwood' to avoid their lot and to find a better, alternative way of life.

It was, therefore, a wide range of people from different backgrounds who came together to make up the Bacaudae. There were deserters and escaped slaves to be sure but also farmers, craftsmen and educated townspeople. What they had in common was a desire to escape the situation they had been born into and find greater freedom to run their own affairs. Some of them may have been refugees from other parts of Gaul, driven from their homes by various barbarian invasions.

The Bacaudae had recognized leaders and some of these are named by Roman writers. In 286 Aurelius wrote: 'Aelianus and Amandus gathered a band of farmers and brigands, whom the Gauls called Bacaudae, and, ravaging the countryside far and wide, assailed many cities.' (Aurelius Victor, a fourth century Roman historian.) Tibatto led the Bacaudae of Armorica during the mid fifth century, while another prominent Gallic Bacaudic leader sought refuge with Attila the Hun. In 449, a man called Basilius led the Bacaudae of northern Spain in a rebellion that saw them killing the bishop of Tarragona and still defying Imperial authority when Visigoths were sent against them five years later.

Military operations

For the most part, the Bacaudae wanted to be left alone and fought defensively against the many attempts by the central authorities to regain control. They did, however, make frequent raids on towns and large estates to secure food and supplies that they could not produce themselves. They also conducted ambushes on the roads to gain plunder. One such ambush in the fourth century resulted in the death of the brother-in-law of the Emperor Valentinian I. The fifth century poet Merobaudes, who himself was involved with attempts to suppress the Bacaudae in Spain, wrote of the rebels of the 'Armorican wilds'. He says that they had fought against the 'efforts of Caesar' and that 'the land was accustomed to conceal within its forests plunder obtained by savage crime'.

Although the Roman armies sent against them encountered significant difficulties, the Bacaudae never had any chance in open battle. Therefore, like modern insurgents, they avoided battle and defended their territory through a series of ambushes, diversions and skirmishes. They would strike when there was a chance of success and melt back into the hills and forests when overwhelming force was brought against them.

Roman authors seemed reluctant to say much about these encounters. Ammianus Marcellinus, for example, says that 'battles less worthy of description were fought throughout various regions of Gaul, which it is superfluous to narrate both because their outcome resulted in nothing worth speaking of and because it is unbecoming to prolong a history with ignoble details'.

Due to their guerrilla tactics, properly defeating the Bacaudae was a near impossible task for the Imperial authorities. One Armorican revolt in 407, which coincided with the invasion of Gaul by the Vandals, took ten years to suppress. Less than twenty years later, Tibatto led another Armorican rebellion. He was defeated and captured by the authorities in 437, but escaped to lead the Bacaudae again in 442. The fact that he was not immediately executed and that he was able to escape hints at some degree of collusion on the part of his captors.

Eventually, as in all long-term insurgencies, some sort of accommodation had to be reached. This was especially true in the fifth century, when all available Imperial manpower had to be concentrated to deal with barbarian invasions and could not afford to be tied up with internal revolts. When Attila invaded Gaul in 451, Armoricans fought alongside Aetius who previously had been their most bitter enemy. It may be that Aetius agreed to some form of local autonomy for the Armorican Bacaudae in exchange for their support. A passage from Zosimus indicates that this may have been the case. It also hints at Bacaudic activity in Britain:

Accordingly the Britons took up arms and, with no consideration of the danger to themselves, freed their own cities from barbarian threat. Likewise all of Armorica and other Gallic provinces followed the Britons' lead. They freed themselves, ejected the Roman magistrates, and set up home rule at their own discretion.

This passage could be interpreted in different ways. Zosimus says that the Britons fought against barbarians not against the central authorities, yet his connection between them and the Armoricans – who clearly were in open rebellion – does give some pause for thought.

It is really not surprising that, when the Franks made a bid to take over Gaul in the late fifth century, they were so easily able to establish kingdoms in former Roman territories when the local population did not support Imperial authority. Initially, the emperors employed barbarian mercenaries to suppress the revolts. The Franks, who came to stay, were probably easier masters to bear than the heavy hand of Imperial bureaucracy. There is no direct evidence of collusion between the Bacaudae and the Franks in Gaul but it is quite likely. In mid fifth century Spain Rechiar, king of the Suebi, apparently made an alliance with the local Bacaudae to help secure his position.

In the Service of Rome

As the third century waned, it may have appeared on the surface that the normal state of affairs had resumed. The Roman army, although still occasionally diverting its attention from frontier defence to support a usurper, was now poised to deal ruthlessly with any attempt by any band of barbarians to raid Roman territory. On the other hand the Germans beyond the Rhine were much stronger than before while the native Gallo-Roman population felt alienated from the Empire at best – in open rebellion at worst.

Although barbarian raids continued into the fourth century, the most obvious route to wealth for an ambitious Frank or Alaman was to serve in the Roman army rather than to risk fighting it. Many did this individually, signing up to join the ranks of the new units of *Auxilia Palatina* which were created by Constantine the Great. Many such units bear names that hint at Frankish origins. Not all of these served in Gaul. Some were stationed as far away as Egypt and the Persian frontier.

Survivors of failed raids were increasingly settled throughout Gaul as *laeti* – prisoners of war who were given abandoned land to farm in return for military service. A panegyric to the Emperor Constantius Chlorus (293–306) praised the benefits of such arrangements: 'Rows of barbarian prisoners... shared out among the inhabitants of your provinces in order to serve them wait to be led to the deserted lands which they must restore to growth... What is more, if they are called up into the army, they hurry to join and are brought to heel by army discipline.'

It was not only Franks who were settled as *laeti* in Gaul. The largest number of military settlers in the province were Sarmatians – a nomadic non-Germanic people from the Middle Danube. Based at Poitiers, an official known as *Praefectus Sarmatarum et Taifalorum Gentilium* (Prefect of Sarmatian and Taifal natives) was responsible for the settlements of *laeti* in Gaul – the terms *gentiles* and *laeti* seemingly being used interchangeably. Under him he had five settlements of Sarmatians based around Paris, Reims, Amiens and Langres; Frankish settlers (*Laetorum Francorum*) at Rennes; and six other settlements (presumably of various Germans) at Chartres, Coutances, Bayeux, Le Mans, Tongres, Auvergne, and along the Lower Rhine.

Three of these other settlements are identified as Suebi which the Romans seemed to have had difficulty differentiating from the Alamanni. One of these (in Normandy) is named *Laetorum Batavorum et gentilium Suevorum* (Batavian *laeti* and Swabian natives). This indicates a mix of peoples. The Batavians were an ancient tribe who, in Tacitus' day, were 'the most conspicuously brave of German tribes... in token of their ancient alliance with us [Rome] they are not subject to the indignity of tribute nor ground down by the tax collector'. By the fourth century the Batavians had long ceased to exist but many senior units in the Roman field army (both cavalry and infantry) were named *Batavii*. This probably had come to mean 'loyal Germans' rather than a specific tribal origin of the recruits. The ancestral homeland of the original Batavians was along the modern Dutch coast and the Rhine delta. This region had come to be occupied by Franks and Frisians in the fourth century – probably absorbing the remnants of the original Batavians.

The Prefect's title assumes a number of Taifal (*Taifali*) settlements under his command. The Taifals were an east Germanic tribe from the Middle Danube, probably related to the Goths. None of the names of the individual settlements give any clues as to how many (if any) were predominantly made up of Taifals. It would seem that many of the *laeti* were groups of resettled prisoners of war from a wide variety of tribal origins which came to form new communities inside the Empire. Some may have been Taifals, others could have been Franks, Alamanni, or from other tribes.

The *Dux Belgicae Secunda*, the military officer responsible for the defence of the Lower Rhine, had five settlements of *laeti* under his command. One of these is identified as Sarmatians and one gives no indication of origin. Two are named as Batavians and the other as *Nervii*. The latter were an ancient tribe from modern Belgium who, like the Batavians, had ceased to exist by the time the *Notitia Dignitatum* was written, their descendants having been absorbed by the Franks. It may be that those settlements named as Batavians and *Nervii* came primarily from Frankish tribes but it is unlikely that they identified themselves as Franks. Any contact with their ancestral homelands would have been severed once they had established new settlements inside Roman territory.

The *laeti* lived in their own self-sufficient communities with men, women and children but they were under Imperial administration and had to provide a certain number of recruits for the Roman army in exchange for their land. It is likely that this obligation was in lieu of the taxes the native Gallo-Romans had to pay, echoing Tacitus' comment about the ancient Batavians who were 'not subject to the indignity of tribute nor ground down by the tax collector'. Most modern historians believe that the *laeti* provided individual recruits to existing Roman units rather than complete contingents under their own leaders.

This arrangement was beneficial to barbarians and Romans alike. The former obtained land inside the Empire with access to its material benefits while still being able to maintain their own communities and way of life. Providing recruits to the Roman army was probably viewed by the *laeti* as less of a burden than it was by the native population. It gave adventurous young men an outlet for their ambition although if they were drawn off to serve in a unit that was then posted to the other ends of Empire it may have been that these men never saw their families again. This sometimes made moving units far beyond their recruiting grounds problematic for the Roman authorities.

Ammianus Marcellinus recounts a mutiny by senior Gallic units in the mid fourth century when orders were given for them to move from Gaul to the east. Quoting an anonymous mutineer from a senior field army unit, Ammianus reports him saying:

We are being driven to the furthest parts of the earth like condemned criminals, and our relations will become slaves to the Alamanni after we have delivered them from that first captivity by desperate battles.

There is no indication that the *laeti* were any more inclined to mutiny than native Roman recruits but increasingly the Roman field armies, like the *limitanei*, were tied to their recruiting grounds. The soldiers had no desire to leave their families, or their smallholdings, for the uncertain adventure of a far-flung offensive.

For the Romans the system of giving Sarmatians and Germans marginal land in exchange for military service gave not only a new source of good recruits but also turned around unproductive land. 'The Chamavi and Frisii (Frankish tribes) now work for me. These vagabonds and pillagers work ceaselessly to bring my land under cultivation... When they are called up into the army they hurry to join and are brought to heel by army discipline.' (Panegyric of Constantine Chlorus)

Archeology reveals something about the *laeti*. A number of graves dated to the fourth century have been found in those areas of northern France where the *laeti* were settled. They reveal men buried with weapons (some of Roman manufacture) alongside women with distinctive Germanic jewellery. Such graves could not contain the remains of native Gallo-Romans as they were not permitted arms and regular soldiers were issued their equipment which would go back into the arsenals when they died.

Many fourth century graves in northern Gaul contain throwing axes which became known as franciscae (singular francisca). These became the hallmark of the Frankish warrior, possibly deriving its name from the Franks or giving it to them. Their use in battle is described by Procopius in the sixth century (see Chapter 10). Some late Roman soldiers carried a hand axe (*securis*) as a sidearm in place of a sword so these graves may contain men buried with their simple sidearm which later evolved into an offensive throwing axe.

These burials do beg the question of whether or not the *laeti* were only resettled prisoners of war who provided individual recruits to the Roman army. If they were then it is reasonable to conclude that the recruit's equipment would have been issued by the state rather than being his personal property. That a man might be interred with weapons suggests that he was more than a simple recruit called to serve in the ranks and files of a standard Roman unit. It is not implausible to conclude that as early as the fourth century some of the Frankish settlements in Gaul were free communities with men owning their own weapons to provide semi-independent allied contingents which fought alongside regular Roman units. Such arrangements became common in the fifth century when units of barbarian allies (*foederati*) served under their own leaders and maintained their distinctive fighting styles rather than being absorbed into existing units of the regular Roman army.

In the fourth century many Franks served in the ranks of the Roman army as individual recruits either from settlements inside Gaul or from beyond the frontier. Some rose to high command. As a barbarian could not hope to aspire to the Imperial throne, Franks and other Germans of ability tended to be trusted by emperors who were ever worried that their best generals might become rivals to power. Bonitus, raised amongst the Frankish *laeti*, was elevated by Constantine the Great to the post of *Magister Militum* (Master of Soldiers) – the highest military rank below the emperor. He played a pivotal role in defeating Constantine's rival Licinius in 324. Bonitus' son Silvanus also rose to high military rank.

Merobaudes, one of the Emperor Julian's most trusted senior commanders in the mid fourth century, was a Frank. Richomer (or Richomeres), another Frank, played a key role in the campaigns against the Goths in 378 and eventually became consul. Richomer died in battle leading the East Roman army again the West Romans who were commanded by his Frankish nephew Arbogast.

Those Franks who reached high office were not entirely free of Imperial pretensions. Silvanus was elevated by the Gallic army to make a bid for the throne and reigned for twenty-eight days. Flavius Magnus Magnentius, who overthrew the Emperor Constans in 350, had a Frankish mother and Romano-British father. He may have been raised amongst the *laeti* of Amiens. Richomer's nephew Arbogast rose to the rank of *Magister Militum* in the West and held supreme power under Valentinian II in the 390s.

By the mid fourth century there were people of Frankish and Alamannic origin settled on Roman territory in Gaul together with Sarmatians and other Germans. Some may have provided formed units of *foederati* but for the most part these settlers provided individuals who served in the ranks of regular Roman army units while a few notable men managed to rise to very high office. These barbarian settlements became increasingly important to the Imperial authorities as the native Gallo-Romans showed no inclination to serve in the army. Many of them either joined or sided with the Bacaudae. Others went to great lengths to avoid being press-ganged, even to the point of cutting off their thumbs so as to be incapable of bearing arms. As the fourth century gave way to the fifth more barbarians were settled as semi-independent *foederati* close to areas of Bacaudic influence with the specific aim of suppressing the rebels. In a Kafkaesque turn of affairs barbarians came to be valued as a better source of recruits than native Gallo-Romans and Roman armies were raised as much to suppress the local population as to protect it.

In the fourth century the majority of Franks lived to the north and east of the Lower Rhine while the Alamanni occupied the east bank of the Upper Rhine in the area known to the Romans as the Agri Decumates. Sometimes the various bands cooperated and sometimes they took opposing sides with some joining the Romans to fight against their countrymen or against other Romans. Leaders would emerge, as we shall see, who were able to extend their authority beyond their immediate followers. They did this through a mix of personal charisma, ruthlessness, and the wealth they gained from their interaction with the Roman Empire.

Chapter 3

Rome's Last Grasp

Thanks to the surviving histories of Ammianus Marcellinus, we know more about the Franks in the mid fourth century than at any other time in their early history. This is paradoxical as at this time the Franks were relatively quiet. After their first appearance in the third century, when the Franks began to take advantage of Rome's weakness, they played only a minor role in Roman affairs in the first half of the fourth century apart from providing valuable soldiers and officers for the army. At this time the Goths on the Lower Danube and the Persians to the east posed the greatest external threats to the Empire. Along the Rhine the Alamanni were the most threatening of the Germanic confederacies although various bands of Franks continued to raid into Gaul.

The vivid descriptions Ammianus gives of the Roman campaigns against the Franks and Alamanni in the 350s makes it worthwhile to examine them in some detail even if the events of the time were not particularly significant from a Frankish point of view. It would take another century before the Franks really came into their own but unfortunately we do not have anything like Ammianus' histories to tell us much about how they managed it.

Ammianus Marcellinus served as a staff officer under the Emperor Julian (331–363) and gives a positive spin to the actions of his commander – the hero of his history. Like most Roman historians Ammianus employed classical stereotypes, partly to show his learning and partly to suit the prejudices of his readers. Therefore, not everything he reports should be taken as given. He was, however, a Roman officer who had seen combat and knew more about actual warfare than most historians either before or after him. His descriptions of the fighting between Romans, Franks and Alamanni are far more realistic than most ancient histories even if they are still laced with a fair degree of poetic licence. This chapter will follow

Ammianus' account of events. Therefore, unless indicated otherwise all quotes will be his.

Raiders and Usurpers

In 354 the Emperor Constantius decided to lead an army against the Alamanni 'who had often made extensive incursions into Roman territories'. After reaching Lake Constance he gave command of the army to Arbetio, his *Magister Equitum* (Master of Horse) with orders to skirt around Lake Constance and to bring the Alamanni to battle.

It all went horribly wrong for the Romans. Arbetio failed to take proper precautions and did not send scouts out in front of his column or, if he did, he did not wait to hear their reports. Presumably the Alamanni did pay more attention to reconnaissance as they were able to ambush the Romans and overwhelm them, killing 'a vast number of common soldiers and ten tribunes'. The scattered Roman survivors were saved by nightfall and managed to regroup in their fortified camps.

> The Alamanni were greatly elated at this event, and advanced with increased boldness, every day coming up to the fortifications of the Romans while the morning mists obscured the light. Drawing their swords they roamed about in every direction, gnashing their teeth, and threatening us with haughty shouts. Then with a sudden sally our *Scutarii* (elite heavy cavalry) rushed forth, and after being stopped for a moment by the resistance of the hostile squadrons, called out all their comrades to join them in the engagement.

Three other senior Roman cavalry units (*Armaturarum*, *Comites* and *Promoti*) then joined the fray.

> These men [the Roman cavalry] ... poured down upon the foe like a torrent, not in a regular line of battle, but in desultory attacks like those of bandits. They put them [the Alamanni] all to flight in a disgraceful manner. Straggling, and hampered by their endeavours to flee, the enemy exposed their unprotected bodies to our weapons, and were slain by repeated blows of sword and spear. Many too

were slain with their horses, and seemed as they lay on their backs to be so entangled as still to be sitting on them. When this was seen, all our men [the Romans] who had previously hesitated to engage in battle with their comrades, poured forth out of the camp. Forgetful of all precautions, they drove before them the mob of barbarians, except those who were saved from destruction by their flight.

This description of the engagement outside the Roman encampment is interesting in that it seems to have been an all-cavalry battle. Had it taken place in Julius Caesar's day we might have expected an elite legion to have led the sally, encouraging others to join in. Although foot soldiers still formed the bulk of all Roman armies the most senior units were now mounted. The *Scutarii*, *Armaturarum*, *Comites* and *Promoti* were the elite of Constantius' *Scholae* (guards) and *Equites Palatini* (palatine cavalry). They were the men whose training and *esprit de corps* made them the best troops in the Roman army.

Most Alamanni tended to fight on foot in formal battle. Yet their best warriors would have owned horses and in the aftermath of their earlier success many probably mounted up to chase down the Roman survivors. Faced by a fortified camp the following morning one might have expected them to dismount if they were thinking of an assault. Most probably the Alamanni did not plan an assault. Ammianus' description of them being killed with their horses when the Roman cavalry sallied out makes it pretty clear that most of the Alamanni were mounted. Perhaps the mounted Alamannic warriors were simply making a demonstration, hoping to cower the frightened survivors of the earlier ambush.

The following year Constantius appointed Silvanus, his *Magister Peditum* (Master of Foot) to take command in Gaul and defend the province from further attacks by the Alamanni and Franks. 'From the long neglect with which these provinces had been treated, the Gauls, having no assistance on which to rely, had borne cruel massacres, with plunder and conflagration, from barbarians who raged throughout their land with impunity.'

Silvanus was the son of Bonitus, one of the Frankish *laeti* who had risen to high command under Constantine the Great in the early years of the fourth century. Silvanus had Frankish blood but had lived his whole life as a Roman. Many of the men he commanded would have had similar backgrounds.

Accusations of treason were trumped up against Silvanus by rivals. Silvanus' officers, many of whom also had Frankish antecedents, rushed to his defence and before long events spiralled out of control. Malarichus, the Frankish commander of the *Gentiles* (a guards unit of German cavalry) and Mallobaudes, tribune of the *Armaturarum* (armoured guards cavalry): 'Spoke out loudly that men devoted to the preservation of the emperor ought not to be circumvented by factions and treachery... Malarichus, alarmed for his own fate and that of his countryman Silvanus, called around him the Franks, of whom at that time there was a great multitude in the palace. In resolute language he laid open and proved the falsehood of the machinations by which their lives were threatened.'

Fearful that the accusations against him would end with execution, Silvanus began to consider appealing to his distant Frankish relatives for support. He was informed, however, that 'the Franks, of whom he himself was a countryman, would put him to death, or else betray him for a bribe'. Seeing no other way out of his predicament he allowed his troops to proclaim him as emperor. His reign lasted barely a month before he was murdered by a band of soldiers who had been bribed by the Emperor Constantius' agents.

> In this way did a general of no slight merit perish, through fear of false accusations heaped on him in his absence by a faction of wicked men, and which drove him to the utmost extremities in order to preserve his safety... Although he could boast of the valorous exploits of his father Bonitus, a man of Frankish extraction... he always feared the Emperor as a prince of wavering and fickle character.

Silvanus' brief usurpation was a small sideshow in the convoluted politics of the later Roman Empire. It is, however, quite significant in our story of how the Franks eventually came to become the masters of Roman Gaul. Although his bloodline was diluted, many Romans would have considered Silvanus to be a Frank. He was supported by other senior officers of Frankish ancestry such as Malarichus and Mallobaudes.

Silvanus' brief flirtation with the idea of seeking support from Franks beyond the frontier was quickly quashed when he learned that the likely outcome would be that they would sell him out. Whatever ancestral ties men like Silvanus had to their distant cousins over the Rhine they had very little in common. On the other hand, many of the Roman soldiers of the Gallic army would have had similar origins to their commander. They therefore rallied round him even to the point of defying the emperor's authority. Others, however, proved far less loyal and were easily swayed to betray and kill Silvanus. Ammianus seems to have had a low opinion of the Gallic soldiery 'whom we knew to be men of doubtful fidelity, and at any time open to change for a sufficient reward'.

The Caesar Julian

The end of Silvanus' brief usurpation removed a threat to Constantius' authority but had the opposite effect on the peace and prosperity of Roman Gaul. 'The Gauls were in a lamentable condition, since no adequate resistance could be made to the barbarians who were now carrying their devastations with fire and sword over the whole country.'

The Emperor Constantius' solution was to appoint his cousin Julian as Caesar (junior emperor) and give him command in Gaul. One could be forgiven for thinking that if Constantius had wanted to restore order in Gaul he would seek out his best general and give him the task. This was not the Roman way. A brilliant commander waging a successful campaign over the barbarians would before long have a much better base from which to mount a coup than Silvanus ever had. Throughout the later Roman Empire usurpers were always seen as a much greater threat than mere barbarian raids. The latter discomforted the provincials and reduced the tax base but the former could end up changing the government. The constant worry that a successful general might make a bid for the throne seriously hampered Rome's ability to deal with her external threats.

Cousin Julian seemed like a safe bet. He had absolutely no military experience and had shown no interest in politics. At the time of his appointment he was studying philosophy in Athens. Presumably Constantius thought that the army would be able to deal with the troublesome Frankish and Alamannic raids with the junior officers running the show under Julian's titular command. It did not quite turn out this way.

In front of an assembly of soldiers Constantius appointed Julian as Caesar on 6 November 355. The soldiers applauded by rattling their shields against their knees which was their way of showing approval. Banging spears against shields was a sign of anger. Both Romans and Germans did this before engaging in battle to intimidate their enemies or if they were in a rebellious mood.

Civil wars had once again left the frontiers open. As the Romans happily slaughtered each other, the Franks in the north and the Alamanni to the south crossed the Rhine to raid or take land for themselves. Often they had been encouraged by the various Roman factions to serve as mercenaries or to attack an opponent's territory. In order to defeat his rival Magnentius, Constantius had granted the Alamanni brothers Vadomar and Gundomar a tract of land on the west bank of the Rhine which at that time was under the usurper's control. Once Magnentius had been defeated the Alamanni had outlived their usefulness and Constantius wanted the land back.

By the time Julian arrived in Gaul much of the Gallic frontier had been overrun and forty-five major towns had fallen. It would be wrong to think of this as a coordinated effort by cohesive groups. For the most part the various bands of Franks and Alamanni operated as small warbands, probably numbering little more than a couple of hundred warriors each. Only very rarely did they cooperate in larger groups which could hope to stand up to a Roman army.

From the perspective of a Roman emperor, barbarian incursions were a nuisance but usurpations could be terminal. Constantius wanted Julian to restore the frontiers of Gaul but he was even more concerned with preventing another rebellion by the Gallic army. Blood ties were not enough to guarantee Julian's loyalty so Constantius did not give him full authority over all the troops in Gaul. For the campaign of 356 Constantius himself led a larger part of the Gallic army and in the following year Barbatio, his *Magister Militum* (master of soldiers) commanded 25,000 troops while Julian only had half as many men.

Julian marched to Vienne on the Rhône where he established his headquarters with the intent of relieving Cologne which had fallen to the

Franks and Autun which was being besieged by them. Autun was a walled city but the walls had fallen into disrepair. A small garrison held out, bolstered by a small body of veteran Roman soldiers. Julian arrived at Autun on 24 June 356 to find the Franks had scattered. He pursued them north towards Auxerre and then on to Troyes. To avoid delay Julian took only a small escort of cataphracts (heavily armoured cavalry modelled on the Sarmatians) and *balistarii*. The term *balistarii* would normally indicate men operating catapults which were known as *ballistae*. Catapults would, however, have been an unlikely escort for a general who wanted to move with speed. There is some evidence to suggest that the Romans had developed an early form of crossbow and a more likely explanation is that Ammianus' *balistarii* were light infantry armed with simple crossbows.

Unlike Arbetio (see heading Raiders and Usurpers on page 36), Julian took proper precautions on his march, sending out advance and flank guards to give him warning of attack. In this way he was able to see off several attacks near Troyes although he was unable to pursue the enemy afterwards as he had no light cavalry with him. When Julian reached Troyes the inhabitants of the city were not convinced that he was the representative of legitimate Roman authority and so at first they refused to open the gates to him. This says something about the appearance of Roman armies of the fourth century when dress and equipment could not be easily distinguished from their barbarian opponents.

Reaching Reims, Julian was reinforced by the troops of the Gallic field army. He marched out to attack a band of Alamanni near *Decem Pagi* (a road station between Metz and Strasbourg). The attack was foiled by an ambush on his rearguard which caused Julian to become more cautious and allowed the raiders to retire unharmed. Julian pushed on to the Rhine to find that Strasbourg, Brumath, Rheinzabern, Seltz, Speyer, Worms and Mainz were all surrounded by bands of Franks and Alamanni who had taken over the countryside even if they left the towns alone. There was a brief battle outside Brumath in which Julian was victorious. After that he recovered Cologne from the Franks and then withdrew to winter quarters at Sens.

After having taken possession of Cologne he (Julian) did not leave it till the Frankish kings began, through fear of him, to abate of their fury, when he contracted a peace with them likely to be of future advantage to the republic.

The campaign of 356 must have been frustrating for Julian. He had chased various small bands of barbarians all over eastern Gaul but although he had received the submission of several Frankish bands, the Alamanni still held most of the southern Rhine frontier in their grip. To make matters worse when Julian retreated into winter quarters in Sens he was attacked and besieged by a band of Alamanni who had learned from deserters that 'he had with him neither the *Scutarii* not the *Gentiles* (senior guards' cavalry units of the *Schola*) who had been dispersed in various towns for the convenience of resupply'. The siege lasted a month but the walls of Sens, which still stand to this day, were too strong for the town to be taken by assault. Eventually the Alamanni withdrew, no thanks to Marcellus, the *Magister Equitum*, who was stationed nearby and made no effort to relieve the siege. Marcellus was later recalled and replaced by Severus who was more cooperative.

After a troubled winter at Sens, Julian resumed the offensive in the spring of 357. The Emperor Constantius sent Barbatio with 25,000 men from Italy to the Upper Rhine in support but relations between Barbatio and Julian were fractious. Julian's plan was to trap the Alamanni in a pincer movement between the two armies and thereby win a decisive battle which would put an end to their aggression. Barbatio, however, showed no inclination to cooperate. Ammianus Marcellinus accuses him of actively undermining Julian.

With 13,000 men Julian pressed on to the Rhine and engaged the Alamanni in a number of skirmish actions. Ammianus tells us how the Romans had to clear roadblocks the enemy had set up through the Vosges mountain passes. Then, as the Romans came down into the plains of Alsace, the Alamanni took refuge on islands 'with which the Rhine is liberally studded'.

Today the Upper Rhine has been channelized and little remains of the meandering branches and wetlands that characterized this part of the river before the 1950s. Older people living in the region tell how it used to be a maze of winding, shallow waterways. These could be navigated relatively easily by those who had local knowledge but would be a barrier to those who did not know the secret ways. In 1945 German soldiers from the region used their knowledge of the area to cross on foot to evade capture by advancing French and American forces.

The Alamanni used this same local knowledge to evade the Romans. Eventually Julian learned from friendly locals that the Rhine was indeed fordable and he ordered a body of lightly armed auxiliaries under the command of Bainobaudes, tribune of the *Cornuti*, to launch a raid. Such small-scale actions were typical of the time. Full-scale battles were far less common as the risk of defeat often led one side or the other to avoid a decisive engagement.

Ammianus' description of the raid is riveting:

> Wading through the shallows and at times supporting themselves on their shields and swimming, they reached a nearby island where they landed and slaughtered everyone they found like sheep, without distinction of age or sex. Then, finding some empty boats, they went on in them, rickety thought they were, and forced their way through a number of similar places... On hearing of this the rest of the Germans, realising that islands offered inadequate protection, conveyed their families and stores and primitive treasure to the further bank of the Rhine.

After clearing the Alamanni from their island refuges Julian pulled back to the foothills of the Vosges and set about rebuilding the fortifications at Saverne which guarded one of the main passes through the mountains from the Rhine Valley into the heartland of Gaul. As he was doing this the Alamanni moved further up river and launched a successful attack on Barbatio. The details of what occurred are quite sketchy and difficult to understand. With 25,000 troops Barbatio should have easily withstood an attack as it is unlikely that the Alamanni could have mustered the same number of warriors as later they were defeated by Julian's 13,000 men. Ammianus says that Barbatio was caught by surprise, routed and pursued back to Augst, losing his baggage to the enemy. He then sent his troops into winter quarters and went back to court 'to frame some charge against the Caesar Julian'.

Having dispersed the larger of the two Roman armies the Germans concentrated their forces to move against Julian. 'Chnodomar and Vestralp, kings of the Alamanni, as well was Urius and Ursicinus together with Serapio, Suomar and Hortar collected their whole strength and advanced towards the city of Strasbourg, believing that the Caesar had retreated for fear of the west, when in fact he was engaged in perfecting his defences (at Saverne to the north-west of Strasbourg).'

The Battle of Strasbourg

Ammianus claims that Alamanni had 35,000 men. Most scholars agree that this is an exaggeration but by how much it is hard to say. Hans Delbrück goes as low as 6–10,000 men which is based on his analysis that this was the most warriors a Germanic tribe could hope to muster. Probably the truth was somewhere between 10,000 and 30,000 men. This was a very large army gathered together by seven kings and ten princes. As the Alamanni had already managed to drive off Barbatio's army of 25,000 it is likely that they had something close to 20,000 warriors but we will never know for certain. The army was made up of 'various peoples, some of whom served as mercenaries and the rest in accordance with pacts of mutual assistance'. Probably the majority fought on foot but the better warriors were mounted and the Alamanni interspersed light infantry amongst the horsemen.

According to Ammianus, Julian had 13,000 'picked troops' in his army. This number is probably fairly accurate and many of the units with Julian are named. These included:

Scutarii and Gentiles - two unit of guards' cavalry (*scholae*). The two units are always mentioned together suggesting a more or less permanent brigading as was the case with most late Roman units.

Cornuti and Bracchiati - the most senior units of *auxilia palatina*, elite troops capable of both special operations as well as fighting in the main battle line. They tended to be brigaded together.

Celtae and Petulantes - Although not mentioned in his description of the battle this pair of *auxilia palatina* are named by Ammianus on several other occasions as part of Julian's army.

Batavi and Heruli – another pair of *auxilia palatina*. The Heruli are not mentioned in the battle but later they, together with the Batavi, are recorded as part of Julian's army.

Primani - A legion which was usually brigaded with the Undecimani. The latter are not named by Ammianus but were most likely present.

Two Moesian Legions - probably the Pannoniciani and Moesiaci, two senior palatine legions that were later detached from Julian's army for an expedition to Britain.

Regii - This unit may have been either a legion or auxilia as one of each is listed in the *Notitia* under the same name. In the battle they supported the Batavi which could indicate they were an auxilia.

Catafractarii - No specific units are named but Ammianus is clear that cataphracts (heavily armoured cavalry lancers) took part in the battle. There were several such *catafractarii* units raised in Gaul which were probably modelled on the Sarmatian cavalry or recruited from Sarmatian *laeti*.

Equites Sagittarii - Light horse archers. No specific units are named.

Balistarii - Possibly light crossbowmen rather than artillery for the reasons already discussed.

If we assume rough numbers of 5–600 men for cavalry and auxiliary units, and 1,000–1,500 for legions (see Appendices I and II) this accounts for around 11,000 of Julian's 13,000 men. Probably additional numbers were made up by a number of foot archers, maybe a couple more cavalry units and possibly one or two more unnamed auxilia.

The Alamanni took three days to cross the Rhine while Julian remained at Saverne without attempting to prevent them. Most probably he wanted a decisive battle to end the Alamannic threat rather than temporarily stopping a new incursion. Julian either had to engage the enemy in open battle or withdraw to central Gaul and admit defeat.

After rebuffing Alamannic envoys offering terms, Julian marched from Saverne towards Strasbourg. The battlefield has not been definitively identified but most likely it took place near Oberhausbergen to the north-east of Strasbourg. Oberhausbergen is about 32km from Saverne along the old Roman road which is close to the twenty-one Roman miles which Ammianus says Julian marched from Saverne before reaching the Alamannic lines.

The Romans formed up on a gently sloping hill from where they could observe the Germans who were arrayed in dense wedges (*cunei*, singular *cuneus*). These were deep attack columns rather than precise wedge formations. There is a low rise to the west of modern Oberhausbergen after which the Rhine Valley is completely flat. To the north (the Roman left) runs the Musaubach stream which is consistent with Ammianus' description of the battlefield. He states that the Alamanni deployed light infantry in ditches and undergrowth on that flank hoping to ambush the Romans there.

After marching more than twenty miles, Julian proposed fortifying a camp and waiting until the next morning before risking battle so that his men would be fresh. His troops, however, were having none of it. They wanted to engage immediately. 'Clashing their spears against their shields to show their eagerness for battle they begged him [Julian] to lead them against an enemy who was already in sight.'

The Romans deployed in two lines with all their cavalry on the right. The *Cornuti* and *Bracchiati* were in the front line of the infantry while the *Primani* along with the *Batavi* and *Regii* were in the rear line. It is likely that archers were deployed behind the front line to shoot over the heads of the spearmen as was the usual late Roman practice. Julian took a position with an escort of 200 cavalry in the centre and Severus commanded the left wing.

Ammianus claims that the Alammanic infantry demanded that the nobles dismount 'and take their stand with them as they were afraid that in the event of a defeat their leaders would have an easy means of escape and leave their wretched followers in the lurch. When he learned of this Chnodomar at once jumped down from his mount and the rest followed his example'. This is reminiscent of the English Wars of the Roses where the nobles were expected to dismount to share the fate of their lesser followers.

As already discussed, it was fairly common Germanic practice for those who had horses to ride into battle and then dismount to fight on foot and it probably had little to do with a fear that the leaders might abandon their followers. Some of the mounted men left their horses behind to fight on foot but from the descriptions of the combat on the Alamannic left wing it seems that some remained on horseback. Chnodomar commanded the left wing. Serapio, who was a young man, commanded a group of light foot deployed in ambush on the right, while presumably Vestralp and the other leaders held the centre.

As the Romans advanced on the Alamanni, Severus on the left suspected an ambush and held back while the rest of the army moved forwards. The first contact happened on the Roman right when the Alamannic cavalry 'threw themselves upon our squadrons of horse with horrible grinding of their teeth and more that their usual fury'. The Roman cataphracts were thrown back when their commander was wounded and took flight, probably taking other cavalry with them. The Roman infantry on that flank held firm but it took an intervention by Julian himself to hold the line.

Meanwhile the Alamanni foot attacked the front line of the Roman centre. The *Cornuti* and *Bracchiati* took the brunt of the initial assault 'intimidating the enemy by their bearing and putting all their strength into their famous war-cry (*barritus*). This is a shout which they raise when the fight is actually at boiling point; it begins with a low murmur and gradually increases in volume till it resounds like the sea dashing against a cliff'.

The battle swayed back and forth with the Alamanni apparently making headway against the first line, requiring an intervention by the *Regii* and *Batavi* from the second line to stabilize the situation in the centre. At the same time the *Cornuti* and *Bracchiati* moved up to block the advance by the victorious Alamanni on the Roman right.

A band of dismounted Alamannic nobles led their followers in a renewed charge against the Roman centre. They succeeded in breaking through only to be blocked by the *Primani* Legion. The *Primani* held their ground. 'Here our troops were drawn up in close formation and in several ranks. They stood as firm as towers and renewed the battle with increased spirit.' Wave upon wave of Alamanni kept up the pressure but they could not make any headway. 'Fresh hosts took the place of the slain till the fires of the dying stupefied them with fear. Then at last they gave way under the stress of disaster and put all their energy into attempts at flight.'

Hard fighting and the judicious use of reserves won the day for the Romans. As was usual with ancient battles the heavy casualties came when one side turned and ran. So it was that, despite the rout of the Roman cavalry on their right and the slogging match in the centre, the Romans only lost 243 men and four officers. One of the officers killed was Bainobaudes of the *Cornuti* who had led the earlier raid on the Rhine islands, another was Innocentius the cataphract commander. Ammianus says that 6,000 Alamanni bodies were counted on the battlefield and that many others died when they tried to swim back across the Rhine. Chnodomar was captured as he tried to escape and he was sent back to Rome where he later died in captivity.

The Romans were not known for their magnanimity in victory and Julian was no exception. He crossed the Rhine and took the fight to the enemy, burning villages and slaughtering the inhabitants until they were so cowed that they would not consider any more raids into Gaul. This mopping up operation lasted another two years by which time the frontiers had been restored and Julian's reputation was riding high with his troops. By 360 Gaul was safe enough that Julian was able to send the *Batavi*, *Heruli* and two Moesian legions to Britain to help defend the island from the Scots and Picts.

Who knows what would have happened had Julian a few more years to re-establish good stable government in Gaul? Fate and the Persians intervened to turn events on their head. In 360 the Emperor Constantius, who had been campaigning on the Danube against the Sarmatians, decided to march against the Persians to restore the Eastern frontier. He ordered Julian to send the *Celtae*, *Petulantes*, *Batavi*, *Heruli*, and 300 men from each of his other units to join the Persian expedition.

Many of the men in Julian's army had been recruited locally, apparently with the promise that they would not have to fight far from home. Many of them would have been Franks and other barbarians from the Gallic *laeti*. When the orders came to move east the army mutinied and proclaimed Julian Emperor. Ironically Julian himself marched east in 361 taking many of these units with him to confront Constantius. Julian became sole emperor later in the year when Constantius died unexpectedly. He then took up the campaign against the Persians in 363 which ended in disaster.

Many of the victors of Strasbourg would never see their western homes again and Julian himself lost his life in a skirmish.

The Franks and Alamanni were cowed for a time by their defeats at Julian's hands in the 350s and the power of the Alamanni was nearly broken. The Alamanni never again posed a serious threat to Rome, nor did the various Alamannic tribes join together for a joint expedition as they had under Chnodomar. Individual bands, however, continued to make incursions across the Rhine to take advantage of perceived Roman weaknesses. The death of Julian provided the first of such an opportunity.

> Meantime the Barbarians beyond the Rhine, who while Julian lived held the Roman name in terror, and were contented to remain quiet in their own territories, as soon as they heard of his death, immediately marched out of their own country, and prepared for a war with the Romans. Valentinian [the new West Roman Emperor and first of that name] on being informed of this, made a proper disposition of his forces, and placed suitable garrisons in all the towns along the Rhine. (Zosimus)

Zosimus goes on to say that Valentinian's military dispositions were not sufficient to prevent a surprise attack. This probably took place in or around 373 as Zosimus says the attack occurred as the East Roman Emperor Valens was preparing to attack Persia. This Persian war lasted from 373 to 375.

> The emperor Valentinian, who resided beyond the Alps, was attacked by a great and unexpected danger. The Germans [probably Alamanni], recollecting their sufferings under the administration of Julian, as soon as they heard of his death, shook off all fear, and resuming their natural audacity, invaded the nations subject to the Roman Empire. Being met by the Emperor, a severe battle ensued, in which the barbarians were victorious. The Roman army dishonourably fled. Valentinian, however, resolved not to save himself by flight; he therefore bore the event of the battle with apparent composure, until he had discovered those, who by their first beginning to fly had caused the disaster. Having at length by

strict inquiry ascertained that the Batavian troops were guilty, he ordered the whole army to assemble... [Valentinian I] commanded the Batavians to be stripped of their arms, and to be sold to a colony as fugitive slaves. Upon this they all prostrated themselves on the ground, and entreated him not to inflict so disgraceful a punishment on his soldiers, promising in future to behave like men and worthy of the Roman name. He complied with their entreaties, requiring them to prove by their actions the sincerity of their intention. They then rose from the ground, armed themselves, and renewed the combat with such alacrity and resolution, that of an immense number of barbarians very few returned to their own country. Thus terminated the war with the Germans. (Zosimus)

In typical Roman fashion once the war was over the defeated enemies became a potential source of valuable recruits for the army.

Valentinian, having favourably disposed the affairs of Germany, made provisions for the future security of the Celtic nations. With this view he levied among the barbarians near the Rhine and the husbandmen in the countries under the Roman dominion a considerable number of young men. These he incorporated with the legionary soldiers, and brought to so good a state of discipline, that from the sole dread of their military skill, during the period of nine years, the nations beyond the Rhine did not dare to make any attempt upon any of the cities belonging to the Romans. (Zosimus)

It is interesting to note that Zosimus differentiates between 'barbarians near the Rhine' and 'husbandmen in the countries under the Roman dominion'. The latter could be interpreted to mean that Valentinian conducted a levy of provincials but given the context it is more likely that Zosimus is referring to barbarians settled as *laeti* in areas under Roman control, differentiating them from barbarian recruits from across the frontier.

Peace on the Rhine did not last long. Valentinian I died in 375 and Gratian became the new West Roman emperor while Valens still ruled the East. In 376 the Goths crossed the Danube forcing Valens to end his war with Persia to deal with them. He called on Gratian to send troops from the West to help him. In 378, the Lentienses, an Alamannic tribe living near the borders of modern Switzerland, took advantage of the situation. As Gratian transferred troops from the Rhine to the Balkans to assist Valens, the Lentienses moved against Colmar on the Roman side of the Rhine. The Lentienses were one of the tribes which had defeated Arbetio in 354. Possibly the memory of this victory counterbalanced the experience of defeat at Strasbourg three years later.

Now the people of the Alamanni, having by treacherous incursions violated the treaty which had been made with them some time before, began to make attempts upon our frontier. This calamity had the following lamentable beginning:

One of this nation (the Lentienses) who was serving among the guards of the emperor, returned home on some private business. Being a very talkative person, when he was continually asked what was doing in the Imperial palace, he told them that Valens [the East Roman Emperor] had sent for Gratian [the West Roman Emperor] to conduct the campaign in the East. The Lentienses greedily swallowed this intelligence... Being so rapid and active in their movements they assembled in predatory bands. When the Rhine was sufficiently frozen over to be passable, in the month of February, they crossed. (Ammianus Marcellinus)

Gratian recalled the troops he had sent to the East and command of the army was given to Mallobaudes. He was one of the Frankish Roman officers who had supported Silvanus (see section Raiders and Usurpers on page 36) and now held the high office of *Comes Domesticorum* (Count of the Household Troops). Ammianus says that he was a king of the Franks, 'a man of great courage and renown in war.'

A battle was fought near Colmar and Ammianus gives us a brief description of it. This is his last account of events on the Rhine frontier and it is the last detailed report we have of the Rhine tribes in battle for more than a century.

A horrid shout was raised by the enemy, and the trumpeters on our side also gave the signal for battle, upon which a fierce engagement began near Colmar. On both sides numbers fell beneath the blows of arrows and hurled javelins... The multitude of the enemy appeared so countless that our [Roman] soldiers, avoiding a conflict with them on the open field, dispersed as best they could among the different narrow paths overgrown with trees. Afterwards [the Romans] stood their ground firmly and, by the boldness of their carriage and the dazzling splendour of their arms when seen from a distance, made the barbarians fear that the Emperor himself was at hand. They [the Lentienses] suddenly turned their backs, still offering occasional resistance, to leave no chance for safety untried. At last they [the Lentienses] were routed with such slaughter that of their whole number, not above 9,000 escaped. These owed their safety to the thickness of the woods. Among the many bold and gallant men who perished was their king Priarius who had been the principal cause of this ruinous war.

In typical Roman fashion, Gratian then ordered a punitive expedition into the high forested hills of the Black Forest – homeland of the Lentienses.

They [the Lentienses] withdrew with speed to their hills, which were almost inaccessible from the steepness of their precipices, and reaching the most inaccessible rocks by a winding path, they conveyed thither their riches and their families, and prepared to defend them with all their might.

Taking 500 picked men from each legion, the Romans sealed off the escape routes and scaled the hills. The Lentienses held their ground, defeating the troops sent against them. When the Romans resorted to blockade in an attempt to starve them out, the Lentienses withdrew deeper into the Black Forest using their local knowledge to find food and avoid destruction. The Romans kept up the pressure and eventually the Lentienses surrendered.

Having by humble supplication obtained mercy, they furnished a reinforcement of the flower of their youth to be mingled with our recruits, and were permitted to retire in safety to their native land.

The defeats of the Alamanni at Strasbourg and Colmar followed a typical pattern. Emboldened by perceived Roman weaknesses strong leaders such as Chnodomar and Priarius gathered sufficient followers to attempt incursions across the Rhine. As we have only Roman accounts to go on we do not know their motivations. Possibly they were looking to seize some Roman territory for themselves or perhaps simply trying to enrich themselves by sacking Roman towns. Once defeated, punishing Roman counter-attacks into their homelands cowed the tribes into submission and forced them to provide recruits for the Roman army without the benefit of Roman land in exchange. For his part in leading the Romans to victory, Mallobaudes the Frank earned the title of *Alamannicus Maximus*.

Frankish Settlement and Resurgence

By capitulating earlier than the Alamanni, the Frankish tribes fared better in the long run. When the Frankish leaders sued for peace after Julian recaptured Cologne in 356, some of them were given land to settle south of the Lower Rhine in modern Flanders. This group became known as the *Salii* (or Salian Franks). Unlike many of the earlier Frankish *laeti*, the Salian Franks seem to have been settled as *foederati* – tribes which lived under their own laws and provided semi-independent contingents for the Roman army rather than individual recruits. The Salian Franks were the people who would eventually take over Roman Gaul for themselves and give it the modern name of France. It is highly unlikely that anyone in the mid fourth century – Roman or Frank – could ever have imagined the eventual outcome.

Although the Franks were quiet for a while after Julian's campaign, as a new generation of young men came of age they took advantage of yet more Roman civil wars to extend their power and influence. In 382 Magnus Maximus (*Macsen Wledig* of Welsh legend) was proclaimed emperor by his British troops. With the backing of soldiers drawn from Britain and never to return, he defeated Gratian, established his capital at Trier and for six years controlled the West. He was eventually defeated by the East Roman Emperor Theodosius in 388. The Theodosian forces included a sizeable contingent of Goths while Maximus drew on the Alamanni as well as Romano-British and Gallic garrisons. Drawing off troops from

Gaul to fight Theodosius in Italy left the Rhine frontier even weaker than before. In a harbinger of things to come, some Franks took advantage of this to expand their power and influence.

At this time we hear of the earliest named Frankish leaders. These were Genobaud, Marcomer and Sunno. They were probably leaders of those Franks still living on the east bank of the Rhine, known as *Francia Rinensis* in some contemporary accounts. Later they came to be called Ripuarian Franks by historians to distinguish them from the Salian Franks who were already settled inside Imperial territory. Like Chnodomar and the princes of the Alamanni, Genobaud, Marcomer and Sunno were powerful warriors who had amassed enough followers to be noted but did not have any sort of hereditary right of rule like later medieval kings. Quoting the fourth century Roman historian Sulpicius Alexander, Gregory of Tours calls them *Duces* (Dukes). In the late Roman world a dux (plural *duces*) was a military commander of *limitanei* on the frontier. This is probably an apt term for the emerging leaders of the Franks whom the Romans would have regarded as frontier military commanders.

The new generation of Rhineland Franks following these three leaders took to the offensive when Magnus Maximus drew the West Roman army from Gaul to Italy to confront Theodosius. The Salian Franks seem not to have been involved and it is quite possible that many of them marched with Maximus into Italy. Later Arbogast, the Frankish *Magister Militum* of the Western Empire, took offensive action against Marcomer and Sunno (see section under Arbogast, Theodosius, Stilicho and Alaric on page 57).

At that time the Franks burst into the province of Germany under Genobaud, Marcomer, and Sunno, their dukes. Having broken through the frontier they slew most of the people and laid waste the fertile districts... The [Roman] military officers to whom Maximus had entrusted his infant son and the defence of the Gauls, assembled an army and met [the Franks] at Cologne. Now the enemy, laden with plunder after devastating the richest parts of the provinces, had crossed the Rhine, leaving a good many of their men on Roman soil all ready to renew their ravages. An attack upon these turned to the advantage of the Romans, and many Franks perished by the sword near Carbonnière (in the forests of the Ardennes) ...

Quintinus [one of the Roman commanders] crossed the Rhine with his army [at Neuss] and at his second camp from the river he found dwellings abandoned by their [Frankish] occupants and great villages deserted. For the Franks pretended to be afraid and retired into the more remote tracts, where they built an *abattis* (rough barricades) on the edge of the woods. And so the cowardly Roman soldiers burned all the dwellings, thinking that to rage against them was the winning of victory, and they passed a wakeful night under the burden of their arms.

At the first glimmer of dawn they entered the wooded country under Quintinus as commander of the battle, and wandered in safety until nearly midday, entangling themselves in the winding paths. At last, when they found everything solidly shut up by great fences, they struggled to make their exit into the marshy fields which were adjacent to the woods. Then the enemy appeared here and there, and sheltered by trunks of trees or standing on the *abattis* as if on the summit of towers, they sent as if from engines a shower of arrows poisoned by the juices of herbs, so that sure death followed even superficial wounds inflicted in places that were not mortal.

Later the [Roman] army was surrounded by the enemy in greater number, and [the Roman army] eagerly rushed into the open places which the Franks had left unoccupied. The horsemen were the first to plunge into the morasses, and the bodies of men and animals fell indiscriminately together as they were overwhelmed by their own confusion. The foot soldiers also who had escaped the hoofs of the horses were impeded by the mud, and extricated themselves with difficulty, and hid again in panic in the woods from which they had struggled before. And so the ranks were thrown into disorder and the legions cut in pieces. Heraclius, tribune of the *Jovinianii* [an elite Legion], and nearly all the officers were slain, when night and the lurking places of the woods offered a safe escape to a few. (Gregory of Tours quoting Sulpicius Alexander)

This action is interesting in that it is the first detailed contemporary account we have of the Franks in combat. It was rare that a Germanic army could stand up to the better trained, organized and disciplined

Romans in open battle. Chnodomar and the Alamanni had learned that to
their cost. Following a tried and tested route the Franks lured the Romans
on to ground of their choosing and then used ambush and terrain to their
advantage. This was how the early Germans had defeated the Romans
in the Teutoburger Forest in the early first century. In 351, the Goths
had destroyed a Roman army at Abritus and killed the Emperor Decius.
This happened when the Romans were lured into difficult marshy terrain
and found themselves helpless to defend themselves against Gothic
arrows backed up by charges from warriors on foot who depended less
on maintaining organized ranks and files than on individual fighting
prowess.

Genobaud, Marcomer, and Sunno's Franks defeated Quintinus by
following a proven way of taking on the Romans and winning. The
reference to 'showers of arrows' is interesting as it is generally assumed
that the western Germanic tribes did really take to archery. Compared
to the sixth century East Romans who placed a very high reliance on
archery it is true to say that the Franks did not do the same, yet it is clear
that missile weapons were part of the Frankish arsenal. We shall look at
this in more detail in Chapter 10.

The Romans valued Frankish contingents in their armies as hand-to-
hand fighters on foot so probably most, or maybe all, Frankish *foederati*
served as such. As Genobaud, Marcomer, and Sunno's men were
defending their homes it is likely that every able-bodied man took part in
the action from wealthy, well-equipped warriors through to lesser men
who fought as best they could. Some of the latter may have formed rear
ranks in a shield-wall while others used bows and arrows from behind
the *abattis* to break up the formations of Romans struggling through
the purpose-made gaps. It may also have been the case that those men
who might normally have fought hand-to-hand in the front ranks took
up bows and arrows as a temporary expedient, later moving into close
combat with the disordered Romans.

Archaeologists have found arrowheads in many western Germanic
graves. Some historians have concluded that these represented hunting
weapons rather than military ones. On the other hand an analysis of
Alamannic graves by Rainer Christlein shows that wealthy men were
buried with hand-to-hand weapons while poorer ones had arrows and

a scramasax (a short single edged sword or long knife) rather than long swords, spears and shields. His conclusion is that those men not of the warrior elite fought as archers while their betters were primarily hand-to-hand fighters.

The use of poisoned arrows by the Franks in this engagement is not attested elsewhere and is impossible to prove or disprove by archaeology. It could well have been made up. As a battlefield tactic poisoned arrows would give no advantage. Archery was most effective in breaking up a formation so it could be more easily destroyed. It did not really matter if an enemy was killed or disabled, what mattered was that he could no longer fight. In modern times it is said that a wounded enemy is better than a dead one as he is not only taken out of the fight but his comrades will try to save him. I am inclined, therefore, to disregard Sulpicius Alexander's account 'of arrows poisoned by the juices of herbs'.

Despite the many Roman descriptions of the Germanic tribes as headstrong and lacking tactical finesse, the Franks and others were just as capable as the Romans in coming up with a good plan and executing it to their advantage as long as the leaders were able to control their followers. This appears to have been what Genobaud, Marcomer, and Sunno were able to do. Setting up barricades to funnel the enemy through gaps which are covered by long-ranged weapons is a relatively sophisticated tactic. It is still used in modern warfare when a minefield might be obviously laid, not so much as to kill those trying to cross it but rather to funnel the enemy through a gap which is well covered by fire.

Arbogast, Theodosius, Stilicho and Alaric

In 388 Magnus Maximus was defeated by the East Roman Emperor Theodosius at Aquileia between modern Venice and Trieste. The political situation in the Western Empire remained precarious, however. Marcomer, and Sunno's Franks remained undefeated although we no longer hear of Genobaud. At this time Arbogast, nephew of the Frank Richomer who had served Rome against the Goths, had risen to the highest military rank in the West Roman Empire.

We would be wrong in assuming that with the Frank Arbogast achieving supreme military command in the West Roman Empire that all of the

Franks gave him their loyal support. Arbogast was probably descended from the earlier Frankish *laeti* and had little in common with those Franks across the Rhine. Just as factional politics caused the Romans to fight amongst themselves as much or more than against barbarian invaders, tribal hatreds, old feuds and rivalry for power meant that the Franks never acted as a cohesive whole until Clovis stamped his authority over them many years later (see Chapter 7). So it was that Sunno and Marcomer were seen by the Romanized Arbogast as enemies rather than as compatriots. Quoting Sulpicius Alexander again, Gregory of Tours tells us:

> Arbogast pursued with heathenish hate the princes of the Franks, Sunno and Marcomer, and hastened to Cologne in the depth of winter, since he knew that all the retreats of Francia could be safely penetrated and ravaged with fire when the woods, left bare and dry by the fall of the leaves, could not conceal men lying in ambush. And so he gathered an army and crossed the Rhine, and devastated the country of the Brictori, near the bank, and also the district which the Chamavi inhabit, and no one met him any where, except that a few of the Ampsivarii and Chatti appeared with Duke Marcomer on the ridges of distant hills.

Later we are told that 'The tyrant Eugenius undertook a military expedition, and hastened to the Rhine to renew in the customary way the old alliances with the kings of the Alamanni and the Franks and to threaten the barbarian nations at that time with a great army.' This implies that some sort of negotiated settlement was eventually reached with the hostile Franks beyond the Rhine. This seems to have been achieved in the usual Roman manner – a strong show of force backed up with gifts and promises of lucrative employment in the Roman army.

Eugenius was Arbogast's puppet emperor whom he had set on the throne in 392 when the youthful Western Emperor Valentinian II attempted to dismiss Arbogast. According to Sulpicius Alexander (again quoted by Gregory of Tours), 'The Emperor Valentinian was shut up in his palace at Vienne and almost reduced to the status of private citizen... Military command was given over to the Frankish allies, and even the civil offices fell under the control of Arbogast's faction.' Valentinian then died in rather dubious circumstances leaving Eugenius and Arbogast in control of the Western Empire. The Eastern Emperor Theodosius had already shown his tendency to intervene in the West whenever a usurper rose up. Therefore Eugenius and Arbogast needed allies not enemies on the Rhine frontier. Patching up their quarrel with the Ripuarian Franks and securing the support of the Alamanni would have been a top priority.

Theodosius was indeed perturbed by Arbogast's *coup d'état* on several accounts. The greatest perhaps was that Arbogast and Eugenius were pagans and there were signs that they might be encouraging a pagan revival. The Christian Theodosius therefore decided that he had to intervene in the West once again to sort things out. Together with Goths from the Balkans and reinforcements from Syria, Theodosius and his general Stilicho marched west in September 394 to defeat Arbogast in a two-day battle that took place in a mountain pass in modern Slovenia through which the river Frigidus flowed (modern Vipava). Many of Arbogast's troops were Franks and Alamanni, both *laeti* and semi-independent allied contingents.

Arbogast's army blocked the pass forcing Theodosius to launch a frontal assault. He used the Goths to do this and they suffered very heavy casualties without achieving any success. Theodosius unexpectedly won the battle on the second day aided by the defection of some of Arbogast's men and a 'divine wind' blowing into the face of the West Roman army. Eugenius was captured and executed while Arbogast committed suicide.

After the Battle of Frigidus, Stilicho became guardian of Theodosius' 9-year-old son Honorius who was proclaimed West Roman Emperor. When Theodosius died in 395 his eldest son, Arcadius, ascended to the Eastern throne. With minors on both thrones Stilicho held supreme military power. His only real rival was Alaric, one of the leaders of Theodosius' Gothic allies. Seeking a better deal for himself and his followers Alaric rebelled, ravaging the Balkans and Greece in an attempt to secure an official appointment from the youthful Arcadius in the East. The full story of Alaric and Stilicho is told in the previous book in this series – *The Goths*.

Theodosius' Gothic allies suffered very heavy casualties at Frigidus and they were on the winning side. Casualties amongst Arbogast's Franks and Alamanni must have been even worse. In normal circumstances they might have expected reprisals from Stilicho as the new power behind the western throne sought to consolidate his power. This did not happen.

As the fifth century dawned Stilicho had his gaze firmly fixed on Alaric in the Balkans and the young East Roman Emperor Arcadius in Constantinople. The Rhine frontier seemed immaterial to the more important and inevitable struggle to follow. Many of the troops previously stationed in Britain and Gaul had been drawn off, first to support Maximus and then to provide manpower for Arbogast and Eugenius. When Alaric invaded Italy in 401 Stilicho withdrew even more troops from the Rhine to defend Italy from Alaric's Goths. He needed the Franks to hold the Rhine for him while he dealt with Alaric so he cut a deal with them.

As the regular Roman garrisons along the Rhine were withdrawn the settlements of Frank, Alamannic and Sarmatian *laeti* took their place. They were supplemented by semi-independent *foederati* such as the Salian Franks whose homeland was on the Roman side of the Rhine in modern Flanders. These people now had as much at stake in defending the Rhine frontier since any new invaders threatened their lands as much as that of the native inhabitants. Stilicho also made treaties with the Ripuarian Franks beyond the frontier, paying and equipping them to hold the east bank of the Rhine on behalf of the Empire.

Chapter 4

Defending the Rhine

The Huns

While the Imperial Roman authorities were fighting it out in Gaul with the Franks, Alamanni, Bacaudae and various usurpers in the mid fourth century, a new deadly threat was emerging in the East. 'Reports spread widely among the [barbarians], that a race of men hitherto unknown had now arisen from a hidden nook of the earth, like a tempest of snows from the high mountains, seizing or destroying everything in its way.' (Ammianus Marcellinus)

These 'hitherto unknown' people were the Huns – a nomadic Asiatic people who were living out on the Eurasian steppe north of the Black Sea. At some point, between 350 and 370, they started moving westward. We do not know why they did this but their westward expansion had a domino effect on the other tribes beyond the Roman frontiers. Some were conquered and absorbed by the Huns, others moved further west looking for new lands. Like water building up behind an inadequate dam, a huge conglomeration of displaced Germanic peoples flooded into the Roman Empire from the late fourth to the early fifth century.

At first the Franks and Alamanni on the Rhine were relatively untroubled by these events thousands of miles to the East. In the 370s, the Huns moved into territory occupied by the Alans (a nomadic people related to the Sarmatians) and Goths (settled Germans) north of the Black Sea. Some were absorbed by the Huns while others fled West to the Lower Danube frontier of the East Roman Empire. Gothic refugees begged for asylum and the Romans granted it as they saw the Goths as a valuable source of recruits for the army. The unscrupulous behaviour of local Roman officials, combined with the closing of the frontier to new arrivals, sparked off a rebellion. The end result was the famous destruction of the East Roman army and the death of the Emperor Valens at the Battle of Adrianople in 378, the full story of which is told in the previous book in this series – *The Goths*.

This was the same year that the Lentienses crossed the Rhine against Colmar (see previous chapter). Their attack had been sparked off when the West Roman Emperor Gratian drew troops from the Rhine to reinforce Valens against the Goths. Over the following decades this pattern would be repeated. Successive Roman emperors and warlords stripped troops from the Rhine to deal with other threats to Italy or the East.

At some point at the end of the fourth century the Huns moved westward again. They moved on to the Hungarian Plain and sent a new wave of Germanic refugees up against the Roman frontiers. As the Huns migrated into central Europe, the first wave of these newly displaced Germans to break over the Roman frontier was led by Radagasius, a Goth, who led his followers into Italy in 405. The composition of Radagasius' force is not known but it was probably a coalition of various Germanic peoples. It included women and children as well as warriors, so it was a migration rather than a raiding force. The army was large enough to require Stilicho to call on thirty units of the Italian field army as well as Hun and Alan auxiliaries to oppose Radagaisus. He also withdrew yet more troops from the Rhine frontier to bolster Italy's defences in order to gather something in the region of 20–25,000 men to engage Radagaisus.

According to the *Notitia Dignitatum* the Italian field army should have contained seven cavalry and thirty-seven infantry units at the end of the fourth century with another twelve cavalry and forty-eight infantry units in the Gallic field army (see Appendices I and II). These were in addition to the border troops stationed along the frontiers. Yet it took Stilicho a great deal of time and effort to gather the thirty units needed to oppose Radagasius, leaving the invaders plenty of time to ravage northern Italy while the Romans marshalled their forces. As far as we know, few Franks were called on to bolster Stilicho's army. Although some regular units of mainly Frankish origin may have been withdrawn from Gaul, it is most probable that Stilicho relied on the Franks to hold the Rhine frontier in place of the Roman troops who were transferred to Italy.

In the end Stilicho decisively defeated Radagaisus near Florence on 23 August 406, incorporating 12,000 of the survivors into his army. Then he fixed his attention firmly on the East oblivious, or unaware, of a new storm gathering to the north and west. In 406 a series of revolts took place in Britain with the British army proclaiming Marcus and Gratian in quick succession as emperor before assassinating their candidates when they did not seem pliant enough. Towards the end of 406 the British army settled on a soldier with the suitably Imperial name of Constantine (Constantine III) who managed to retain their approval. He then crossed the channel to establish himself in northern Gaul.

Meanwhile Stilicho became embroiled in a dispute with Constantinople over control of the Balkans. Parts of the Balkan provinces had previously belonged to the Western Empire but had been transferred to the East several years earlier. Stilicho wanted them back as they were a prime recruiting ground for soldiers. Additionally, it would give him territory he could offer Alaric in order to finally come to a lasting settlement with his troublesome Goths.

The Vandals

The Goths and Alans were not the only barbarians displaced by the Huns. As Radagaisus burst over the Alpine passes into Italy, large numbers of Germanic Vandals and Suebi together with many non-Germanic Alans were moving westward towards the Rhine.

Unsurprisingly the arrival of the Vandals and their allies on the east bank of the Rhine led to conflict as the Franks and Alamanni attempted to close their borders. The last thing they wanted was a new group of migrants knocking on their door for a piece of their hard-won territories. There were probably many small engagements as groups of new arrivals tried their luck only to be repulsed. Most of these have gone unrecorded but at some point there was a major battle between the Vandals and the Ripuarian Franks. Fragments of the contemporary writer Renatus Profuturus Frigeridus, preserved by Gregory of Tours, say that the Vandals were on the brink of a catastrophic defeat at the hands of the Franks. Their King Godegisel was killed in the fighting but at the last minute the Vandals were saved by the timely intervention of a force of Alans under Respendial who 'turned the army of his people from the Rhine, since the Vandals were getting the worse of the war with the Franks, having lost their king Godegisel, and about 20,000 of the army, and all the Vandals would have been exterminated if the army of the Alans had not come to their aid in time'.

This battle probably took place sometime in the summer of 406 and it allowed the Vandals and their Suebi and Alan allies to move into Ripuarian Frankish territory on the Middle Rhine. Although they had won a path to the Roman frontier the new migrants must have been in a fairly desperate state. Unable to grow or harvest crops and with no supply bases to call on, it would have been a monumental task to keep their people and livestock alive. If they managed to move up to the Rhine in the autumn of 406 the Vandals may have been able to take in some of the crops the Franks had harvested but this would at best only keep starvation at bay for a few months.

In the pre-industrial age no sensible army moved in winter. Without the benefit of preserved food, mass production and mechanized transport, any movement of large groups in winter would inevitably lead to utter disaster. Yet on the last day of 406 a huge horde of Vandals, Suebi and Alans crossed the Rhine to enter Roman Gaul. What on earth persuaded them to do this when all sensible armies would have been in winter quarters awaiting the onset of the spring campaigning season?

The traditional view is that the winter was so cold that the Rhine froze over giving the invaders the possibility to cross on a wide front. Although the Rhine remains open all year round in present times, it has frozen over in the past and it is not impossible that it froze in the winter of 406/7. Ammianus recorded that the Lentienses crossed the frozen Rhine in February 378. If the river had again frozen over in 406/7, whether the ice would have been thick enough for tens of thousands of people with their wagons and baggage to cross is another matter. There are no contemporary accounts to support the idea of a crossing on ice, despite the fact that it has become a relatively accepted popular image.

The Vandals and their allies were not a sensible army. They were desperate people on the move seeking a new homeland. Near starvation, their only hope of survival was to cross into Roman territory and seize the grain stores of the cities over the Rhine. Waiting on the east bank over winter with no food supplies would have resulted in catastrophe. Whether or not the Rhine froze would have been immaterial. There were bridges they could use and makeshift boats and rafts could have ferried them across the river.

As far as we can tell, the only serious resistance to the crossing of the Rhine by the Vandals, Suebi and Alans came from the Franks. Once they had been defeated, thanks to the timely intervention of the Alans as quoted above, Gaul was nearly defenceless.

In order to understand how easily the Vandals, Alans and Suebi crossed the Rhine once they had defeated the Franks on the east bank we need to appreciate the Roman system of defence as previously described in Chapter 2. The frontiers were defended by *limitanei* (soldiers defending the frontier fortifications) or *riparenses* (soldiers defending the rivers). These men occupied strongpoints along the frontiers and patrolled the borders. Deployed in relatively small detachments they were able to deter or intervene to deal with small-scale incursions but were neither expected nor able to deal with a major invasion. To think of them in modern terms they were more like a border force or home guard than an army capable of offensive action, even though many of the units could trace their heritage back to the famed legions of previous centuries. Backing them up, in the Western Empire, there were two main field armies, one was based in Italy and the other in Gaul. Each of these field armies were, on paper, about 20–30,000 strong. It was their job to intervene once the frontiers had been breached to defeat the invaders and restore order.

This was the theoretical principle of defence but in reality the field armies in the fifth century were more occupied supporting various political interests than they were in defending the Empire from external threats. Stilicho had the support of the Italian field army but not that of Gaul. When Constantine III crossed over from Britain in early 407 much of the Gallic field army went over to him. Many other units had been drawn off to Italy to fight against Radagaisus and Alaric.

The Gallic field army was commanded by the *Magister Equitum intra Gallias* who in theory had 12 cavalry and 48 infantry units at his disposal with unit strengths probably averaging out at roughly 500 men each. We have already seen how Stilicho struggled to field an army of thirty units to fight Radagasius and so we should not assume that the *Magister Equitum's* entire force could be quickly and easily deployed. Furthermore, many of these units would have been severely weakened after their defeats in the civil wars and may well not have been anything like at full strength.

The defence of the Middle Rhine, where the Vandals crossed, fell to the *Dux Mogontiacensis* (Duke of Mainz). According to the *Notitia Dignitatum* he had eleven prefects under his command. The units commanded by these prefects and their home stations are recorded as:

Praefectus militum Pacensium, at Saletio (Selz)
Praefectus militum Menapiorum, at Tabernis (Saverne)
Praefectus militum Anderetianorum, at Vico Iulio (Germersheim)
Praefectus militum Vindicum, at Nemetis (Speyer)
Praefectus militum Martensium, at Alta Ripa (Altrip)
Praefectus militum Secundae Flaviae, at Vangiones (Worms)
Praefectus militum Armigerorum, at Mogontiacum (Mainz)
Praefectus militum Bingensium, at Bingio (Bingen)
Praefectus militum Balistariorum, at Bodobrica (Boppard)
Praefectus militum Defensorum, at Confluentes (Koblenz)
Praefectus militum Acincensium, at Antonaco (Andernach)

Some of these units are also listed under the Gallic field army which may indicate that they had been pulled back from the Rhine frontier. Alternatively it could also mean that a few units of the field army such as the *Menapi* and *Armigeri* (legions assigned to the Gallic field army – see Appendix I) had been sent to reinforce the frontier. As the trend had been to strip the frontiers to bolster the field armies it seems that the first possibility is the most likely.

These units probably only contained a few hundred men each. While they could hold the walls of a fortified strongpoint and mount patrols, there could never have been any possibility that these dispersed garrisons could block a crossing of the frontier by many thousand warriors, even if the latter were weakened by hunger and bogged down with their families and chattels. At best all these men could hope for would be to hold out behind their fortifications while the barbarians moved past to be dealt with by the field army at a later date.

There was also a Rhine fleet, the *Classis Germanica*, which patrolled the river and was an integral part of the Roman defensive system. We do not know how large it was but Ammianus Marcellinus tells us that a squadron of forty ships was used against the Alamanni in 359. If the

Rhine had been frozen or partially frozen then it would have prevented any ships from intercepting the invaders. The *Classis Germanica* seems to have disappeared after the Vandal invasion as there is no mention of it in the *Notitia Dignitatum*.

So if the *Dux Mogontiacensis* and his border force were never expected to hold back a major invasion what did the Gallic field army do? Apparently very little.

In the fourth century the Gallic capital had been at Trier on the Rhine but by the fifth century it had moved to Arles at the mouth of the Rhône in the south. The Rhine had been abandoned psychologically if not yet in reality. It was held more through treaties with the Franks and barbarian settlements rather than strong garrisons of Roman soldiers. From Arles the focus of the Imperial Gallic authorities was far more towards Italy and the Mediterranean than to the far away northern frontier.

An explanation for the apparent inaction by the Gallic army rests in the convoluted Imperial politics of the time. On paper the Gallic army should have had enough men to deal with the barbarian incursion across the Rhine just as it had in the fourth century. However, as the Vandals and their allies were crossing into Gaul from Germany so too was Constantine III crossing from Britain. Unloved and run-down by Stilicho, much of the Gallic army threw in its lot with Constantine and their main worry was to hold their own against the Imperial authorities with the barbarian incursion a secondary concern. Most of the military might of the Western Empire resided under Stilicho's command in Italy. He was about to embark on a war with the Eastern Empire over control of Illyricum. So what did he do when he learned that the barbarians were overrunning Gaul and that Constantine III was doing his best to contain them?

Naturally he did what any late Roman potentate would do. He sent an army to Gaul to destroy Constantine. A usurper was after all a far greater threat to Stilicho's power than a mere barbarian invasion. Stilicho's army, led by the Goth Sarus, was defeated leaving Constantine in control of Britain and Gaul with Spain also recognizing his authority. So it was that rather than concentrating their forces to defeat a foreign invader, the Romans fought amongst themselves and left Gaul open to the Vandals and their allies. Many Franks probably sided with Constantine to defend their holdings against Sarus as well as against the Vandals, Alans and Suebi.

A Funeral Pyre

In this age of Twitter, we could be forgiven for thinking that we invented the art of the short sound bite in modern times. However the ancient Romans were just as happy as we are to condense complex ideas to 140 characters or less. So it is that the Gallo–Roman Bishop Orientus gives us a wonderful line that encapsulates the impact of the Vandal migration: 'All Gaul was filled with the smoke of a single funeral pyre.' Deconstructing exactly what happened to create this 'funeral pyre' is difficult if not impossible to discern.

In all likelihood, the Vandals, Suebi and Alans crossed the Rhine on a fairly wide front with Mainz as their main crossing point. It is the first town mentioned by St Jerome (see quote below) and there was a good Roman bridge over the river at this point, the remains of which can still be seen today. Mainz was near the southernmost boundary of Ripuarian Frankish territory after which there was a stretch of river under contention. Further south the Alamanni held sway while the Burgundians were pushing into the buffer zone between them. After defeating the Franks in the summer of 406 the Vandals and their allies would naturally have moved into the contested border regions. As winter set in, bringing the prospect of starvation, they would have been well aware that Roman Mainz would have been well stocked with provisions.

Mainz possibly fell without a fight, the garrison of the *Praefectus militum Armigerorum* either fleeing or having already been withdrawn before the crossing took place. After capturing Mainz the Vandals would have been able to supply themselves and contemplate moving on beyond the frontier where the towns had no garrisons at all. St Jerome lists the towns that fell to the barbarians in an evocative letter written in 409 in which he warns of the coming of the Antichrist:

Savage tribes in countless numbers have overrun all parts of Gaul. The whole country between the Alps and the Pyrenees, between the Rhine and the Ocean, has been laid waste by hordes of Quadi,

Vandals, Sarmatians, Alans, Gepids, Heruls, Saxons, Burgundians, Alamanni and – alas for the commonweal – even hostile Pannonians.

The once noble city of Mainz has been captured and destroyed. In its church many thousands have been massacred. The people of Worms after standing a long siege have been extirpated. The powerful city of Rheims, the Ambiani, the Altrebatae [Amiens and Arras], the Belgians on the skirts of the world, Tournai, Spires, and Strasbourg have fallen to the Germans: while the provinces of Aquitaine and of the Nine Nations, of Lyons and of Narbonne are with the exception of a few cities one universal scene of desolation. And those which the sword spares without, famine ravages within. I cannot speak without tears of Toulouse which has been kept from failing hitherto by the merits of its reverend bishop Exuperius.

Even the Spains are on the brink of ruin and tremble daily as they recall the invasion of the Cimbri; and, while others suffer misfortunes once in actual fact, they suffer them continually in anticipation.

In most cases there seems to have been little or no opposition apart from the siege of Worms which may have been undertaken by Burgundians rather than Vandals, Suebi or Alans. We need to view the list of towns with a pinch of salt. We mostly have the writings of early Christian bishops to go on and the stories that survive often mix fact and legend. For example, Bishop Nicasius of Reims was allegedly killed by the Vandals and the city pillaged. However, another version of the story has Nicasius being killed by the Huns half a century later and yet another has him dying of smallpox. One thing is quite clear and that is that much of Gaul fell to the ravages of the new invaders in the aftermath of the Rhine crossing.

Like migrants risking all to cross the Mediterranean today in order to get into Europe, the Vandals, Alans and Suebi were desperate, impoverished and seeking a better life for themselves and their families. The very fact that they made their move in the depths of midwinter shows just how desperate they were. Each Roman town they took gave them enough supplies for a brief period and then they would have to move on again, probably splitting up into small bands to range over a wide swathe of territory.

Later, in 451 when the Huns moved into Gaul, many of the Gallic towns closed their gates and resisted the onslaught. Then Aetius, the most important man in the Roman Empire at the time, saw Gaul as his power base. In 407 Stilicho cared little for Gaul and the inhabitants felt cut off and excluded from Imperial power. As the Vandals approached their towns the Romans inside the walls probably knew that the Imperial armies were unlikely to come to their rescue and so opening their gates may have been seen as the lesser of evils. Many fled and joined the Bacaudae.

Jerome says that Strasbourg fell to the barbarians. This town lies well to the south of Mainz and it is opposite the Alamannic heartland which the Vandals and their allies seemed to have bypassed. The modern German-speaking inhabitants of Alsace, of which Strasbourg is the most important city, are the descendants of the ancient Alamanni who expanded their territory to include both sides of the Upper Rhine in the late fourth and early fifth centuries.

It is possible that the migrating Suebi crossed the Rhine further south near Strasbourg in league with their Alamannic cousins. Then the Alamanni, like the Burgundians at Worms, took advantage of the general confusion to take over Strasbourg and all of the Upper Rhine Valley, while the Suebi moved on. It could also be that the Suebi bypassed Alamannic territory to the north to cross the Rhine near Mainz together with the Alans and Vandals. The new migrants had already suffered a near defeat at the hands of the Franks (quoted above) and it is unlikely that they would have wanted to take on the Alamanni as well in their attempt to reach the Rhine.

The Suebi and Alamanni were closely related and some of the early Suebic clans described by Tacitus ended up forming the Alamanni while others retained a separate identity. Their modern descendants live together in the German state of Baden-Würtemburg, the Swabians in Würtemburg and the Alamanni in Baden as well as Alsace and parts of Switzerland. To an outsider they may seem more or less the same and it was no different in ancient times. Gregory of Tours mixes up the Suebi and Alamanni in his brief description of the migration: 'The Vandals left their own country and burst into the Gauls under King Gunderic. And when the Gauls had been thoroughly laid waste they made for the Spains. The Suebi, that is, Alamanni, following them, seized Galicia.' On another occasion Gregory mixes up the Alamanni and Alans. That a near contemporary was not clear on who was whom gives some idea of the utter confusion at the time of this migration.

The *Notitia Dignitatum* has a section for a *Comes Argentoratensis*, (Count of Strasbourg) but assigns him no troops, no officials and no towns. In the late fourth century Strasbourg and the Upper Rhine into northern Switzerland, was held by the *Legio VIII Augusta Pia Fedelis Constans*. This is probably the same unit named in the *Notitia* as the *Octavani* which was part to the Italian field army. Maybe this was one of the units withdrawn by Stilicho to help him against Radagasius leaving Strasbourg open for the Alamanni to take. As Stilicho concluded a number of treaties with the Alamanni as well as the Franks to hold the Rhine for him, then it is also possible that Strasbourg was part of the deal.

It is interesting that Jerome mentions Saxons in his list of the Germanic barbarians who overran Gaul in 406–7. We tend to think only of the Saxons in relation to their raids and eventual settlement of Britain. Britain was not the only place to feel the effect of Saxon seaborne raids launched from the coasts of modern northern Germany and Denmark. Saxon raiders had been active in the North Sea and English Channel for several years before 407. The *Notitia Dignitatum* lists a command of the *Comes Litoris Saxonici per Britanniam* (Count of the Saxon Shore of Britain) who defended the east coast of Britain against them. Several bands of seaborne Saxons also penetrated the rivers of western France and some established settlements there. Jerome was describing the general state of Gaul at the time of the Vandal crossing of the Rhine and it would seem that many other Germanic peoples decided to take advantage of Roman Gaul's weakness to seize bits of it for themselves.

Going back to Jerome's list of invaders, the Sarmatians and Alans were probably one and the same. There may have been some Heruls and Gepids swept up in the Vandal migration but as both these East German tribes remained well beyond the frontier for another century his inclusion of them is either an exaggeration or refers to smaller bands that may have decided to move into Gaul while the bulk of their people remained behind. This leaves the 'Pannonians'. Pannonia is the region south of the Danube, before the bend, that includes parts of modern Austria, Hungary and Slovenia. This was Roman territory and as Jerome's lamentation implies, some of the Roman inhabitants of this oft ravaged region decided to throw in their lot with the migrants as a better option than remaining loyal to the Empire which had failed to protect them. In 405 Radagasius and his horde crossed through Pannonia on their way to Italy. The Pannonian peasants would have taken the brunt of these invasions and their livelihoods destroyed.

As Roman power receded the Imperial authorities were hard-pressed to uphold the interests of the aristocracy let alone protect the poorer elements of society. This led to the endemic Bacaudae uprisings previously described. Other hard-pressed Roman provincials probably decided that they would be better off joining up with the invaders rather than passively accepting their depredations. When the Gothic refugees took up arms against Rome in 376 they were certainly joined by disaffected Romans and the same was probably the case in 406/7. If so the Pannonians mentioned by Jerome may have been provincial Romans who had thrown their lot in with the invaders.

Constantine III

As far as we can tell, from 407 to 409, the Vandal/Alan/Suebi invaders ravaged much of northern Gaul. They do not seem to have stayed long in any one place. Most likely they split up into relatively small bands taking undefended towns and ravaging the countryside to feed their followers. The Burgundians took and held Worms as did the Alamanni with Strasbourg.

What then of the Franks? It would seem as though the Ripuarians held true to their agreement with Stilicho to defend the frontier from the new invaders. After a near victory over the Vandals in which they killed the Vandal king they were defeated by a timely intervention by the Alans. The Salian Franks who occupied lands on both sides of the Lower Rhine in modern Flanders must also have been troubled by the Vandal migration as would the various settlements of *laeti*.

If Jerome is correct in saying that Amiens, Arras and Tournai fell to the Vandals then these cities were under the influence, if not direct control, of either Salian Franks or settlements of *laeti*. We know nothing about how these cities fell to the Vandals but it is hard to imagine that the

Franks simply sat aside and let it happen. Even if they were tempted to ignore their agreements with Rome they were unlikely to passively cede their hard-won territory to a group of impoverished migrants. We can only imagine the various skirmishes and sieges which would have pitted Franks, acting in their own interests as well as in the name of Rome, defending their patch against the Vandals, Alans and Suebi. Possibly there was a degree of collusion with some Franks agreeing to supply the invaders if they moved on and it is also possible that some ambitious young Franks joined up with the Vandals to seek new adventures. We have no evidence one way or the other to know what really happened.

What we do know is that Stilicho was otherwise occupied when the Vandals, Alans and Suebi moved into Gaul. It fell to Constantine III to restore some semblance of order when he crossed from Britain into Gaul in 407. Zosimus recounts his actions:

The Vandals, uniting with the Alans and the Suebi, crossed (the Rhine), and plundered the countries beyond the Alps. Having there occasioned great slaughter they likewise became so formidable even to the armies in Britain, that they were compelled, through fear of their proceeding as far as that country, to choose several usurpers, as Marcus, Gratian, and after them Constantine.

A furious engagement ensued between them in which the Romans gained the victory, and killed most of the barbarians. Yet by not pursuing those who fled, by which means they might have put to death every man, they gave them opportunity to rally, and by collecting an additional number of barbarians, to assume once more a fighting posture. For this cause, Constantine placed guards in these places, that those tribes should not have so free access into Gaul. He likewise secured the Rhine, which had been neglected since the time of the Emperor Julian.

Having thus arranged affairs throughout all Gaul, he decorated his eldest son, Constans, with the habit of a Caesar, and sent him into Spain. For he wished to obtain the absolute sovereignty of that country, not only through the desire of enlarging his own dominions, but of diminishing the power of the relations of Honorius (who were of Spanish origin).

The British field army at this time was not large, probably no more than 4–6000 men. However most of the Gallic army, which was probably dispersed over several towns, came over to Constantine although for a time Arles remained loyal to Stilicho and the Emperor Honorius. It is most probable that the majority of the Frankish settlers living in Roman Gaul joined Constantine and fought alongside him. If we accept Zosimus' account, Constantine III engaged the Vandals in battle, defeated them, but failed to destroy them. Given a free hand perhaps Constantine could have finished the job but he had to turn his attention south to deal with the army Stilicho had sent against him under the Goth Sarus.

Constantine defeated Sarus' army, probably with the aid of many Franks. Zosimus' account leads us to believe that the Vandal coalition was licking its wounds in northern parts of Gaul leaving Constantine to turn his attention to Spain. Unfortunately for him Gerontius, one of his generals whom he had sent to Spain, took exception to the appointment of a rival and rose up in revolt. With Constantine's attention thus turned towards Spain and Italy the Vandals were able to break loose from the frontier regions where they had been previously constrained.

> The greater part of his [Constantine's] army being in Spain, the barbarians beyond the Rhine made such unbounded incursions over every province, as to reduce not only the Britons, but some of the other Celtic nations also, to the necessity of revolting from the Empire and living no longer under the Roman laws but as they themselves pleased. The Britons therefore took up arms, and incurred many dangerous enterprises for their own protection [against the Saxons], until they had freed their cities from the barbarians who besieged them. In a similar manner, the whole of Armorica, with other provinces of Gaul, delivered themselves by the same means; expelling the Roman magistrates and erecting a government, such as they pleased, of their own. (Zosimus)

Here we have a story not only of barbarian depredations but more interestingly another story of local inhabitants taking matters into their own hands in despair of official protection. The last remnants of the British field army left Britain with Constantine and the inhabitants had no choice but to look to their own interests without any prospect of help from the authorities whether these were in Italy or Gaul. Armorica (roughly modern Brittany and parts of Normandy) became a centre of the Bacaudae who defied Imperial control for decades.

Picking up Zosimus' narrative we learn that:

> Thus happened this revolt or defection of Britain and the Celtic nations, when Constantine usurped the Empire, by whose negligent government the barbarians were emboldened to commit such devastations. In the meantime, Alaric [the leader of the Goths], finding that he could not procure a peace on the conditions which he proposed, nor had received any hostages, once more attacked Rome, and threatened to storm it if the citizens refused to join with him against the Emperor Honorius.

Stilicho was executed by Honorius on 22 August 408. The convoluted politics which led to this are described in the previous volume of this series – *The Goths*. Stilicho's fall from grace was no doubt tied to his failure to keep Gaul under Honorius' control. Following Stilicho's demise Alaric's Goths were at the walls of Rome and the Vandals, Alans and Suebi crossed into Spain. Constantine III had the Gallic field army under his command supplemented by the troops he had withdrawn from Britain as well as his Frankish allies. In the immediate aftermath of Stilicho's execution there was no one of his stature to lead the army of Italy to defend Rome against Alaric, let alone intervene in the affairs of Gaul.

Therefore, as the first decade of the fifth century came to a close, Italy was in chaos, Alaric's Goths sacked Rome in 410, and Britain had been abandoned. Spain was tenuously held by the usurper Gerontius and invaded by the Vandals, Alans and Suebi. Devastated and with large swathes of the countryside under the control of the Bacaudae, Franks, Alamanni and Burgundians, Gaul had the only Roman leader capable of restoring any semblance of Roman control. In this Constantine III was supported by the Franks.

It did not last long. In 411 Gerontius left Spain for Gaul in an attempt to depose Constantine. Gerontius defeated Constantine's son at

Vienne and then moved down the Rhône to besiege the father at Arles. Gerontius' troops mutinied and Gerontius fled back to Spain where he was eventually killed. The legitimate West Roman Emperor Honorius had meanwhile appointed Constantius as Stilicho's successor. Alaric died shortly after his sack of Rome in 410 and his successor Ataulf was looking for a new homeland for his Gothic followers. The Imperial authorities saw a possible solution to both the Goths rampaging through Italy and Constantine's usurpation in Gaul. Honorius' General Constantius led the Roman army of Italy against Constantine III while setting Ataulf's Goths against the Vandals and their allies in Spain.

Both actions were successful. Constantine III was executed and after four years of semi-independence Gaul was brought back under Honorius' jurisdiction. Then Ataulf's Goths moved into southern Gaul with Roman encouragement. Together with some Burgundians and Alans, the Goths defeated yet another Roman usurper in 414 and then made their way via Narbonne to take Barcelona, seriously weakening the Vandals and their allies in the process.

More than happy with the results, the Imperial authorities recalled the Goths to Gaul in 418 and gave them the province of *Aquitania Secunda*, centred on Toulouse and the Garonne Valley. We have very little detail on the terms of this settlement. In all likelihood the Romans had no idea that they were creating what would become the Visigothic Kingdom. Most probably they thought that they were billeting a Romano-Gothic army on relatively unimportant lands far from the centre of Imperial power where the Goths could act as a bulwark between the rebellious Bacaudae to the north and the Vandals to the south.

As the second decade of the fifth century came to an end much of northern Gaul on the Roman side of the Rhine was occupied by Frankish settlements. The Franks had kept to their treaties with Rome and as far as we can tell they defended the Rhine frontier with as much or more vigour than their Roman allies. After the passing of the Vandals and their allies into Spain we can only assume that the Franks reoccupied whatever territory they had lost to them in 407–9 and had taken advantage of the confusion to expand it a bit.

The Alamanni had taken Strasbourg and much of the west bank of the Upper Rhine while the Burgundians held Worms and a section of the Middle Rhine. South-west Gaul had been ceded to the Goths while the Bacaudae held Brittany and were being reinforced by refugees from Britain. The Imperial authorities established a colony of Alans around Orléans. They were given land in exchange for keeping the Bacaudae in check and to act as a bulwark against a number of Saxons who had settled the Lower Loire Valley. All of these settlements were under nominal Roman control but control was at arm's length. The centre of real Roman power in Gaul was centred at Arles at the mouth of the Rhône. From Arles the Gallo-Roman authorities had their attention firmly fixed on Italy rather than the Gallic interior or the distant Rhine frontier.

Chapter 5

Aetius and Attila

Aetius

From the 420s the affairs of Gaul and of the Franks were dominated for three decades by the Roman warlord Flavius Aetius (391–454). Aetius spent his childhood as a hostage, first of the Goths and later of the Huns. He developed a close relationship with the Huns and relied on them for support in a series of civil wars from which he emerged as the most powerful man in the West Roman Empire. Unlike Stilicho who had tended to ignore Gaul, Aetius set himself the task of establishing his power base there, defending it from internal and external threats.

When the Emperor Honorius died in 423, Aetius raised an army of Huns (allegedly and improbably 60,000 of them) to support the usurper Joannes. By the time Aetius arrived in Italy, Joannes had been deposed and the 7-year-old Valentinian III was on the throne with his mother Galla Placidia the power behind it. A general with an army of Huns at his back was still a force to be reckoned with so Galla Placidia bought Aetius off with a command in Gaul and gold for his Hun followers.

With the support of the Huns, Aetius built up his power in Gaul. In 429 he assassinated the *Magister Militum* Felix and assumed his place. When Galla Placidia insisted on giving the position of supreme military command to Boniface, the Count of Africa, Aetius refused to give it up and marched on Italy to confront Boniface. Aetius lost the initial battle near Rimini in 432 and was forced to flee to seek refuge amongst the Huns beyond the frontier. Boniface, however, was mortally wounded and the following year Aeitus returned with another Hun army at his back to assume supreme power. For the next eighteen years Aetius concentrated on defending Gaul, waging successful campaigns against the Goths, Burgundians, Franks and Bacaudae.

As described in the previous chapter, the Franks had held more or less true to their treaties with Rome to help defend the Rhine frontier against

Plate 2: A copy of the signet ring from the grave of the Frankish King Childeric. He was buried at Tournai *c.*,481 along with a treasure which was stolen in the nineteenth century. (*Monnaie de Paris*)

Plate 1: Barbarian captives taken by the Romans on the Middle Rhine frontier in the first century AD – possibly from one of the tribes which eventually formed the Franks. Tacitus described some early Germans fighting nearly naked apart from short cloaks like the figure on the left. He probably came to such a conclusion from seeing prisoners of war or monuments like this one rather than from first-hand experience of Germans in battle. (*Landesmuseum, Mainz*)

Plate 3: Amongst the lost treasures from Childeric's grave were 300 gold and garnet bees. Napoleon Bonaparte had copies of them sewn into his coronation robe to link his rule to that of the ancient Frankish kings. (*Bibliothèque Nationale, Paris*)

Plate 4: The fourth century tombstone of Lepontius, a Roman soldier on the Upper Rhine frontier. His round shield, spear and long sword have more in common with a Germanic warrior's equipment than that of a Roman soldier of previous centuries. He may well have been of Alamannic origin. His plumed helmet bears no resemblance to any known styles but this may simply be due to the crude sculpting. The cockerel standard in the background is more reminiscent of ancient Gallic symbols than Imperial Roman ones. (*Musée Archéologique, Strasbourg*)

Plate 5: A silver disc from the horse harness of an Alamannic noble of the late sixth–early seventh century. The engraved warrior has a classical Roman appearance but his pose, spear, helmet and shield bear a striking resemblance to those of Lepontius. (*Musée Archéologique, Strasbourg*)

Plate 6: The head of a dragon standard (*draco*) which the Romans originally adopted from the Sarmatians for their cavalry units. With a cloth windsock attached to the gilded head it became a common standard for most later Roman units and was also used by several Germanic peoples. It is not known if the Franks carried such standards but Frankish units of *Foederati* in the Roman army probably did. (*Landesmuseum Mainz*)

Plate 7: A rare depiction of a Frankish warrior on a gravestone from Niederdollendorf on the Rhine near modern Bonn. His short single edged sword (scramasax) is clearly shown if exaggerated. He appears to be combing his hair. Combs have been found in many Frankish graves and hairstyles were an important way of demonstrating allegiance to a particular group. The curved serpent above his head is reminiscent of the draco standard and is also a common design painted on late Roman shields. (*Landesmusem Bonn*)

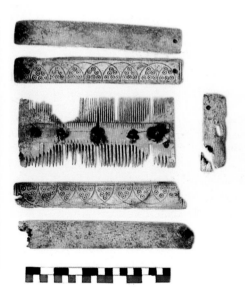

Plate 8: Combs have been found in Frankish and Alamannic graves of both men and women. They were clearly very important personal items. This ornate bone comb is from an Alamannic grave in Alsace. (*Musée Archéologique, Strasbourg*)

Plate 9: Both the Franks and Alamanni had very similar weapons and equipment. These come from fifth-sixth century Alamannic graves from Niedernai-Kirchbeuhl in Alsace. The long iron shaft of an angon is in the foreground. The shape of the angon head indicates an armour or shield piercing capability. The small barbs at the base of the head made it difficult to pull out once it had hit an opponent. Alongside the angon is a francisca head, long sword and scabbard fitting, as well as a number of conventional spearheads. (*Musée Archéologique, Strasbourg*)

Plate 10: Modern reconstructions of Frankish shields. Made of wood they were covered and edged with leather. The faces were probably painted and were often decorated with metal studs and fastenings which helped to hold the inner hand grip. Wealthier warriors may also have used additional metal decorations. (*Musée des Tees Barbares, Marle*)

Plate 11: The central hand grip of Frankish shields were covered by prominent iron bosses. These gave the shields an offensive capability. (*Landesmuseum Mainz*)

Plate 12: This protruding shield boss would have been a very effective offensive weapon when thrust against an opponent. (*Musée Saint–Loup, Troyes*)

Plate 13: A reconstruction of a Roman patrol ship of the *Classis Germanica* based on wrecks found at Mainz. These small craft played a vital role in attempting to stop raids across the Rhine. Forty of them are recorded in action against the Alamanni in 359. (*Museum of Ancient Seafaring, Mainz*)

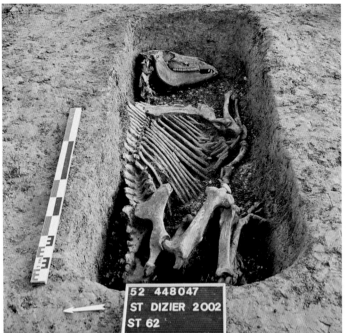

Plate 14: The graves of many Frankish warriors contain items of horse furniture. There have also been a number of finds of horses buried nearby human graves such as this one at St Dizier between Troyes and Metz. There were also horses buried alongside the tomb of Childeric. (*Musée de Saint-Dizier*)

Plate 15: A recreation of an alliance being formed between two Frankish war leaders. The painted designs on the shields are conjectural but are based on motifs found in sculpture and jewellery. There are contemporary references to shields being painted but none as to what designs may have been used. Ordinary warriors would have had much simpler designs or perhaps just plain colours. (*Musée des Temps Barbares, Marle*)

Plate 16: A sixth century silvered Frankish belt buckle proclaiming the owner's Christian faith. A few Franks were Christians before Clovis' baptism *c.*,500 but most converted afterwards. (*Musée des Temps Barbares, Marle*)

Plate 17: A recreation of fourth century negotiations between a Roman dux (frontier commander) and a Frankish chieftain seeking land in exchange for providing troops for the Roman army. Most of the Frankish settlements inside Roman territory came about in this way rather by conquest. (*Musée des Temps Barbares, Marle*)

Plate 18: Re-enactors equipped as fourth–fifth century Roman soldiers. Franks, Burgundians, Sarmatians and Alamanni provided most of the recruits for the later Roman army in Gaul. (*Musée des Temps Barbares, Marle*)

Plate 19: A reconstruction of the arms and armour of a fully equipped sixth-seventh century Frankish warrior. Chain mail was the most common form of body armour in the west but examples of lamellar construction like this have been found in Frankish and Alamannic graves. This style had eastern origins and was formed by lacing small plates onto a leather or fabric backing. (*Musée des Temps Barbares, Marle*)

Plate 20: This magnificent helmet is a reconstruction of one found in a late sixth century Alamannic grave at Niederstozingen. The lamellar style may have been influenced by contact with eastern troops during the Alamannic invasions of Italy in the sixth century. (*Landesmuseum Württemberg, Stuttgart*)

Plate 21: A reconstructed Frankish village rebuilt on the site of an original Salian Frankish settlement in northern France close to modern Laon. (*Musée des Temps Barbares, Marle*)

Plate 22: The formidable walls of Sens were built by the Romans in the third century although the additions at the top are medieval. It was behind these walls where Julian withstood an Alamannic siege in the winter of 356/7. (*Sens, France*)

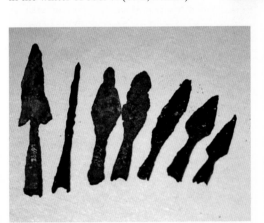

Plate 23: A number of arrowheads from Alamannic graves. Some poorer men were buried with bows and arrows, others with a francisca and short sword. Angons and long swords are mainly found in the graves of wealthier men. (*Musée Archéologique, Strasbourg*)

Plate 24: This gilded helmet is typical of the style worn by most Roman soldiers in the fourth–fifth centuries. It is made of two half-bowls held together by a central reinforcing ridge over the crown. Although this example is missing its cheek pieces, these would have been laced to the bowl as was the neck guard. Nose guards were common with other helmet types of the time but unusual with this style. As much of their military equipment came for Roman sources, this style of helmet would have been worn by some Franks. (*Munich Archeological Museum*)

Plate 25: The curved head of this fifth century francisca is a classic example of the Frankish throwing axe. (*Musée des Temps Barbares, Marle*)

Plate 26: An ivory relief showing scenes from the life of St Remi. The bottom panel shows the bishop baptizing Clovis. (*Musée de Picardie, Amiens*)

Plate 27: This impressive horde of coins was buried by its Roman owners in central France when they fled civil wars and barbarian attacks in the third century. Many such hordes dated to this time have been found all over France indicating the chaotic state of Gaul in the third century. (*Musée Saint-Loup, Troyes*)

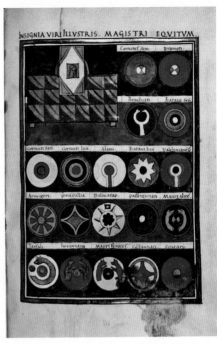

Plate 28: The insignia of the Roman *Magister Officiorum* showing the *fabricae* (arms factories) he controlled. The shields may be those of the *Scholae* (guards' cavalry) which he also commanded. There were only five units of *Scholae* in the West (seven in the East) so the identification of the seven shields with the units of the western *Scholae* cannot be certain. (*Notitia Dignitatum*)

Plate 29: The insignia of the Roman *Magister Equitum* (commander of horse) showing the shield designs of the most senior cavalry units in the fourth-fifth century Roman army. (*Notitia Dignitatum*)

Plate 30: A modern reconstruction of a wealthy sixth-seventh century Frankish warrior based on archaeological finds. A well accoutred man such as this probably also owned body armour and would have ridden a horse into battle even if he later dismounted to fight on foot. There are records of Franks wearing their long hair braided in front like this man but most would have shaved their beards, some leaving a moustache. (*Musée des Temps Barbares, Marle*)

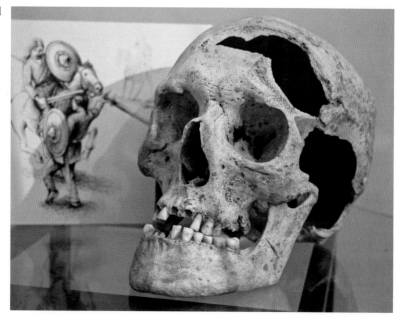

Plate 31: The skull of an Alamannic warrior who was cut down by a sword blow to the head, probably from a mounted enemy. (*Musée Archéologique, Strasbourg*)

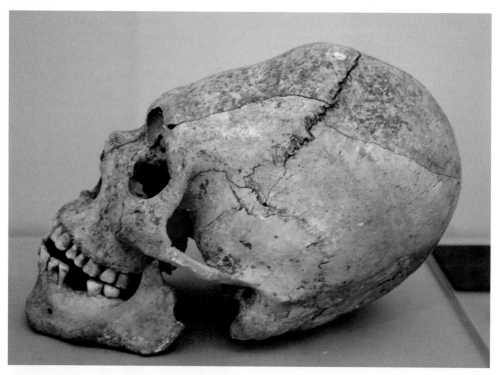

Plate 32: This fifth century Alamannic skull was deliberately deformed by a practice introduced by the Huns amongst whom skull deformation was fairly widespread. It was very unusual amongst the German tribes except for those who came under Hun domination. This find may indicate that the Alamanni allied with the Huns in the 450s or it may be that someone who had grown up amongst the Huns later ended up amongst the Alamanni. (*Musée Archéologique, Strasbourg*)

Plate 33: A sixth century Alamannic helmet from Baldenheim in Alsace. The iron bowl was silvered and reinforced with decorated bronze panels. The bronze cheek pieces were also decorated with an intricate pattern. The original helmet would have been lined with leather and may well have had a mail neck guard. (*Musée Archéologique, Strasbourg*)

Plate 34: An array of fifth century Gallo-Roman and Frankish grave goods from Soissons. Syagrius had his capital at Soissons until he was defeated by Clovis. (*Musée St Leger, Soissons*)

Plate 35: Reconstructions of the style of dress worn by Alamannic women in the fifth-seventh centuries. (*Musée des Temps Barbares, Marle*)

Plate 36: The still intact Roman Imperial Palace at Trier. In the fourth century Trier was the centre of Roman power in Gaul and was the occasional seat of emperors and usurpers. As the Middle Rhine came under increasing pressure from the Franks, the Romans transferred their Gallic capital to Arles in Provence. (*Aula Palatina, Trier, Germany*)

Plate 37: Although the Franks were noted foot warriors, many Frankish graves contain items of horse furniture. These silvered accoutrements held the leather straps of a wealthy Frankish warrior's horse. (*Landesmuseum, Trier*)

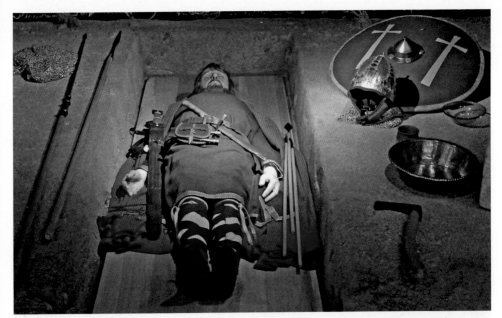

Plate 38: A reconstruction of the grave of a high-status Frankish warrior whose burial at Bad Kreuznach-Planing, near Mainz, has been dated to around 525. He was buried with the full equipment of the best warriors of the time. This includes: chain mail shirt, angon and conventional spear on his right; helmet with mail neck guard, shield and francisca on his left; long sword and three javelins by his body; a scramasax (short sword) and dagger in his belt. The Christian crosses on his shield are conjectural and are taken from decorations on his helmet.

Plate 39: The Bad Kreuznach-Planing helmet. This helmet style probably originated from amongst the Sarmatians on the Middle Danube and was widely adopted by the Franks, Alamanni, Burgundians and Romans in the fifth-sixth centuries. The original had a chain mail neck guard. (*Landesmuseum Mainz*)

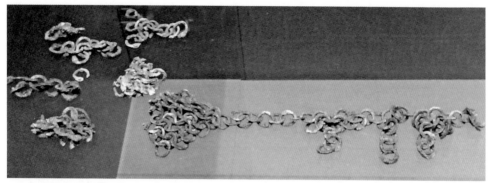

Plate 40: Fragments of chain mail body armour and helmet neck guard found in the Bad Kreuznach-Planing grave. (*Landesmuseum, Mainz*)

Plate 41: The grave of a late fifth century Frankish warrior from northern France. His weapons include a long sword on his left side, a francisca, and a conventional spear. (*Musée des Temps Barbares, Marle*)

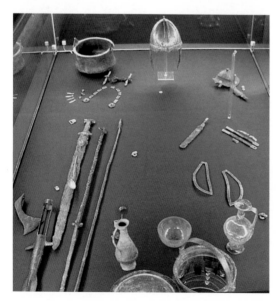

Plate 42: The grave goods of a high-status early sixth century Frankish warrior from Krefeld-Gellep, near Düsseldorf. He was buried with the full panoply of war including angon, francisca, long sword, helmet and horse furnishings. (*Burg Linn Museum*)

the Vandals, Alans and Suebi. They had shown their worth as allies with a vested interest in defending their own territories in Flanders and on the east bank of the Middle Rhine. It was only natural that they would ally themselves with the most powerful Roman commander in Gaul even when that person was a usurper. Therefore, the Franks found themselves supporting a series of Gallic or British claimants to the throne including Magnus Maximus, Eugenius and Constantine III.

The Roman politics of the early fifth century were extremely confused and it must have been difficult for the various bands of Franks to know if they were fighting for the legitimate Imperial authority or against it. Probably it did not matter to them. The Romans may have had ideas of the enduring Roman state and the legitimacy of emperors but the Franks and other Germans did not. To them an oath of allegiance was binding and personal. So a Frankish warrior's oath to fight for Constantine III would have been made because he saw in Constantine a man worth following who could help protect his land and family and give him just reward for his allegiance. The convoluted politics of Ravenna (the West Roman capital) and Constantinople (the Eastern one) would have seemed far away and much less important than the strength of a warlord closer to home.

This had been the situation for decades as the legitimate West Roman authorities turned their attention away from Gaul to focus on Italy and the East. This changed when Aetius came on the scene. He treated Gaul almost as his personal fiefdom and spent all his efforts to keep it secure. No doubt many Franks saw in Aetius a man they could follow and they joined his army just as the previous generation joined Constantine III. Yet Aetius' personal presence and the fact that Gaul was his priority made it difficult for other Franks. Unlike Stilicho, who needed Frankish allies to hold the Rhine while his attention was turned elsewhere, Aetius had large numbers of Huns supporting him. Individual Frankish recruits would no doubt have been welcomed but Aetius did not have to rely on the more independent settlements. Those Franks who had taken the opportunity of civil wars and invasions to expand their power and influence suddenly found themselves facing a new Roman warlord who possibly needed them less then they needed him. To Aetius the Franks were subjects while for decades the Franks had been independent power brokers. Inevitably this led to conflict.

Aetius sought to establish his authority over as much of Gaul as he could. The Goths held Aquitaine in the south-west, the Salian Franks held Flanders, much of the west bank of the Rhine was occupied by Burgundians and Alamanni while the Ripuarian Franks were on the east bank of the Middle Rhine. In those areas of nominal Roman control many citizens had gone over to the Bacaudae. Armorica had almost become a semi-independent Bacaudic territory reinforced by refugees from Britain who gave the region its modern name – Brittany.

Hun allies were used by Aetius to ruthlessly break the power of the Burgundians on the Middle Rhine and he resettled the survivors in modern Burgundy. The destruction of the Burgundian kingdom of Worms by Aetius' Huns became the subject of heroic legends that formed the base of the *Nibelungenlied* and Wagner's *Ring Cycle*. This event is recounted frustratingly briefly in the chronicle of Prosper:

> Aetius crushed in battle Gundicharius, the king of the Burgundians living within Gaul, and gave him the peace he asked for. But Gundicharius did not enjoy that peace for long, since the Huns utterly destroyed him and his people.

Aetius' greatest concern was the Bacaudae and he did his best to bring them under some sort of control and break their power base in Armorica. This was not an easy task as increasing numbers of Gallo-Roman citizens had joined them. Most probably the Bacaudae saw themselves as Romans, doing their best to survive at a time when Imperial control had all but disappeared. Civic society had broken down and various barbarians had displaced many of the Roman inhabitants of Gaul, Britain and Spain. Powerful landowners fortified their estates and offered some protection to the locals, planting the seeds of the feudal system that would emerge in later centuries. Bishops held sway over the cities with ecclesiastical power filling part of the vacuum left by the absence of effective civil administration.

As more and more people fled the fields and the cities to join the Bacaudae or to seek the protection of aristocratic landowners, Aetius was faced with a shrinking tax base from which to pay his troops. Like the nobles of pre-revolutionary modern France and the super-rich of today's global society, the aristocracy were able to evade or avoid taxes and the burden increasingly fell on those least able to pay it. It was this situation which made the Bacaudae a greater threat to Aetius' grip on Gaul than the various bands of barbarians. The latter could be given land in exchange for military service but maintaining the regular Roman army required coin raised through taxation to pay them. As long as the Bacaudae provided a viable alternative to staying put and paying taxes, Aetius had a problem maintaining the troops he needed to hold Gaul.

So it was that Aetius used his Hun allies, together with Alans and other barbarians, to wage war on the inhabitants of Gaul who had joined the Bacaudae. Instead of serving to protect the people who paid for it, the Roman army, composed almost entirely of non-Romans, was used to suppress them.

> Gaul withdrew from Roman society, following Tibatto, leader of the rebellion [in 435]. During this outbreak nearly all the slaves of Gaul conspired with the Bacaudae. [In 437] the uprising of the Bacaudae quieted down after Tibatto was captured and the rest of the leaders of the revolt were either taken or captured. (The Gallic Chronicle of 452)

This campaign, led by Aetius' Lieutenant Litorius, may have secured a temporary success but Tibatto later escaped and if the Bacaudae had been temporarily cowed, they were not destroyed. Furthermore, nothing was done to fix the underlying causes of the endemic rebellions. In the years that followed, British refugees fleeing the chaos which resulted from the end of Roman rule in Britain, bolstered and strengthened the Bacaudae of Armorica and they remained a force to contend with until well beyond the end of the West Roman Empire.

The Visigoths

As we saw in the previous chapter the Goths, who had sacked Rome in 410, were given land to settle in south-western France after campaigning as a surrogate Roman army against the Vandals in Spain. They established a semi-independent kingdom centred on Toulouse and came to be known as the Visigoths to distinguish them from the other Goths who still lived across the frontier at this time. This latter group of Goths would eventually come to be known as the Ostrogoths or eastern Goths.

From 418 to 451, under the leadership of Theodoric I, Alaric's illegitimate son, the Visigoths established themselves in relative harmony with the local inhabitants. Many of the Gallo-Romans would have found their circumstances enhanced rather than diminished by their new Visigothic rulers. The aristocrats continued to enjoy their cultured lifestyle and quite probably benefited from a reduction in taxation. The writings of Sidonius Apollinaris, a Gallo-Roman aristocrat who lived at this time, give us a sense of the continuation of a lifestyle that would have seemed familiar to Romans of Augustus' day, even if the political situation had radically changed.

Visigothic warriors occasionally served as Roman auxiliaries and allies campaigning against the Vandals and Suebi in Spain. At other times the Visigoths flexed their muscles and tried to expand their holdings in Gaul at Roman expense. They attacked but failed to capture Arles in 425 and again in 430. These may have been attempts by independent bands to strike out on their own rather than a deliberate effort by King Theodoric to expand his realm.

The first Visigoth attack on Arles coincided with the death of Honorius and the conflict between Aetius, Felix and Boniface. Bands of Visigoths may have taken the opportunity of Roman civil war to expand their influence as the Franks and others had done in previous civil wars. In 429 the Vandals crossed from Spain into Africa and ten years later they captured Carthage, taking with it the vital grain supplies to Italy. The remaining Roman power in the West now lay in the hands of Aeitus in Gaul.

Between 436 and 439 the conflict between the Visigoths and Romans became more serious. Although Aetius had been a hostage with Alaric's Goths as a child and had a Gothic wife, he did not display any pro-Gothic leanings. Attempts by the Visigoths to expand their holdings in Gaul were a direct challenge to his power and authority and he did not let them go unchecked.

When the Visigoths again attacked Arles and laid siege to Narbonne, Aetius sent his General Litorius, with an army of Huns at his back, to drive the Visigoths back to Toulouse and restore the status quo. During this campaign there was a fascinating incident when Avitus, a Gallo-Roman aristocrat – former *Magister Militum* and future emperor – had to defend his fortified estate, not from the Goths but from pillaging Huns serving as the Roman army which Litorius had previously led against the Bacaudae.

> Litorius, elated by the conquest of the Armoricans was hurrying his Scythian [Hun] horsemen against the Gothic host through the land of the Arvernian and they with raid and fire and sword and barbarity and pillage were destroying all things near them, betraying and making void the name of peace. A servant of Avitus was wounded by one of these, more savage than his fellows, soon to be wounded in turn. The victim [Avitus' servant] fell and falling commended his woeful fate to the vengeance of his absent master. As he died he carried with him to the Stygian stream a hopeful forecast of the revenge that was to come. Rumour brought knowledge of the dastardly deed to our leader [Avitus] as he kept his ward of towers and gates, regardful of the frightened populace...
>
> At length he [Avitus] dashes forward, shouting again and again for his arms. [His men] bring him his corselet, still clotted with gore, his lance blunted by wounds dealt upon the barbarians and his sword notched by unceasing slaughter. He cases his legs in greaves and puts upon his head a gleaming helmet, here on a golden crest-base rises aloft, darting an angry flash from on high. Next he mounts his charge and tearing the gates from their hinges he rushes forth. (Sidonius Apollinaris)

The image of a former Roman general (shortly to become emperor) fighting against Hun soldiers in a Roman army who were campaigning against the Armorican Bacaudae and the Visigoths, perfectly captures the confused loyalties of fifth century Gaul. Many Romans had become enemies of the state by joining the Bacaudae to escape the heavy hand of taxation, while Roman armies were made up of Huns, Alans, Franks and other barbarians. The Gallo-Roman aristocrats, such as Avitus, fortified their villas and provided some protection to the local inhabitants as the above passage shows.

Those aristocrats who found their estates in regions controlled by the Visigoths did not seemed unduly perturbed by Gothic ascendancy. Not only did they make accommodation with the new overlords, many of them – such as Avitus – actively supported them. Some may have seen close cooperation with the Goths as a means to power or as a bulwark against the shifting politics of the Imperial court. The same was probably true in regions controlled by the Franks.

Conflict with the Franks

A panegyric to Aetius in 446 gives a tantalizing hint of conflict between the Romans and Franks. 'The Rhine has bestowed pacts making the wintery world Rome's servant, and content to be guided by western reins, rejoices that the Tiber's domain swells for it from both sides.' The writer was Flavius Merobaudes, a Roman officer who saw action in Spain against the Bacaudae and was probably a descendant of the Frankish general of the same name (see Chapter 2). The passage implies a restoration of order along both banks of the Rhine which could have been a result of a campaign, a new treaty, or a combination of both.

As the Franks are not mentioned specifically, the above passage could easily refer to Aetius' destruction of the Burgundian kingdom on the Rhine in 436 and their resettlement in modern Burgundy as *foederati* in 443. The Ripuarian Franks, however, continued to flex their muscles at Rome's expense. In the early 440s they sacked the former Imperial capital of Trier. A few years later Aetius was minting coins in that city. Therefore it is reasonable to assume that Aetius retook Trier and established a new treaty with the Ripuarian Franks in which, once again, the Franks undertook to hold the Rhine as Roman allies. It is unlikely that Aetius won a victory over the Ripuarian Franks as otherwise Merobaudes' panegyric would have lauded it. Most probably the Franks sacked Trier, took what they wanted and then retired back over the Rhine as Aetius moved in to pick up the pieces.

For the most part the Salian Franks in Flanders seem to have been more or less content to hold on to their lands under nominal Roman sovereignty without pushing their luck too much. The arrangement suited both parties as the Salians provided good recruits for the Roman army in return for land inside the Empire. This gave them access to the wealth and benefits of Roman civilization without the heavy burden of taxation which wore down the native Gallo-Romans.

While most ambitious Salian Frankish warriors sought to increase their wealth and influence through service in the Roman army, it is not unreasonable to assume that others looked to expanding their hold over neighbouring territories. We learn from Sidonius Apollinaris that a band of Salian Franks made a move on Arras in the late 440s or early 450. This led to conflict with Aetius' troops led by the future Emperor Majorian. In a panegyric to Majorian, Sidonius portrays this as a great Roman victory but it would seem as though it was nothing more than Roman troops breaking up a Frankish wedding party. This leads us to wonder if the Salian Franks had indeed attacked Arras or whether it was simply a large band of them gathering for a celebration.

A yellow-haired bridegroom was marrying a young bride of like colouring. Well, these revellers, they say, he [Majorian] laid low. Time after time his helmet rang with the blows and his hauberk with their protecting scales kept off the thrust of spears until the enemy were forced to turn and flee. Then might be seen the jumbled adornments of the nuptials gleaming red in the wagons. Captured salvers and viands flung together pell-mell and servants crowned with fragrant garlands carrying wine-bowls on their oily top-knots. (Sidonius Apollinaris)

Possibly the Frankish wedding party was more like a large group of uninvited guests rather than an invasion force. Their gathering may have caused the Imperial authorities to panic and take action against them. The leader of these Franks was Chlogio (also Clodio or Chlodio). Gregory of Tours has this to say of him:

They say also that Chlogio, a man of ability and high rank among his people, was king of the Franks then, and he dwelt at the stronghold of Dispargum which is within the borders of [Tongres in modern Belgium]. Chlogio sent spies to the city of Cambrai, and they went everywhere, and he himself followed and overcame the Romans and seized the city, in which he dwelt for a short time, and he seized the land as far as the river Somme. Certain authorities assert that king Merovech, whose son was Childeric, was of the family of Chlogio.

Putting together the snippets we have from Sidonius Apollinaris, Gregory of Tours and others, it would seem that Chlogio was an emerging leader of the Salian Franks who was doing his best to assert greater dominance over the Roman cities of northern Gaul and in the process, increase his influence over the other Salian Franks. It appears as though this brought him into conflict with Aetius but such conflict resulted in minor skirmishes rather than all-out war. We will hear more of Chlogio's descendants in the next chapter.

The Appearance of the Franks

The above quote from Sidonius is the first description we have of the Franks' physical appearance. For the most part the Romans gave generic, unflattering descriptions of the various Germanic peoples and, apart from Tacitus, made little effort to distinguish one tribe from the other. To the Romans they were all tall, blonde, pale skinned, savage and half-naked, or dressed in furs and skins. Sidonius does follow these stereotypes and his yellow-haired Franks with 'oily top-knots' may be just that. The top-knots hark back to the Suebian knot described by Tacitus (see Chapter 1) and so may be a classical convention rather than an actual description.

In a later passage Sidonius gives another, more detailed, description of Frankish warriors. Here he not only gives us a glimpse of their appearance but also of their fighting methods. Comparing them to monsters which the youthful Majorian had managed to subdue he says that the Franks had a distinctive hairstyle which involved drawing their hair forward over their heads, exposing the backs of their necks. He goes on to say:

Their eyes are faint and pale, with a glimmer of greyish blue. Their faces are shaved all round, and instead of beards they have thin moustaches which they run through with a comb. Close fitting garments confine the long limbs of the men; they are drawn up high so as to expose the knees, and a broad belt supports their narrow

waist. It is their sport to send axes hurling through the vast void
and know beforehand where the blow will fall, to whirl their shields,
to outstrip with leaps and bounds the spears they have hurled, and
reach the enemy first. Even in boyhood's years the love of fighting
is full grown. Should they chance to be sore pressed by numbers, or
by the luck of the ground, death may overwhelm them but not fear.
Unconquerable they stand their ground and their courage well-nigh
outlives their lives.

The Salian Franks had been settled inside Roman territory for several
generations. Their clothes and equipment would have come from Roman
sources, modified to suit their tastes and to distinguish them from the
Gallo-Romans amongst whom they lived. It would seem as though most
of the barbarian peoples who set themselves up inside Roman territory
sought some means to distinguish themselves. One way of doing this was
to adopt distinctive hairstyles.

Long hair became a particular distinction of the various Germans.
The later Frankish monarchs became known as the 'long-haired kings'.
Depictions of the Goths show them with long hair and Vandal laws in
Africa forbade their subject Roman males from growing their hair.
The Frankish, Gothic and Vandal men also tended to shave their faces,
sometimes leaving a moustache while most Romans of the time wore
short beards and short hair. Sidonius' description of top-knots and hair
drawn towards the front, leaving the back of the neck exposed, may well
have been a distinctive fifth century Frankish hairstyle.

In a later letter to a friend (AD 470), Sidonius describes the Frankish
Prince Sigismer on his way to the palace of his future Burgundian father-
in-law at Lyons:

You who are so fond of looking at arms and armed men, I can
only imagine your delight if you could have seen the young prince
Sigismer on his way to the palace... decked out in the fashion of
his nation. Before him went a horse gaily caparisoned. Other horses
laden with flashing jewels preceded or followed him. But the most
gracious sight of the procession was the prince himself marching on
foot amid his runners and footmen, clad in gleaming scarlet, ruddy

gold and pure white silk. His fair hair, glowing cheeks and white skin matched the colours of such bright dress.

The chiefs and companions who escorted him presented an aspect terrifying even in peacetime. Their feet from toe to ankle were laced in hairy shoes. Their knees, shins and calves were uncovered. Above this was a tight-fitting many-coloured garment, drawn up high and hardly descending to their bare elbows – the sleeves covering only the upper part of the arm. They wore green mantles with crimson borders. Their swords suspended from their shoulders by baldrics pressed against sides girded with studded deerskins.

No small part of their adornment consisted of their arms. In their hands they grasped barbed spears and throwing axes. Their left sides were guarded by shields which flashed bright with golden bosses and silvery borders, betraying their wealth and good taste.

This letter is particularly interesting on a number of counts. There is, for example, a hint of uniformity in the description of the green and crimson cloaks as well as the shields adorned with gold and silver. This might be expected in the *comitatus* of a successful prince who would have presented his followers with gifts to display his wealth and power. Gifts of clothing were often presented to allies by the Romans and it is reasonable to assume that Germanic warlords did the same. The 'barbed spears' and 'throwing axes' are confirmed by other writers as well as by archaeological evidence (see Chapter 10). Then we have the horses. Although Sigismer and his entourage chose to parade on foot, they had horses and no doubt would have used them in battle from time to time if the circumstances were suitable.

As a final thought, one cannot help but wonder if this Sigismer, arriving at the Burgundian court, could have been one of the historical inspirations for the legendary Siegfried who did the same in the *Nibelungenlied* and Wagner's *Ring Cycle*.

Attila

We saw in the previous chapter that the westward migration of the Huns in the 370s pushed the Goths over the Danube and that their later expansion into modern Hungary sent the Vandals, Alans and Suebi over the Rhine. In the early decades of the fifth century the Huns, then settled in modern Hungary, were ruled by Rua. He supported Aetius, giving him Hun allies which enabled him to emerge supreme in the various civil wars and to assert his authority over Gaul. Rua died in 434 to be succeeded by his sons Bleda and Attila.

The sixth century Romano–Gothic historian Jordanes tells the tale of Attila's rise to power:

> After [Rua's] death Attila succeeded to the throne of the Huns, together with his brother Bleda. In order that he might first be equal to the expedition he was preparing, he sought to increase his strength by murder. Thus he proceeded from the destruction of his own kindred to the menace of all others. But though he increased his power by this shameful means, yet by the balance of justice he received the hideous consequences of his own cruelty. Now when his brother Bleda, who ruled over a great part of the Huns, had been slain by his treachery, Attila united all the people under his own rule.

For most of the early part of his reign, Attila maintained relatively good relations with Aetius and the West while building up his power and prestige, primarily at the expense of the East Romans. Ruling over a polyglot empire of subject and allied tribes, Attila's power rested on his ability to reward his followers with increasing amounts of wealth and glory. To this end he invaded the East Roman Empire in 440. After laying waste to the Balkan frontier provinces he defeated several Roman armies that were sent against him. When he was checked by the walls of Constantinople he concluded a treaty which increased the tribute previously paid to his Huns to keep the peace.

When the Eastern Emperor Theodosius II died in 450, and his successor Marcian refused to pay the tribute, Attila had two choices: go to war against the Eastern Empire again or find another source of wealth. He therefore decided to turn against the Western Empire in the knowledge that there was probably little more he could extract from the East. It must also have rankled that while the Visigoths, Vandals, Franks, Alans and Burgundians all had land within Roman territory and were able to enjoy the fruits of Roman civilization, the Huns were excluded. Despite years of faithful service with the West and many successful campaigns against the East, the Huns were still kept beyond the frontiers.

So Attila set his sights on the West Roman Empire. The reasons why the Huns suddenly turned against the West Romans with whom they had long been allies are complex and convoluted. A wide variety of causes, some quite trivial, sparked off the conflict.

First of these was the new Eastern Emperor Marcian's policy of ending the ruinous extortion extracted by the Huns in exchange for keeping the peace. Perhaps Attila's most obvious response would have been to renew war against the Eastern Empire but what would that have achieved? There was probably not a copper plate worth having anywhere in the Balkans that had not already been looted. Yet safe behind the walls of Constantinople the true riches of the East were beyond Attila's grasp. He could have sought to occupy land in the Balkans as the Goths had done in the previous century but after so many decades of continuous warfare the land was probably not worth holding. In any case the Huns were nomads, not farmers.

Gaul on the other hand offered potential as Aetius wrestled with the many barbarians and restless natives for control. From Attila's point of view a successful campaign in Gaul in which he might supplant one or another of the various petty rival fiefdoms surely seemed a more profitable enterprise than once again descending on the devastated Balkans.

A possible claim to a legitimate holding for Attila within the Western Empire came from a rather unlikely source. Honoria, the sister of the Western Emperor Valentinian III, became involved in a love scandal at court. Her lover was executed and Honoria was set to be married off to a rather dull Roman senator to keep her from causing more trouble. In 450 Honoria appealed to Attila for help sending him her ring as a token. Attila took this as a promise of marriage and demanded half of the Western Empire as a dowry. In moving against the West he could do so, not simply as an invader but as someone claiming his right as the emperor's future brother-in-law.

Meanwhile the Salian Franks were fighting amongst themselves over leadership following Chlogio's death at the end of the 440s. According to Priscus, Chlogio's eldest son sought assistance from Attila to claim his inheritance. A younger brother who had been adopted by Aetius during an earlier Frankish embassy to Rome sought his adopted father's help.

> Attila's excuse for war against the Franks was the death of their king and the disagreement of his children over the rule, the elder who decided to bring Attila in as his ally, and the younger, Aetius. I saw this boy when he was at Rome on an embassy, a lad without down on his cheeks as yet and with fair hair so long that it poured down his shoulders. Aetius had made him his adopted son. (Priscus)

It may be that Chlogio's younger son was the semi-legendary Merovech who gave his name to the Frankish Merovingian dynasty which later came to rule Gaul. The case for this was made by French scholars in the early eighteenth century and was taken up by Sir Edward Gibbon. There are, however, no primary sources to back it up. Very little is known about Merovech. According to Gregory of Tours: 'Some say that Merovech, the father of Childeric, was descended from Chlogio.' *The Chronicle of Fredegar* relates a legend in which Merovech was conceived when Chlogio's wife went swimming and was impregnated by a sea monster.

Chlogio died around 450 and Childeric was in his prime in the 460s. It is technically possible that Priscus' unnamed Frankish princes could have been Chlogio's sons and one of them could have been Merovech. We will never know for certain. It may well be that Merovech is an entirely mythical character and that perhaps Childeric was the young prince adopted by Aetius. What we do know is that one of the Frankish princes – the one adopted by Aetius – led a Frankish contingent which fought with the Romans against Attila. Other Franks, maybe Ripuarians or the followers of Chlogio's elder son, or maybe both, sided with the Huns.

Another reason for Attila to consider an invasion of Gaul came from the Vandals in Africa who encouraged the Huns to move against the Visigoths of south-western France.

> When Geiseric, king of the Vandals, learned that Attila's mind was bent on the devastation of the world, he incited him by many gifts to make war on the Visigoths, for he was afraid that Theodoric, king of the Visigoths, would avenge the injury done to his daughter. She

had been joined in wedlock with Huneric, Geiseric's son, and at first was happy in this union. But afterwards he was cruel even to his own children, and because of the mere suspicion that she was attempting to poison him, he cut off her nose and mutilated her ears. He sent her back to her father in Gaul thus despoiled of her natural charms. So the wretched girl presented a pitiable aspect ever after, and the cruelty which would stir even strangers still more surely incited her father to vengeance. (Jordanes)

Concerned that Theodoric would lead the Visigoths against him to avenge his daughter's honour, Geiseric sought an alliance with the Huns. He probably hoped that if the Huns threatened the Visigoths the latter would be in no position to wage war on him. From Attila's point of view he saw an opportunity to supplant the Visigoths in southern Gaul while establishing a client kingdom of Franks in the north by supporting the eldest of Chlogio's sons.

Attila was of two minds and at a loss which he should attack first, [the East or West Roman Empires]. But it seemed better to him to enter on the greater war and to march against the West, since his fight there would not be only against the Italians but also against the Goths and Franks. Against the Italians so as to seize Honoria along with her money, and against the Goths in order to earn the gratitude of Geiseric, the Vandal king. Attila's excuse for war against the Franks was the death of their king and the disagreement of his children over the rule. (Priscus)

So it was that Attila's Huns invaded Gaul, supported by many Germanic tribes, including Franks and probably some Alamanni as well. Although the Alamanni are not specifically mentioned in any contemporary sources, a number of Alamannic graves from this time have revealed artificially deformed skulls. This practice, which involved binding the head when a child, originated amongst the Huns for high-status individuals. It was not practised amongst the Germanic tribes other than at the time of Hun overlordship.

Attila made his move in the spring of 451 when Aetius was in Italy, leaving Gaul more or less undefended apart from the Franks on the Rhine. A large number of Franks had chosen to throw in their lot with Attila. Whatever remained of the regular Roman forces in Gaul had been run-down or ignored for a generation. For more than twenty years Aetius had relied on Huns and Alans to secure his authority against the Visigoths, Franks, Burgundians and Bacaudae. With the Huns suddenly his opponents, Aetius had to turn to his former enemies for support.

Aetius managed to convince the Visigoths that they would be better off by siding with him rather than simply defending their territory against the Hun onslaught. He also had Merovech's Franks at his back, if it was indeed the legendary founder of the Merovingian dynasty who had sought Aetius' help against his older brother.

According to Jordanes:

> He [Aetius] assembled warriors from everywhere to meet [the Huns] on equal terms. Now these were his auxiliaries: Franks, Sarmatians, Armoricans, Liticians, Burgundians, Saxons, Riparians, Olibriones (once Romans soldiers and now the flower of the allied forces), and some other Celtic or German tribes.

Interestingly, no mention is made of any Roman troops raised in France. Were there any? Sidonius Apollinaris recounts that Aetius moved from Italy to Gaul with only 'a thin meagre force of auxiliaries without regular troops'. It is unclear why more troops from the Italian field army were not released. Quite possibly Emperor Valentinian III did not want to leave Italy undefended, or he did not trust Aetius to have command of too many Roman troops in case he was tempted to stage a coup. Although the men following Aetius into Gaul would have been good troops there were clearly very few of them – not enough to stop Attila without allies.

According to the *Notitia Dignitatum*, the field army of the *Magister Equitem Intra Gallias* (see Appendix 1) contained twelve vexillations of cavalry, ten legions, fifteen *auxilia palatina*, and ten *pseudocomitatenses* – units brought in from frontier garrisons. On paper this should have provided at least 25,000 men. Furthermore, there were significant numbers of troops still listed as guarding the Rhine frontier in the early fifth century. What had happened to them?

The Rhine frontier collapsed following the migration of the Vandals, Alans and Suebi in 407 and had largely been replaced by settlements of Franks, Alamanni and Burgundians. Throughout the 430s and 440s Aetius had relied on Hun and Alan allies rather than the Gallic field army to deal with his enemies and it is quite probable that many of the native Gallo-Roman soldiers had either joined or were sympathetic to the Bacaudae. By 451 the Roman army in Gaul had probably been reduced both in numbers and quality to render it almost useless as a field force. Certainly the ease at which Attila captured many Gallic towns is evidence of the paucity of quality troops that could have resisted him. That said, there must have been at least some half-decent Roman soldiers available in Gaul to swell the numbers of Roman troops Aetius could call on. The '*Riparians*' in Jordanes' description may have been either Ripuarian Franks or *riparenses*. The latter were Roman militia, descended from the old legions, who defended river frontiers. As the Ripuarian Franks sided with Attila the latter is perhaps the most likely explanation.

When Jordanes speaks of 'Sarmatians' he is probably referring to the Alan colony settled around Orléans in the aftermath of the Vandal crossing of the Rhine. The Alans were a Sarmatian people who were famous for their heavy cavalry lancers. Led by Sangiban, the Alans of Orléans provided unenthusiastic support for Aetius against Attila.

The Armoricans (from modern Brittany) were either Bacaudae, recent immigrants from Britain, or a combination of both. The Armorican Bacaudae had been one of Aetius' chief opponents in previous years and possibly he had made a deal with them to provide a contingent in exchange for being left alone to manage their own affairs.

Burgundians, settled in Gaul, were the survivors of Aetius' earlier campaign against them and while they had no more cause than the Visigoths or Armoricans to support Aetius, their defeat had come at the hands of the Huns and perhaps they chose the lesser of two evils. In any case their resettlement in modern Burgundy had come with the proviso that their men had to serve in the Roman army.

The Liticians and Olibrones mentioned by Jordanes are a puzzle. Possibly they could have been *laeti*. It is also likely that Aetius' army would have been augmented by the private armies of the powerful Gallic landowners. Throughout the fifth and sixth centuries powerful magnates built up their own private military units to protect their holdings as Imperial power receded. Coming to be known as *bucellarii*, these units owed their allegiance to their employer rather than the Imperial authorities. Perhaps Jordanes' enigmatic 'Olibriones' could have been similar troops, especially as he says that they were previously Roman soldiers.

Most of these contingents were *foederati*, men from a variety of nations who had been given land or pay in return for service in the Roman army. They fought in their native style but were technically part of the Roman army rather than independent allies. They would have been equipped largely from Roman arms factories and may have been almost indistinguishable in appearance from more regular Roman troops even though they fought under their own leaders and were not integrated into regular units.

The Battle on the Catalaunian Plains

In the spring of 451 Attila marched east towards the Rhine. In addition to his Huns he had contingents of Franks, Gepids, Ostrogoths (eastern Goths), Rugians, Thuringians, Scirians and probably Alamanni. After securing alliances with the Visigoths, Burgundians, Armoricans and some of the Salian Franks, Aetius moved north to stop him.

Aetius was faced with a nearly insurmountable problem. The men who had been the backbone of his armies for over twenty years were now his opponents. If he lost Gaul he would lose everything and he had to turn to his former enemies for help. The coalition that he was able to cobble together to stop Attila was very much a marriage of convenience. He had no desire to see the Visigoths or Franks become even more powerful but he had no choice but to seek their help. He would strive to ensure that once the battle was won he would do what he could to prevent them from exploiting any victory. He had to stop Attila but he probably did not want Hun power to be completely broken. The Huns provided a useful counterbalance to the Visigoths and Franks. No doubt he hoped to be able to draw on their support again, once Gaul was safe.

Aetius' strategy, therefore, was to defeat Attila but to ensure that in doing so he was still the most powerful warlord in Gaul. He would need to use allies to help him do this but he had no intention of letting them profit too much by their support.

The clash between Aetius and Attila took place on 20 June 451 probably near Troyes in modern Champagne where the flat 'Catalaunian' plains are dominated by a long ridge now called Montgueux. 'The armies met... in the Catalaunian plains. The battlefield was a plain rising by a sharp slope to a ridge, which both armies sought to gain; for advantage of position is a great help.' (Jordanes)

Aetius' Visigothic vanguard drove Attila's covering force from the Montgueux ridge and then he deployed his army on the plains below with the Visigoths on the right, Alans in the centre and Romans on the left. Aetius' Frankish contingent was probably deployed with the other nominally Roman contingents on the left.

Attila attacked with his Huns in the centre and his Germanic allies on both flanks – his left dominated by Ostrogoths while the Gepid king commanded his right. We do not know where Attila's Frankish allies were deployed nor how they fared in the battle. It is quite possible that they were alongside the Gepids facing Aetius' Frankish contingent.

Hand to hand they clashed in battle, and the fight grew fierce, confused, monstrous, unrelenting – a fight whose like no ancient time has ever recorded. There such deeds were done that a brave man who missed this marvellous spectacle could not hope to see anything so wonderful all his life long. For, if we may believe our elders, a brook flowing between low banks through the plain was greatly increased by blood from the wounds of the slain. It was not flooded by showers, as brooks usually rise, but was swollen by a strange stream and turned into a torrent by the increase of blood. Those whose wounds drove them to slake their parching thirst drank water mingled with gore. In their wretched plight they were forced to drink what they thought was the blood they had poured from their own wounds. (Jordanes)

Although we do not know what happened on Aetius' left where his Franks were probably stationed, it is clear that the Visigoths on the other flank came under immense pressure. The Visigothic King Theodoric rode up and down the line to steady his men and keep the shield wall intact as they faced the Ostrogoths while the Huns began to threaten their left flank. As he was doing so, disaster struck.

> While riding by to encourage his army, Theodoric was thrown from his horse and trampled under foot by his own men, thus ending his days at a ripe old age. But others say he was slain by the spear of Andag of the host of the Ostrogoths. (Jordanes)

At that moment Thorismund, Theodoric's son, intervened to save the day.

> [Thorismund's Visigoths] fell upon the horde of the Huns and nearly slew Attila. But he prudently took flight and straightway shut himself and his companions within the barriers of the camp, which he had fortified with wagons. (Jordanes)

The fighting raged on over the plains as dusk fell and the Huns fell back to their wagon laager. Evidence for an orderly withdrawal rather than a rout is hinted at in Jordanes' description of intense combat right up to the Hun wagons:

> As he [Thorismund] was fighting bravely, someone wounded him in the head and dragged him from his horse. Then he was rescued by the watchful care of his followers and withdrew from the fierce conflict.

Our only near contemporary source, Jordanes, mentions only the actions by the Goths on both sides so we have no idea of how the Franks fared. The Huns fought as mounted archers and it is probable that many of Attila's east Germanic allies such as the Gepids and Ostrogoths had relatively large numbers of horsemen alongside spearmen and archers on foot. After more than three decades of settlement in south-western Gaul the Visigoths were probably well-equipped from Roman arms factories and many would have owned horses. In all likelihood the main Visigothic contingent dismounted and formed a shield wall to fend off attacks by the Hun horse archers although it may be that Thorismund's contingent would have been mounted to deliver the battle-winning charge on Aetius' right flank.

What then of the Franks and other western Germans such as the Alamanni and Burgundians? The traditional view is that they would have fought on foot as most of the Alamanni had done at the Battle of Strasbourg (see Chapter 3). Grave finds show many warriors were buried with spears, franciscae, short swords, and shields with prominent central bosses which could be used offensively as well as for protection. This is consistent with the equipment of warriors fighting on foot and Sidonius Apollinaris' description of Frankish fighting methods quoted above (see *The Appearance of the Franks*). On the other hand, horse burials have also been discovered and the graves of wealthier Frankish and Alamannic men often contained items of horse furniture while those of poorer men had bows and arrows.

A Frankish army on home ground where all able-bodied men could be called on probably had a mix of troop types. The mainstay of the army would have been good warriors who tended to fight on foot. The wealthier of them would have had horses but they would not have been a separate cavalry arm. The mounted Frankish warriors would often dismount to fight on foot as Chnodomar's Alamanni had done against Julian. Poorer men supported their betters with archery and, when the situation required it, other men may also have used bows and arrows as Genobaud, Marcomer, and Sunno's men did in the previous century (see Chapter 3).

The Frankish contingents following both Aetius and Attila would have been bands of picked men rather than tribal levies. Many of them may have owned or appropriated horses but probably most dismounted to fight on foot on the Catalaunian Plains, especially those on Aetius' side as he fought a defensive battle. As Attila's army was primarily a cavalry army it is possible that those of his Franks, Alamanni and Thuringians who had horses may have remained mounted. On the other hand, a body of good warriors on foot would have been more useful auxiliaries for an army with a high preponderance of horsemen.

On the defensive Aetius' Franks would have formed a shield wall, perhaps alongside the Burgundians and Roman infantry. On the attack the Franks tended to surge forward in a dense column which Tacitus and Ammianus described as a wedge (*cuneus*). These wedge formations should not be taken too literally. The *cuneus* was more like an attack column with the leader front and centre surrounded by his household warriors. As the column surged forward the leader and his best men would have advanced more quickly while those on the vulnerable flanks held back. By the time they reached the enemy, the formation would have resembled a rough wedge. Sidonius' description of 'whirling shields' and men running into close combat behind a volley of throwing axes and spears, tends to indicate a relatively loose formation which allowed each individual warrior to wield his weapons to best effect with the most enthusiastic surging forward.

Nightfall put an end to the fighting. Attila was defeated but his army was not destroyed. The victorious but exhausted Roman army camped on the field, apparently quite close to the Huns as on the following day a shower of arrows from the Roman camp was able to keep the Huns at bay. Then, surprisingly, Aetius allowed Attila to retreat rather than launching an assault to finish him off.

When the battle was finished, Aetius said to Thorismund: 'Make haste and return swiftly to your native land, for fear you lose your father's kingdom because of your brother.' The latter, on hearing this, departed speedily with the intention of anticipating his brother, and seizing his father's throne first. At the same time Aetius by a stratagem caused the king of the Franks to flee. When they had gone, Aetius took the spoils of the battle and returned victoriously to his country with much booty. And Attila retreated with a few men. Not long after Aquileia was captured by the Huns and burned and altogether destroyed. Italy was overrun and plundered. Thorismund, whom we have mentioned above, overcame the Alans in battle, and was himself defeated later on by his brothers, after many quarrels and battles, and put to death. (Gregory of Tours)

Gregory's account, which is backed up by Jordanes, may or may not be true. Thorismund's position was precarious as he was later killed by his younger brother Theodoric II who in turn was assassinated later by another brother – Euric. So the Gothic heir apparent had every reason to depart the field quickly and get back to Toulouse to secure his throne. It is even possible that the Goths and Franks departed against Aetius' wishes and the above stories were invented to add greater nobility to their tales.

There is, however, one other version of events recounted in the seventh century *Chronicle of Fredegar*. Here we are told that Aetius promised the Huns and Goths half of Gaul each for defending it against the other. Then he extorted 10,000 gold solidi from both of them. *Fredegar* asserts that, rather than letting the Huns go, Aetius with Romans and Franks pursued them into the lands of the Thuringians (east of the Middle Rhine).

Whatever the truth of the matter, Attila was able to withdraw from the field in relatively good order and make it back across the Rhine to his heartland in Pannonia. He was still strong enough to invade Italy the following year. Many modern historians have criticized Aetius for not destroying Attila's army when he had the chance. After taking heavy casualties, and facing an inevitable break-up of his temporary alliance, Aetius probably had no choice. Even if he was not motivated by a strategic desire to keep the Huns as a counterbalance to Visigothic and Frankish power he was probably wise to give his enemy a line of retreat rather than force another costly engagement.

Three years after the battle on the Catalaunian Plains most of the main protagonists were dead. Theodoric, king of the Visigoths, died on the field, his successor Thorismund was then assassinated by his brother Theodoric II in 453. Attila died that same year and his Germanic subjects rose up to defeat the Huns at the Battle of Nedao in 454. Aetius also met his death in 454 – killed by the ungrateful Emperor Valentinian III who saw his warlord as a threat.

Chapter 6

The End of Roman Gaul

The Fall of the West

Attila's defeat on the Catalaunian Plains was a significant moment in the history of Europe. We cannot know what might have happened had Attila won. Quite possibly much would have been destroyed which ended up being preserved. Equally possibly Attila may have come to some arrangement with Ravenna and established a kingdom for himself within the Western Empire. Had this been the case he may well have settled down to rule it in much the same way as the Franks did later. The Huns, however, had far less respect for Greco-Roman civilization than the Franks. Had the Huns been able to carve out a kingdom in Gaul then the course of European history surely would have changed significantly.

Aetius' nominal victory in 451 did not preserve Roman power in Gaul. When Aetius was assassinated the various Gallic factions jostled with each other for power and influence. In the south-west the Visigoths expanded into Spain, taking advantage of the vacuum left by the earlier Vandal departure to Africa. Some bands also pushed northwards into the Loire Valley as others threatened Provence. Theodoric II who had supplanted his brother Thorismund shortly after the Catalaunian Plains was in turn assassinated by his younger brother Euric in 466.

The Bacaudae remained endemic throughout Gaul and their stronghold in Armorica remained free of Imperial control. Refugees from Britain, fleeing the Saxons, began to join them.

> Now Euric, king of the Visigoths, perceived the frequent change of Roman emperors and strove to hold Gaul by his own right. The Emperor heard of it and asked the Britons for aid. Their King Riothamus came with twelve thousand men into the state of the Bituriges [Bourges in central France] by the way of Ocean... Euric

came against them with an innumerable army, and after a long fight he routed Riothamus, king of the Britons, before the Romans could join him. (Jordanes)

We know little about Riothamus. He, and the exploits of his men, are tied up in the heroic Arthurian legends. Most likely he was a Romano-British warlord who was losing ground at home and took the opportunity to make a bid for power in Gaul just as Magnus Maximus and Constantine III had done before. What we do know is that the Celtic language survived in Brittany into modern times, most likely due to an influx of British migrants who gave the region its modern name.

In the aftermath of Aetius' assassination, Valentinian III was in turn killed by Aetius' bodyguards. In 455 the Gallo-Roman Avitus was proclaimed emperor with the support of the Visigoths. He was deposed the following year by Ricimer who had risen to become the Western Empire's most powerful warlord, making and breaking emperors for the next two decades.

Shortly after Aetius' death a Romano-Gallic warlord by the name of Aegidius was beginning to make his presence felt. According to Priscus, Aegidius had served under Aetius and continued to command some of the remnants of Aetius' army in northern Gaul, probably with the continuing support of many of the Salian Franks. He also had the backing of the Emperor Majorian who had been placed on the western throne by Ricimer in 457. In 458 Aegidius took Lyons from the Burgundians and later fought against the Visigoths at Arles and Orléans. In the latter battle he was supported by many Franks and Gregory of Tours says that the Franks proclaimed Aegidius as their king.

This coincided with Ricimer's deposition of the West Roman Emperor Majorian. His replacement was Libius Severus whose sovereignty Aegidius did not recognize. Aegidius was not the only one who paid no attention to Ricimer's new emperor. Another Gallo-Roman warlord, by the name of Paul – possibly one of Aegidius' former officers – is recorded as acting independently with Frankish support against the Saxons on the Loire. These Saxons were led by Eadwacer, often mistakenly equated with the Scirian Odoacer who deposed the last West Roman emperor in 476. Another independent Gallo-Roman war leader, or more correctly

Franco-Roman, was Arbogast who controlled the west bank of the Rhine around Trier and Cologne. He was possibly descended from the Frank of the same name who had fought at the Battle of Frigidus (see Chapter 3).

By the mid-460s the West Roman Empire had effectively broken up. Britain had long ago been abandoned; Africa was held by the Vandals; and the Visigoths were expanding into Spain while other parts were held by the Suebi who had broken from the Vandals when the latter crossed into Africa. Only Italy remained under the sway of whomever Ricimer put on the throne at Ravenna. A brief resurgence of hope for the Gallo-Romans died with Avitus and Majorian. Gaul was being carved up amongst the various warring factions including those Romans, like Aegidius, who had broken from Ravenna even if none of them proclaimed themselves emperor as their predecessors would have done. Only a brief strip of modern Provence, centred on Arles, remained under Imperial control. That Aegidius accepted the title of King of the Franks from his Frankish followers shows how much the balance of power had shifted. Kingship of the Franks was now more influential than the hollow title of West Roman Emperor.

Aegidius died in 464. Four years later the West and East Roman Empires combined their forces in an attempt to reconquer Africa from the Vandals. As many as 1,000 ships, carrying an army of at least 20,000 soldiers, set sail from Constantinople for Sicily where the intent was to link up with the West Romans and then capture Carthage. It did not go well for the Romans. At the Battle of Mercurium, off the tip of what is now called Cap Bon in modern Tunisia, the Vandal fleet destroyed the Roman armada. Grain supplies from Africa were essential for the survival of the West. If Rome and Constantinople had been able to retake Africa from the Vandals then the West could possibly have survived. Without it, the rump of the Western Empire was doomed.

In 475 Orestes, Attila's former Roman secretary, made his son Romulus Augustulus emperor with the backing of Herul, Rugian, Scirian and Thuringian mercenaries. These men were now what constituted the Roman army of Italy. Under the leadership of Odoacer, they rose in revolt the following year, killed Orestes and on 4 September 476 deposed Romulus, effectively ending the West Roman Empire forever.

Childeric

As Roman Gaul was slipping further into chaos one leader of the Franks became increasingly prominent. This was Childeric who may have been the grandson of Chlogio or possibly his son (see previous chapter). We know more of Childeric than most fifth century Frankish leaders thanks to the discovery of his grave at Tournai in 1653. Although many of the artefacts were stolen they were documented shortly after their discovery. Childeric was buried with the sort of weaponry and jewellery which was typical for the grave of a prominent fifth century Frank. These included a francisca (throwing axe), sword fittings, gold buckles, arm rings, broaches, and decorations from horse harnesses. What sets this grave aside from all others is a signet ring with the inscription *Childerici Regis* (belonging to King Childeric).

This is archaeological confirmation of the fact that from the mid fifth century the most prominent Frankish leaders had taken the title of *Rex* (King) while Gregory of Tours referred to the fourth century leaders as *Duces* (Dukes).

Childeric's rise to prominence did not start out auspiciously.

Childeric was excessively wanton and being king of the Franks he began to dishonour their daughters. They were angry with him on this account and took his kingdom from him. And when he learned that they wished also to kill him he hastened to Thuringia, leaving there a man who was dear to him to calm their furious tempers [Wiomad]. He arranged also for a sign when he should be able to return to his country, that is, they divided a gold piece between them and Childeric took one half and his friend kept the other part, saying: 'Whenever I send you this part and the joined parts make one coin, then you shall return securely to your native place.'

Accordingly Childeric went off to Thuringia and remained in hiding with King Basinus and Basina his wife. The Franks, after he was driven out, with one accord selected as king Aegidius, whom we have mentioned before as the commander of the troops sent by the Republic [Rome]. And when he [Aegidius] was in the eighth year of his reign over them that faithful friend [Wiomad] secretly won the good will of the Franks and sent messengers to Childeric with the part of the divided coin which he had kept, and Childeric learned by this sure sign that he was wanted by the Franks, and returned from Thuringia at their request and was restored to his kingdom...

Basina, whom we have mentioned above, left her husband and came to Childeric. And when he asked anxiously for what reason she had come so far to see him it is said that she answered: 'I know your worth,' said she, 'and that you are very strong, and therefore I have come to live with you. For let me tell you that if I had known of any one more worthy than you in parts beyond the sea I should certainly have sought to live with him.' And he was glad and united her to him in marriage. And she conceived and bore a son and called his name Clovis. He was a great and distinguished warrior. (Gregory of Tours)

Disentangling fact from fiction and legend in the above quote is not easy. One interpretation is that Childeric's father (possibly the legendary Merovech) led the Franks who supported Aetius against Attila. Dying shortly after the battle on the Catalaunian Plains his son Childeric took over the leadership of the band of Franks who could claim victory over the Huns and also those Franks who had supported the elder of Chlogio's sons. The prestige gained from this victory would have attracted more followers. When Aegidius took over the remnants of the Roman army in northern Gaul he may have seen Childeric more as a rival than an ally. If Childeric had been abusing his power, as Gregory says, then Aegidius took the opportunity to drive him into exile, accepting the proclamation of the grateful Salian Franks to become their king.

Gregory says that Childeric took refuge amongst the Thuringians. These were one of the Germanic tribes who had supported Attila in 451. In Childeric's time they were living to the east of the Middle Rhine beyond the Ripuarian Franks. If Gregory's story is to be believed, Childeric seduced Basina, wife of the Thuringian King Basinus, and took her with him back to Gaul. Some modern historians doubt this tale, suggesting that Childeric may have gone to Tongres rather than Thuringia. As Gregory occasionally confused Alans with Alamanni, we have reason to doubt his absolute accuracy when it comes to names with similar alliteration. The same could be said about Childeric's wife Basina. Gregory's assertion that Childeric took her from the Thuringian King Basinus may again have been no more than a conclusion based on the similarity of their names.

Going all the way over the Rhine to seek refuge with a tribe he or his father had previously been in conflict with does seem a little unlikely. Joining with another group of Salian Franks in Tongres makes more sense as we know that in Childeric's time the Franks were not a united people. Some supported Childeric, some supported Aegidius, while others would have done their best to stay out of it.

Wherever he went, the eight years of Childeric's exile more or less coincided with the ascension of the Emperor Majorian whom Aegidius' supported (457) and Aegidius' death in 464 or 465. With Aegidius out of the way the field was open for Childeric to make his return:

> Childeric fought a battle at Orléans [against the Visigoths]. Odoacer [Eadwacer] with the Saxons came to Angers. At that time a great plague destroyed the people. Aegidius died and left a son, Syagrius by name. On his death [Eadwacer] received hostages from Angers and other places. The Britons were driven from Bourges by the Goths, and many were slain at the village of Déols [in the central Loire Valley]. Count Paul with the Romans and Franks made war on the Goths and took booty. When [Eadwacer] came to Angers, King Childeric came on the following day. He slew Count Paul and took the city...
>
> After this war was waged between the Saxons and the Romans the Saxons fled... Their islands were captured and ravaged by the Franks, and many were slain. In the ninth month of that year, there was an earthquake. [Eadwacer] made an alliance with Childeric, and they subdued the Alamanni. (Gregory of Tours)

Gregory of Tours wrote his history more than 100 years after Childeric and his version of events is not corroborated by any contemporary accounts. The signet ring found in the grave at Tournai confirms that Childeric was a king of the Franks but we know nothing for certain about his rise to power nor what sort of power he held. In addition to the above-quoted campaign against the Saxons, there was a battle fought near Orléans in

463 just before Aegidius' death. There the Visigoths were defeated by an army commanded either by Childeric (according to Gregory of Tours) or Aegidius (according to the contemporary Spanish chronicler Hydatius).

> In Armorica, Frederic, the brother of King Theodoric II [of the Visigoths], rose up against Aegidius, count and *Magister Militum*, a man who enjoyed an excellent reputation and who pleased God with his good works. Frederic and his men were defeated and killed. (Hydatius)

As this battle took place before Aegidius' death it is more likely that he commanded the army which defeated the Visigoths at Orléans. It is not impossible that Childeric was involved, either cooperating with Aegidius, or making his bid to return from exile supported by a different group of Franks from those following Aegidius. It is also possible that Childeric never really went into exile at all and acted as a subordinate to Aegidius until the latter's death.

Whomever commanded, was the victorious army at Orléans Roman or Frankish? The answer is probably both. Aegidius was a Roman but he had broken with the Emperor Libius Severus, no longer held any Imperial command and would have been regarded as a rebel by the Imperial authorities in Ravenna. On the other hand he was acknowledged by some Salian Franks as their king. If Childeric had commanded at Orléans he may have done so a pseudo-Roman general. Any 'Roman' army in northern Gaul at this time would have been primarily composed of Franks along with recruits from the remaining settlements of *laeti*. This would have been the case whether Aegidius or Childeric commanded it. It may well have been that the Battle of Orléans in 463 was part of a Roman civil war fought through surrogates – the Visigoths acting against Aegidius on behalf of the West Roman Emperor Severus to destroy a rebel, and the Franks in support of Aegidius.

In the two decades following Aegidius' death in the mid-460s Childeric consolidated his power over the old Roman province of *Belgica Secunda* which included the cities of Reims, Cambrai, Soissons and Tournai. In doing so he not only brought many of the Salian Franks under his control but he also won the support of key bishops who held sway over the Gallo-

Romans in the absence of temporal Roman power. When he died in the early 480s Childeric had laid the foundations of the Frankish kingdom which his son Clovis would carve out of Roman Gaul.

The exact date of Childeric's death and Clovis' ascension is not precisely known. Childeric's grave was discovered in the 1600s long before radiocarbon dating although the coins found there give some indication that he must have died in the 480s. A discovery of Frankish burial pits in 1983, only 20m from Childeric's grave, revealed ten horse skeletons dated to around 490, give or take a decade or two. Such a lavish sacrifice would have been appropriate for a royal funeral and so it is quite likely that these horses were interred at more or less the same time as Childeric. Lacking any firmer evidence it is probable that Childeric died in the early 480s. The traditionally accepted date is 481 although some modern historians place it a few years later.

The Last Roman

Aegidius was succeeded by Syagrius who may have been his son. What was it that Syagrius inherited? A popular interpretation is that he ruled over a Roman kingdom in northern Gaul which survived beyond the fall of the West Roman Empire. This version imagines a Gallo-Roman state ruled by Syagrius surrounded by Salian Franks to the north; Britons and Bacaudae to the west; Goths to the South; and Ripuarian Franks, Burgundians and Alamanni to the east. Modern historians tend to cast doubt on the romantic idea of an enduring Gallo-Roman kingdom beyond the end of the Western Empire.

Unlike Aegidius, Syagrius was not an acknowledged king of the Franks, nor did he hold any Imperial Roman title. He probably inherited those elements of Aegidius' army which did not go over to Childeric. This made him a power to be reckoned with but did not give him a kingdom. His power was his army, not land nor people who acknowledged his authority and provided a solid tax base. His army was mostly probably composed of Franks and *laeti* as much or more than Gallo-Romans. Most of the latter had either little military worth or had gone over to the Bacaudae.

There is a counterargument to this which comes from the sixth century East Roman historian Procopius describing the state of fifth century Gaul:

as time went on, the Visigoths forced their way into the Roman Empire and seized all Spain and the portion of Gaul lying beyond the Rhône River and made them subject and tributary to themselves. By that time it so happened that the Arborychi [Armoricans] had become soldiers of the Romans. The Germans [Franks] wishing to make this people subject to themselves, since their territory adjoined their own and they had changed the government under which they had lived from of old, began to plunder their land and, being eager to make war, marched against them with their whole people. But the Arborychi proved their valour and loyalty to the Romans and showed themselves brave men in this war, and since the Germans were not able to overcome them by force, they wished to win them over and make the two peoples kin by intermarriage. This suggestion the Arborychi received not at all unwillingly; for both, as it happened, were Christians. And in this way they were united into one people, and came to have great power.

Now other Roman soldiers had been stationed at the frontiers of Gaul to serve as guards. And these soldiers, having no means of returning to Rome, and at the same time being unwilling to yield to their enemy [the Visigoths] who were Arians, gave themselves, together with their military standards and the land which they had long been guarding for the Romans, to the Arborychi and Germans. They handed down to their offspring all the customs of their fathers, which were thus preserved, and this people has held them in sufficient reverence to guard them even up to my time. For even at the present day they are clearly recognised as belonging to the legions to which they were assigned when they served in ancient times, and they always carry their own standards when they enter battle, and always follow the customs of their fathers. And they preserve the dress of the Romans in every particular, even as regards their shoes.

Procopius had no first-hand experience of Gaul but he wrote at a time when the Franks were making advances into northern Italy and fought against the East Roman army (see Chapter 9). So he did have some knowledge of the Franks a century later than the time he was writing about. Procopius' reference to the Arborychi (most likely the Britons of Armorica) being loyal to Rome possibly derives to the fact that a contingent of Armoricans fought for Aetius on the Catalaunian Plains. That he claims they later joined up with the Christian Franks must refer to the time after Clovis' conversion (see Chapter 7).

It may have been that some Roman soldiers remained active in Gaul beyond the fall of the Western Empire, taking service with whomever could pay them or at least give them the means to support themselves. Since the time of Diocletian (284–305) sons were obliged to follow their fathers' profession so the son of a soldier would become a soldier when he came of age. Assuming that Syagrius took over his father's army then it is quite likely that he had a number of men descended from the remnants of the Imperial Gallic army in addition to Franks and other barbarians such as the Alan settlers near Orléans. There is evidence that Gallo and Hispano-Romans fought for the Visigoths. If Procopius is correct then others joined up with the Armoricans and Franks. That these men still formed identifiable Roman units carrying the standards of long defunct legions seems more than a little fanciful although clothing and hairstyles may have set them apart from the Franks – at least initially.

It is tempting to take a romanticized view of Syagrius taking a last stand for Roman civilization in Gaul like his legendary contemporary Arthur in Britain. Gregory of Tours says that Syagrius 'had his seat in the city of Soissons'. This has caused some people to imagine a Gallo-Roman Kingdom of Soissons ruled by Syagrius from Aegidius' death for a decade beyond the fall of the West Roman Empire, which held out against the barbarian hordes. Unfortunately this is not very likely. Gregory possibly inflated Syagrius' power in order to make his defeat by the Franks more noteworthy.

Syagrius may have been a Roman but he did not have a recognized Roman command or title. Thanks to the troops who went over to him on Aegidius' death, he held sway over a patch of northern Gaul, based on Soissons, against Childeric and other warlords. This army may have had a number of Gallo-Roman soldiers, as discussed above, but many others would have been Franks, Alans and possibly Saxons as well.

In a letter to Syagrius, Sidonius Apollinaris makes much of his ability to speak the Frankish language:

You are the great-grandson of a consul, and in the male line too... I am therefore inexpressibly amazed that you have quickly acquired a knowledge of the German tongue with such ease. And yet I know that your boyhood had a good schooling in liberal studies and I know that you often declaimed with spirit and eloquence before your professor of oratory. This being so, I would like you to tell me how you have managed to absorb so swiftly into your inner being the exact sounds of an alien race. So now after reading Virgil under the schoolmaster's cane and toiling and working through the rich fluency of [Cicero] you burst forth before my eyes like a young falcon from an old nest.

It is not surprising that Sidonius – a slightly pompous classicist who looked back wistfully to Roman civilization of previous centuries – would have been confused by Syagrius' ability to speak German. Yet this was the new reality. Being able to recite Virgil or Cicero would have been of little use to Syagrius as he tried to hold on to his patch of northern Gaul. Being able to speak to his Frankish soldiers in their own language, however, would have been a great asset. Sidonius' image of a 'new falcon from an old nest' is quite apt. The old nest was the bygone days of Roman power, the new falcon appreciated that power in northern Gaul now rested with the Franks.

Syagrius' power probably only extended as far as the reach of the soldiers who followed him. He may have been a Gallo-Roman warlord but he did not rule a Gallo-Roman kingdom distinct from the other parts of Gaul controlled by Germanic kings or the Bacaudae. His army was probably just as Frankish as that commanded by Childeric, and his son Clovis who succeeded him. Theirs was probably just as Roman as Syagrius'. What Childeric and Clovis had, which Syagrius lacked, was that they were recognized as kings of the Salian Franks and could draw on a much deeper base of support.

In the fifth year of [Clovis'] reign [around 486] Syagrius, king of the Romans, son of Aegidius, had his seat in the city of Soissons which Aegidius, who has been mentioned before, once held. Clovis came against him with Ragnachar, his kinsman, because he [Ragnachar] used to possess the kingdom. They [Clovis and Ragnachar] demanded battle. Syagrius did not delay nor was he afraid to resist. And so they fought against each other and Syagrius, seeing his army crushed, turned his back and fled swiftly to King Alaric [Alaric II, king of the Visigoths] at Toulouse. Clovis sent to Alaric to send him back, otherwise he [Alaric] was to know that Clovis would make war on him for his refusal. Alaric was afraid that he would incur the anger of the Franks on account of Syagrius, seeing it is the fashion of the Goths to be terrified, and so he surrendered Syagrius in chains to Clovis' envoys. Clovis took him and gave orders to put him under guard. When he [Clovis] had got his kingdom he directed that Syagrius be executed secretly. (Gregory of Tours)

So it was a decade after the fall of the West Roman Empire, that the last Gallo-Roman warlord was defeated by the Franks led by Clovis son of Childeric – after whom later French kings took the name of 'Louis'. From this point onwards control of Gaul was no longer a struggle between Romans and Germans but rather between competing Germanic kingdoms.

Clovis King of the Franks

Clovis' victory over Syagrius is often referred to as the Battle of Soissons based on Gregory of Tours' assertion that Soissons was Syagrius' headquarters. As Soissons contained a Roman armoury and was well protected by walls it may well have been Syagrius' main base. Even so, we do not know where the battle took place, nor the numbers of troops involved nor how they fought. Even the date is in question – 486 is the traditional date but analysis by some modern historians suggest it may have been later than that, perhaps in the early 490s. At this later date the attention of the Visigothic King Alaric II was fixed on Italy in support of Theodoric the Ostrogoth against Odoacer, the self-proclaimed King of Italy who had overthrown the last West Roman emperor.

As Syagrius fled to the Visigoths after his defeat it may be that he had been supported by them, perhaps relying on Visigothic allies to supplement his locally recruited Franks, Alans and Gallo-Romans. If this is true then the diversion of Visigoths to Italy in 490 may have provided the opportunity for Clovis to make his move.

The Visigoths at this time held sway over south-western France and were expanding their influence into Spain at the expense of the Suebi and Hispano-Romans. The Armorican Bacaudae and Britons ran their own affairs in modern Brittany. The Alamanni held both banks of the Upper Rhine while the Burgundians controlled that part of modern France which we now call Burgundy.

Clovis may have been the most powerful Frank in the last decade of the fifth century but he did not yet have the allegiance of all his kinsfolk. The Ripuarian Franks, who had taken over Cologne and much of the Middle Rhine, did not acknowledge his sovereignty, nor did all of the Salian Franks of modern Belgium and northern France. There is an interesting passage in Gregory of Tours which gives us an indication of this. Clovis was supported by Ragnachar of Cambrai against Syagrius but he also called on other Franks, not all of whom heeded the call.

> When [Clovis] had fought with Syagrius, Chararic had been summoned to help Clovis, but stood at a distance, aiding neither side, but awaiting the outcome, in order to form a league of friendship with him to whom victory came. For this reason Clovis was angry, and went out against him. He entrapped and captured him and his son also, and kept them in prison, and gave them the tonsure [forced them to cut their hair and become priests] ... When Chararic complained of his degradation and wept, it is said that his son remarked: 'It was on green wood,' said he, 'that these twigs were cut, and they are not altogether withered. They will shoot out quickly, and be able to grow. May he perish as swiftly who has done this.' This utterance was reported to the ears of Clovis, namely, that they were threatening to let their hair grow back and kill him. So [Clovis] ordered them both to be put to death. When they were dead, he took their kingdom with the treasures and people. (Gregory of Tours)

Ragnachar of Cambrai had supported Clovis against Syagrius. Gregory of Tours tells us that Clovis rewarded his followers with gold bracelets and belts but that they were of gilded bronze not pure gold. Despite Ragnachar's loyalty Clovis did not want any rivals. He bribed Ragnachar's followers with the false gold and they handed Ragnachar over to Clovis along with his brother Ricchar.

> Clovis said to Ragnachar: 'Why have you humiliated our family in permitting yourself to be bound? It would have been better for you to die.' Raising his axe [Clovis] dashed it against [Ragnachar's] head. Then Clovis turned to Ragnachar's brother and said: 'If you had aided your brother, he would not have been bound.' In the same way he smote [Ricchar] with his axe and killed him. After their death their betrayers perceived that the gold which they had received from the king was false. When they told the king of this, it is said that he answered: 'Rightly,' said he. 'Does he receive this kind of gold, who of his own will brings his own master to death? It ought to suffice them that they were alive and were not put to death, to mourn amid torments the wicked betrayal of their masters.' When they heard this, they prayed for mercy, saying it was enough for them if they were allowed to live. The kings named above were kinsmen of Clovis, and their brother Rignomer was also slain by Clovis' order... When they were dead Clovis received all their kingdom and treasures. Having killed many other kings and his nearest relatives, of whom he was jealous lest they take the kingdom from him, he extended his rule over all the Gauls. (Gregory of Tours)

Clovis' ruthless assertion of control over the Franks was typical of both Roman and German leaders of the age. Roman emperors happily murdered their rivals and their rivals families. The same was true of the Gothic kings. Thorismund, the Visigothic hero at the Battle on the Catalaunian Plains was killed by his brother Theodoric. He in turn was done away with by another brother – Euric. The later medieval concepts of the divine right of kings and hereditary royal families were still some way off. Leaders in the fifth century emerged if they could attract enough followers and reward them with the fruits of victory. Kingship was awarded to the most powerful men and had to be maintained with the kind of ruthlessness Clovis demonstrated. Many of the men who had followed his father Childeric would initially have supported the young Clovis. Their continued loyalty, however, would only have lasted as long as Clovis appeared to be a winner. His victory over Syagrius, and execution of his rival relatives, cemented Clovis' position as the pre-eminent warlord in northern Gaul and laid the foundations of the Merovingian dynasty.

Although a pagan, Clovis was careful to cultivate the Roman bishops. After 476 there was no longer a West Roman emperor and Clovis' victory over Syagrius had removed the last Gallo-Roman warlord even if Syagrius held no Imperial command. In the absence of temporal authorities, the Romans of northern Gaul looked to their bishops for leadership. For most of the latter part of the fifth century the bishops of the larger cities provided much more than spiritual guidance to the inhabitants of their sees.

The number of warriors Clovis could call on would have been relatively small compared to the armies of the later Roman Empire. He had enough men to stand up to rivals but not enough to keep down a rebellious population which considerably outnumbered the Franks. By keeping the bishops on side Clovis could concentrate on defeating his Germanic rivals while the bishops ensured the acceptance of their flocks to Clovis' suzerainty.

There is a parallel in relatively modern times. After the English conquest of New France in North America the new English protestant rulers allowed the local population to practise their Roman Catholic religion without interference. As a result, the original inhabitants of what is now Quebec in Canada, looked to their clergy for leadership, carrying on much as they had done before the conquest. When the United States invaded Canada in 1776 and again in 1812 the French Canadians supported the status quo, ignoring the blandishments of the Americans to throw off the English yoke.

Clovis' policy of seeking the support of the Christian bishops of northern Gaul, rather than sacking their cities and taking their riches, had a similar effect. That Clovis was a pagan was no greater problem for the Gallo-Roman bishops than English Protestantism was for the catholic clerics of New France in the late eighteenth century. In some ways it was an advantage, as we shall see in the next chapter.

Chapter 7

From Gaul to Francia

A Matter of Faith

Unlike the Franks, the fifth century Goths and Vandals were Christians. They followed the teachings of Bishop Arius whose followers converted many of the east German tribes in the fourth century. In simple layman's terms Arius believed that Jesus was a man created by God the Father. He was from God but Jesus and the Father were not the same being. Others held that the Trinity of the Father, Son and Holy Ghost were one and the same with no differentiation or hierarchy between them.

The subtle nuances surrounding the nature of the Trinity resulted in the deaths of thousands of believers on both sides as the various adherents of one idea or the other persecuted their opponents with fanatical fervour. The Council of Nicaea in 325 attempted to draw a line under the controversy, defining the relationship of the Son and Father as 'of the same substance'. As a result, the idea that the Father, Son and Holy Ghost were the same being became known as the Nicene belief, and from this we get the Nicene Creed, which is today the official doctrine of the Roman Catholic Church.

The Nicaean Council did not settle the matter. Furious, frequently deadly, debates continued as the Roman Empire became consumed with the relationship between Jesus and God the Father. In 381 the Arian version of Christianity was finally declared heretical and the Nicene Creed became the only acceptable interpretation of Christianity for Romans. The Goths and Vandals, however, still held to the Arian version of Christianity. This put up an impenetrable barrier between them and the Roman populace over which they ruled. The heretic Arians were seen by the ecclesiastical authorities as a much greater threat than mere pagans. The former was a threat to the authority of the Church while pagans would no doubt later convert to the true faith. Therefore collusion between the pagan Franks and Christian bishops of northern Gaul was possible while the same did not happen in Spain or North Africa where the Arian Goths and Vandals held sway.

For the Goths and Vandals their Arian-Christian religion became a central part of their identity – setting them apart from the Romans. The same cannot be said for Clovis or his pagan Frankish followers. Pagan beliefs were more personal than the state-controlled Christianity which emerged in the latter years of the Roman Empire. Some of Clovis' followers would have been Gallo-Roman Christians and he respected the power of the Christian bishops – using them to consolidate his rule over the Gallo-Roman population of the lands he controlled. Without holding strong Arian beliefs it was relatively easy for the Franks to convert to the Catholic, or Nicaean, version of Christianity.

Clovis probably converted to Christianity at some point in the last decade of the fifth century. In the 490s he was engaged in a war with the pagan Alamanni on the Rhine. The Chronicle of St Denis gives an account of Clovis' conversion linking it to this war and the influence of his Christian wife Clotilda.

At this time the King [Clovis] was yet in the errors of his idolatry and went to war with the Alamanni, since he wished to render them subject. Long was the battle and many were slain on one side or the other. The Franks fought to win glory and renown, the Alamanni to save life and freedom. When the King at length saw the slaughter of his people and the boldness of his foes, he had greater expectation of disaster than of victory. He looked up to heaven humbly, and spoke thus: 'Most mighty God, whom my queen Clothilde [Clotilda] worships and adores with heart and soul, I pledge you perpetual service unto your faith, if only you give me now the victory over my enemies.

Instantly when he had said this, his men were filled with burning valour, and a great fear smote his enemies, so that they turned their backs and fled the battle; and victory remained with the King and with the Franks. The king of the Alamanni was slain; and as for the Alamanni, seeing themselves discomfited and that their king had fallen, they yielded themselves to Chlodovocar [Clovis] and his Franks, and became his subjects.

The King returned after this victory into Frankland. He went to Rheims, and told the Queen what had befallen; and they together gave thanks unto Our Lord. The King made his confession of faith from his heart, and with right good will. The Queen, who was wondrously overjoyed at the conversion of her lord, went at once to Saint Remi [Bishop Remigius after whom the modern city of Reims takes its modern name]. Straightway he [Remi] hastened to the palace to teach the King the way by which he could come unto God, for his mind was still in doubt about it. He [Remigius] presented himself boldly before Clovis, although a little while before he [the bishop] had not dared to come before him.

When St. Remi had preached to the King the Christian faith and taught him the way of the Cross, and when the King had known what the faith was, Clovis promised fervently that he would henceforth never serve any save the all-powerful God. After that he said he would put to the test and try the hearts and wills of his chieftains and lesser people: for he would convert them more easily if they were converted by pleasant means and by mild words, than if they were driven to it by force; and this method seemed best to St. Remi. The folk and the chieftains were assembled by the command of the King. He arose in the midst of them, and spoke to this effect: 'Lords of the Franks, it seems to me highly profitable that you should know first of all what are those gods which you worship. For we are certain of their falsity: and we come right freely into the knowledge of Him who is the true God. Know of a surety that this same God which I preach to you has given victory over your enemies in the recent battle against the Alamanni. Lift, therefore, your hearts in just hope; and ask the sovereign defender, that He give to you all that you desire – that He saved our souls and gave us victory over our enemies.' When the King, full of faith, had thus preached to and admonished his people, one and all banished from their hearts all unbelief, and recognised their creator.

When shortly afterward Chlodovocar [Clovis] set out for the church for baptism, St. Remi prepared a great procession. The streets of Rheims were hung with banners and tapestry... Then came the bishop leading the King by the hand, next the Queen with the multitude. Whilst on the way the King asked of the bishop, if this was the Kingdom of Heaven which he had promised him. 'Not so,' replied the prelate; 'it is the road that leads to it.'

... After having made his profession of the orthodox faith, the King is plunged thrice in the waters of baptism. Then in the name of the holy and indivisible Trinity – Father, Son, and Holy Ghost – the prelate consecrated him with the divine unction. Two sisters of the King and 3000 fighting men of the Franks and a great number of women and children were likewise baptised...

The King showed vast zeal for his new faith. He built a splendid church at Paris, called St. Genevieve, where later he and Clothilde [Clovis' wife] were buried. Faith and religion and zeal for justice were pursued by him all the days of his life. Certain Franks still held to paganism, and found a leader in Prince Ragnachairus [Ragnachar] but he was presently delivered up in fetters to Clovis who put him to death. Thus all the Frankish people were converted and baptised by the merits of St. Remi....

At this time there came to Clovis messengers from Anastasius, the [East Roman] Emperor at Constantinople, who brought him presents from their master, and letters whereof the effect was, that it pleased the Emperor and the Senators that he [Clovis] be made a 'Friend of the Emperor,' and a Patrician and Consul of the Romans. When the King had read these letters, he arrayed himself in the robe of a senator, which the Emperor had sent to him. He mounted upon his charger; and thus he went to the public square before the church of St. Martin; and then he gave great gifts to the people. From this day he was always called 'Consul' and 'Augustus.'

We do not have to accept this version of events as entirely accurate. The very close parallel to the Roman Emperor Constantine's acceptance of Christ at the Battle of Milvian Bridge (AD 312) leaves more than a little doubt as to its absolute veracity. Clovis' execution of Ragnachar possibly happened before his conversion but his Christian wife Clotilda (also Chrodechildis, Clotilde or Clothild) probably had a great influence.

Clotilda was a Burgundian who did her best to bring her husband to Christianity. This is what Gregory of Tours has to say of it:

> He [Clovis] had a first-born son by queen Clotilda, and as his wife wished to consecrate him in baptism, she tried unceasingly to persuade her husband, saying: 'The gods you worship are nothing, and they will be unable to help themselves or any one else...'
>
> The boy, whom they named Ingomer, died after being baptised... At this the king was violently angry, and reproached the queen harshly, saying: 'If the boy had been dedicated in the name of my gods he would certainly have lived. Since he was baptised in the name of your God, he could not live at all...'
>
> After this she bore another son, whom she named Chlodomar at baptism; and when he fell sick, the king said: 'It is impossible that anything else should happen to him than happened to his brother, namely, that being baptised in the name of your Christ, should die at once.' But through the prayers of his mother, and the Lord's command, he became well.
>
> The queen did not cease to urge him to recognise the true God and cease worshipping idols. But he could not be influenced in any way to this belief, until at last a war arose with the Alamanni, in which he was driven by necessity to confess what before he had of his free will denied. It came about that as the two armies were fighting fiercely, there was much slaughter, and Clovis' army began to be in danger of destruction. He saw it and raised his eyes to heaven, and with remorse in his heart he burst into tears and cried: 'Jesus Christ, whom Clotilda asserts to be the son of the living God, who art said to give aid to those in distress, and to bestow victory on those who hope in thee, I beseech the glory of thy aid, with the vow that if thou wilt grant me victory over these enemies, and I shall know that power which she says that people dedicated in thy name have had from thee, I will believe in thee and be baptised in thy name. For I have invoked my own gods but, as I find, they have withdrawn from aiding me; and therefore I believe that they possess no power, since they do not help those who obey them. I now call upon thee, I desire to believe thee only let me be rescued from my adversaries.'

When he said thus, the Alamanni turned their backs, and began to disperse in flight. And when they saw that their king was killed, they submitted to the dominion of Clovis.

Then the queen asked Saint Remi, bishop of Rheims, to summon Clovis secretly, urging him to introduce the king to the word of salvation. And the bishop sent for him secretly and began to urge him to believe in the true God, maker of heaven and earth, and to cease worshipping idols, which could help neither themselves nor any one else...

Whatever actually happened is shrouded in legend and religious propaganda. It may well have been that Clovis accepted Christianity some time before actually being baptized. This would not have been unusual as Constantine the Great turned to Christianity relatively early in his reign but was only baptized on his deathbed. Such a delay would have allowed Clovis to hedge his bets, appearing Christian to the Gallo-Romans while avoiding alienating his pagan Frankish followers.

What we know for certain is that Clovis converted to the Nicaean version of Christianity at some point at the end of the fifth century or early sixth. In doing so many or most of his followers did the same thing. Whether it was his wife's influence or an attempt to rally his Christian soldiers in his war against the Alamanni, Clovis' conversion bridged any remaining gaps between his Frankish warriors and the Christian Gallo-Romans. From this point on Clovis was not only the most powerful temporal power – he also could be seen as defending the true (Nicaean) faith against the heretical Arian Goths.

Clovis Secures the North

Although Clovis was destined to be the conqueror of Roman Gaul, at the time of his conversion to Christianity it was the Goths who seemed most likely to succeed. The Visigoths held south-western France and were expanding into Spain. In 493 the Ostrogoth, Theodoric the Great, took Italy from Odoacer and began to spread his influence through a series of marital alliances with the various other Germanic kings, including Clovis whose sister Audefleda was married off to Theodoric himself.

To the Goths, Clovis must have appeared to be no more than one of many other Germanic kings holding the north and east of Gaul. In the immediate aftermath of Clovis' victory over Syagrius (whom the Visigoths had supported), a peace was patched up between them and Clovis' Franks. This allowed the Goths (both Visi- and Ostro-) to concentrate on Italy and Spain. It also gave Clovis the opportunity to focus his attention on the north while the southern borders of his territory were relatively secure.

We do not know when Clovis did away with his rivals Ragnachar, Ricchar, Rignomer and Chararic to assert his full authority over the Salian Franks. The natural assumption is that he did this immediately after defeating Syagrius. The story that Chararic and his son were initially forced to become Christian priests could indicate a time after Clovis' conversion a decade or so later. The chronicle of St Denis (quoted above) is quite specific in saying that Ragnachar remained a pagan and the other pagan Franks rallied around him until Clovis defeated them. As the actual date of Clovis' victory over Syagrius is in some doubt we can only assume that from the mid-480s through to the 490s Clovis concentrated on winning over or destroying any Frankish rivals in the aftermath of Syagrius' defeat. He will have taken on some of these immediately, leaving others until he had greater support – including that of the Church.

Having accomplished supremacy over the Salian Franks, Clovis needed other victories to secure the loyalty of his executed rivals followers. This initially resulted in the previously described campaign against the Alamanni which may have resulted in Clovis' conversion to Catholic Christianity. He also had campaigned against the Thuringians to the east of the Ripuarian Franks on the other side of the Rhine. We are told by Gregory of Tours that Clovis secured an alliance with Sigibert, king of the Ripuarian Franks of Cologne. Sigibert was wounded in the leg at the Battle of Tolbiac (Zülpich) in which he and Clovis defeated the Alamanni. This earned him the nickname of 'Sigibert the Lame'. The traditionally accepted date for this battle is 496.

Zülpich is not far from Cologne in the heartland of the Ripuarian Franks – a long way from Alamannic holdings on the Upper Rhine. It is most likely, therefore that Sigibert called on Clovis to help him defend his territory and it was a defensive campaign rather than a war of conquest.

The end result, however, was the destruction of the Alamanni and their absorption into the Frankish kingdoms. There are records from the early sixth century which mention an influx of Alamannic refugees into the Ostrogothic Kingdom of Italy in 508. No doubt the Battle of Tolbiac did not bring about the immediate destruction of the Alamanni, especially if it had been a victory over an invading army. It would have taken the Franks some time to consolidate their victory with other unrecorded battles and mopping up operations in the Alamannic homeland to the south. These may well have continued well into the next century until the remaining Alamanni accepted Frankish hegemony. This could account for the record of Alammanic refugees a decade after the battle.

Clovis got the credit for victory over the Alamanni at Tolbiac, thanks to his reputed conversion to Christianity on the eve of battle. It is more likely that Sigibert and the Ripuarians would have borne the brunt of the fighting and conducted most of the follow-up operations against the Alamanni as they shared a border with them, while the Salians were far away in modern Belgium and northern France. Clovis may well have given continuing support but his main focus was elsewhere – looking south towards the Visigoths and Burgundians.

The Burgundians

We saw in Chapter 4 how the Burgundians had moved into Roman territory on the Middle Rhine in the early fifth century. Their kingdom, centred on Worms, was destroyed by Aeitus' Huns in the mid-430s and they were resettled as *foederati* into that part of modern France we now call Burgundy. In the last years of Roman Gaul the Burgundians were a power to be reckoned with. The Burgundian Prince Gundobad rose up to become a powerful Roman warlord, making and breaking West Roman emperors in the early 470s. Seeing no future in the dying embers of Roman Italy he returned to Gaul in 473 to take over kingship of the Burgundians. Initially Gundobad had to share power with his brothers: Godegisel, Chilperic and Godomar. This did not last long.

Gundobad killed his brother Chilperic with the sword, and sank his wife in water with a stone tied to her neck. His two daughters he condemned to exile. The older of these, who became a nun, was called Chrona, and the younger Clotilda. And as Clovis often sent embassies to Burgundy, the maiden Clotilda was found by his envoys. And when they saw that she was of good bearing and wise, and learned that she was of the family of the king, they reported this to King Clovis. He sent an embassy to Gundobad without delay asking her in marriage. Gundobad was afraid to refuse and so surrendered her to [Clovis'] men. They took the girl and brought her swiftly to the king. The king was very glad when he saw her, and married her, having already, by a concubine, a son named Theodoric [or Theuderic].

We do not know what happened to Godomar but Godegisel sought an alliance with Clovis. His marriage to Clotilda would have ensured Clovis' enmity to Gundobad who had killed his wife's parents.

At that time [*c.*,500] the brothers Gundobad and Godegisel were kings of the country about the Rhône and the Saône together with the province of Marseilles. And they, as well as their people, belonged to the Arian sect. And since they were fighting with each other, Godegisel, hearing of the victories of King Clovis, sent an embassy to him secretly, saying: 'If you will give me aid in attacking my brother [Gundobad]... I will pay you every year whatever tribute you yourself wish to impose.'

Clovis accepted this offer gladly, and promised aid whenever need should ask. And at a time agreed upon he marched his army against Gundobad... And these three, namely, Clovis, Gundobad and Godegisel, were marching their armies to the same point. They came with all their warlike equipment to the stronghold named Dijon... Godegisel joined Clovis, and both armies crushed the people of Gundobad. (Gregory of Tours)

Gundobad later rallied his forces to defeat Godegisel. Besieged in Vienne, Godegisel sought refuge in the Arian church where he was killed by Gundobad's men. Godegisel had a number of Franks fighting for him. These Gundobad sent in exile to the Visigoths. Then he set about asserting his authority by killing off all the Gallo-Roman senators who had supported Godegisel.

> He [Gundobad] restored to his own dominion all the region which is now called Burgundy. He established milder laws for the Burgundians lest they should oppress the Romans. (Gregory of Tours).

Some sort of peace was patched up between Clovis and Gundobad. How this was arranged, or what the terms were, is not known. It may well have been that Gundobad agreed to some form of tribute, perhaps including military support to Clovis and some sort of acknowledgement of his overlordship.

What we do know is that in the first few years of the sixth century Clovis turned his attention to the Visigoths in south-western France. Why he did this when he had not yet managed to subdue the Burgundians is not known. Perhaps the Visigoths made the first move causing Clovis to patch up a peace with Gundobad in exchange for support against the Visigoths. Perhaps the former Roman warlord Gundobad had proved too strong and an alliance with him against the Visigoths seemed a better bet than continuing the war with the Burgundians. The latter is the most likely conclusion as there are few records of the Visigoths making aggressive moves against the Franks other than to secure their northern border. If anything the opposite was true as the Visigoths were looking south towards Spain and King Alaric II was having a tough time maintaining his authority over his nobles.

The End of the Visigoths in Gaul

In the 490s, as the Franks were campaigning against the Thuringians, Alamanni and Burgundians, the Visigoths of Aquitaine (south-western France) were expanding into Spain where there was a power vacuum. Of the Vandals, Alans and Suebi who had crossed the Rhine in 407 to eventually settle in Spain (see Chapter 4) only the Suebi remained. The Alans had been destroyed by the Visigoths and in 429 the Vandals crossed into Africa. Over the following decades the Suebi were worn down and weakened in almost constant warfare with the Visigoths.

There are very few records of the Visigothic expansion from France into Spain. A contemporary Spanish Chronicle has a brief entry in 494 which simply states, 'the Goths entered Spain.' A second entry for 497 adds: 'the Goths acquired settlements in Spain.'

As far as we can tell this expansion into Spain was not a deliberate shift away from the Visigothic power centre in Aquitaine. More probably it was the result of younger warriors and those less favoured, striking out on their own to seek greater glory and riches. The royal court remained at Toulouse and seemed to have had its work cut out to impose authority on ambitious Visigothic warriors.

As the Visigoths were thinning out into Spain, Clovis would have seen the opportunity this presented. Having patched up a peace with Gundobad's Burgundians, and with the continuing support of Sigibert the Lame, he struck south against the Visigoths. Relations between the Franks and Visigoths had never been good. From the time of Childeric there had been a sort of phoney war between the two peoples which occasionally broke out into open conflict. There are records of the Visigoths taking Saintes from the Franks in 496 and two years later the Franks took Bordeaux from the Visigoths. This was at the time when Clovis was engaged against the Alamanni and Burgundians and so he patched up some sort of temporary armistice with King Alaric II in 502. By 507 the Alamanni had been conquered and peace secured with the Burgundians. So it was that Clovis took the offensive against the Visigoths supported by Sigibert the Lame's Ripuarian Franks and Gundobad's Burgundians.

The Visigothic King Alaric II sent urgent pleas for help to Theodoric, the Ostrogothic king of Italy, while doing his best to delay the Franks without engaging them in decisive battle. In a letter preserved in the records of Cassiodorus (a Roman serving King Theodoric), Theodoric gave the following reply to Alaric:

Surrounded as you are by an innumerable multitude of subjects, and strong in the remembrance of their having turned back Attila, still do not fight with Clovis. War is a terrible thing, and a terrible risk. The long peace may have softened the hearts of your people, and your soldiers from want of practice may have lost the habit of working together on the battlefield. Before blood is shed, draw back if possible. We are sending ambassadors to the King of the Franks to try to prevent this war between our relatives [Theodoric was married to Clovis' sister]; and the ambassadors whom we are sending to you will go on to Gundobad, King of the Burgundians, to get him to interpose on behalf of peace. Your enemy will be mine also.

Theodoric also wrote to Clovis in an attempt to avert war:

The affinities of kings ought to keep their subjects from the plague of war. We are grieved to hear of the paltry causes which are giving rise to rumours of war between you and our son Alaric, rumours which gladden the hearts of the enemies of both of you. Let me say with all frankness, but with all affection, just what I think. It is the act of a passionate man to get his troops ready for action at the first embassy which he sends. Instead of that refer the matter to our arbitration. It would be a delight to me to choose men capable of mediating between you. What would you yourselves think of me if I could hear unmoved of your murderous intentions towards one another? Away with this conflict, in which one of you will probably be utterly destroyed. Throw away the sword which you wield for my humiliation. By what right do I thus threaten you? By the right of a father and a friend. He who shall despise this advice of ours will have to reckon us and our friends as his adversaries. I send two ambassadors to you, as I have to my son Alaric, and hope that they may be able so to arrange matters that no alien malignity may sow the seeds of dissension between you, and that your nations, which under your fathers have long enjoyed the blessings of peace, may not now be laid waste by sudden collision. You ought to believe him who, as you know, has rejoiced in your prosperity. No true friend is he who launches his associates, unwarned, into the headlong dangers of war.

Before the Ostrogoths could come to his aid or diplomatic interventions could dissuade either Clovis or Gundobad, Alaric was forced to give battle by his own men who were incensed that their king took no decisive action against the Franks while their lands were being plundered. The battle fought at Vouillé, near Poitiers, determined the future of France but unfortunately we know very little about it. Theodoric's attempted alliance with Gundobad's Burgundians did not materialize. Instead they fought alongside the Franks. With the Visigoths spread over the vast area of southern France and much of Spain it is unlikely that Alaric could have called on every Gothic warrior in his kingdom while Clovis had all his followers to hand along with Burgundian and Ripuarian allies.

> King Clovis met with Alaric, king of the Goths, in the plain of Vouillé at the tenth milestone from Poitiers, and while the one army was for fighting at a distance the other tried to come to close combat. And when the Goths had fled as was their custom, King Clovis won the victory by God's aid. He had to help him the son of Sigibert the Lame, named Chloderic. This Sigibert was lame from a wound in the leg, received in a battle with the Alamanni near the town of Zülpich. Now when the king had put the Goths to flight and slain king Alaric, two of the enemy suddenly appeared and struck at him with their lances, one on each side. But he was saved from death by the help of his coat of mail as well as by his fast horse.
>
> …From this battle Amalaric, son of Alaric, fled to Spain and wisely seized his father's kingdom. Clovis sent his son Theuderic to Clermont by way of Albi and Rodez. He went, and brought under his father's dominion the cities from the boundaries of the Goths to the limit of the Burgundians. When Clovis had spent the winter in Bordeaux and taken all the treasures of Alaric at Toulouse, he went to Angoulême. And the Lord gave him such grace that the walls fell down of their own accord when he gazed at them. Then he drove the Goths out and brought the city under his own dominion. (Gregory of Tours)

Unfortunately we know little more than this about what actually took place at the Battle of Vouillé. The same is true for all the other battles and campaigns of Clovis' reign previously described. There are, however, a number of clues in the above quote which hint at how the Franks and Goths may have fought.

Gregory says that one army tried to fight at a distance while the other tried to come to close combat. Visigothic fighting methods are fully described in the previous book in this series *The Goths*. Many of them would have fought on horseback in the Roman way. Armed with javelins as well as swords and spears they would tend to harass their enemy from a distance, sometimes feigning flight to draw on their opponents and then closing in for the kill when their enemies were disordered. Therefore it would have been the Visigoths who attempted to fight at a distance, supporting Gregory's statement that the 'Goths fled as was their custom'.

As previously described, the mainstay of Frankish armies were men on foot who fought primarily hand-to-hand, neatly matching Gregory's statement that 'the other tried to come to close combat'. The Burgundians fought in a similar manner. Many of the more notable Frankish and Burgundian warriors may have ridden into battle and then some or all may have dismounted to fight on foot. In the pursuit they would have mounted up again and Gregory's comment that Clovis was saved by his armour and fast horse is consistent with this. Chapter 10 will discuss Frankish fighting methods in more detail.

Clovis' victory at Vouillé resulted in the end of the Visigothic Kingdom in south-western France. From this point onwards, the Visigoths concentrated on carving out a new realm in Spain. His victory left Clovis the most powerful king in Gaul but he did not rule it all. The Goths held on to a strip of the southern coast thanks to the intervention of the Ostrogoths in Provence. The Armorican Bacaudae and new British migrants remained fiercely independent in Brittany and the Burgundians still ran their own affairs as did the Ripuarian Franks of the Middle Rhine. As a catholic Christian, Clovis was able to secure an alliance with the East Roman Empire which was becoming increasingly troubled by the power of the Arian Ostrogoths in Italy. To counter this, the Emperor Anastasius gave Clovis the title of Consul in 508. Gregory of Tours goes as far as to say that Anastasius recognized him as co-emperor.

King of all the Franks

Before he died, Clovis brought the Ripuarians under his sway in a typically brutal way as Gregory of Tours describes:

When King Clovis was dwelling at Paris he sent secretly to the son of Sigibert [Chloderic] saying: 'Behold your father has become an old man and limps in his weak foot. If he should die,' said he, 'Of due right his kingdom would be yours together with our friendship.' Led on by greed the son plotted to kill his father. And when his father went out from the city of Cologne and crossed the Rhine... his son sent assassins in against him, and killed him there, in the idea that he would get his kingdom... He sent messengers to king Clovis to tell about his father's death, and to say: 'My father is dead, and I have his treasures in my possession, and also his kingdom. Send men to me, and I shall gladly transmit to you from his treasures whatever pleases you.'

Clovis replied: 'I thank you for your good will, and I ask that you show the treasures to my men who come, and after that you shall possess all yourself.' When they came, he showed his father's treasures... When he did so, and was much bent over, one of them lifted his hand and dashed his battle axe against his head, and so in a shameful manner he incurred the death which he had brought on his father. Clovis heard that Sigibert and his son had been slain and came to the place and summoned all the people, saying... 'Chloderic, son of my kinsman, was in pursuit of his own father asserting that I wished him killed... when he was opening the treasures, he was slain himself... Now I know nothing at all of these matters. For I cannot shed the blood of my own kinsmen... But since this has happened, I give you my advice. If it seems acceptable; turn to me, that you may be under my protection.'

They listened to this, and giving applause with both shields and voices, they raised him on a shield, and made him king over them. He received Sigibert's kingdom with his treasures, and placed the people, too, under his rule. For God was laying his enemies low every day under his hand, and was increasing his kingdom, because he walked with an upright heart before him, and did what was pleasing in his eyes.

Having established himself as king of the Franks and ruler of much of Roman Gaul through murder and conquest, Clovis set about consolidating his position in much the same way as a Roman usurper might have done. He turned his attention to legal, administrative and ecclesiastical matters. He published laws aimed at bringing his subjects together and filling the vacuum left by the end of Roman rule. As the prelude to the *Lex Salica* (the laws of the Salian Franks) states:

With God's help it pleased the Franks and their nobility and they agreed that they ought to prohibit all escalations of quarrels for the preservation of enthusiasm for peace amongst themselves. Because they excelled other neighbouring peoples by force of arms, so they should excel themselves in legal authority with the result that criminal cases might be concluded in a manner appropriate to the type of complaint.

In 511 Clovis convened the First Council of Orléans, bringing together thirty-two bishops to decide on ecclesiastical matters in the aftermath of his conquest of the Arian Visigoths in Aquitaine. Any remaining semblance of civilization in post-Roman Gaul stemmed from the bishops and the moral authority they held over their flocks. By embracing them and including them in his councils Clovis was sowing the seeds for the medieval Kingdom of France which he more or less created.

When Clovis died he was buried in Paris as a Christian king in marked contrast to his father Childeric's pagan interment. The traditionally accepted date of his death is 511, the same year as the Council of Orléans, although some modern historians have argued for a later date.

In just over two decades Clovis had risen from one among many relatively minor rulers in northern Gaul to become king over Franks, Romans and Alamanni; and consul of Rome. He was also one of the most powerful men in the post-Roman West, sharing that distinction with his contemporaries Theodoric the Ostrogoth in Italy and Thrasamund the Vandal king of Africa, all of whom were connected by marriage. Clovis laid the foundation of the Merovingian dynasty (named after his legendary ancestor Merovech) and turned Roman Gaul into Francia, Frankreich, or France.

Clovis' Sons

Clovis was succeeded by his wife Clotilda and four sons: Theuderic, Childebert, Chlodomar and Chlothar. When Clovis died, his kingdom was divided up amongst his sons, possibly due to Clotilda's influence in order to prevent Theuderic (the eldest and born to a concubine) from cutting out her three children.

This seemed to work reasonably well at first although later it created enduring problems. Each of the sons of Clovis used the base they inherited to expand Frankish power against external rather than internal enemies, while Clotilda held a unifying influence.

Theuderic, supported by his half-brother Chlothar, attacked the Thuringians to the east of the Rhine. Gregory gives an interesting (if typically short) account of a battle fought between them. It is noteworthy that the Thuringians were most worried about Frankish horsemen.

> The Thuringians prepared stratagems against the coming of the Franks. They dug pits in the plain where the fight was to take place, and covering the openings with thick turf they made it seem a level plain. So when they began to fight, many of the Frankish horsemen fell into these pits and it was a great obstacle to them, but when this stratagem was perceived they began to be on their guard. When finally the Thuringians saw that they were being fiercely cut to pieces and when their King Hermenfred had taken to flight, they turned their backs [and fled]... The victory being won [the Franks] took possession of that country and brought it under their control. (Gregory of Tours)

Although the Franks were noted for their foot warriors armed with throwing axes (franciscae) and throwing spears (angons), by 520 the host Theuderic and Chlothar could muster was not a tribal warband. Now in control of much of Gaul, many the men who followed them would have come from a variety of backgrounds. Some may have been descended from Syagrius' followers and the various settlements of Sarmatian *laeti* (see Chapter 2). Many of such men would have preferred mounted combat and many Franks would have had the land and means to maintain good cavalry mounts. The Thuringians, on the other hand, lived to the east of the Rhine. Their homeland amongst the hills and forests of Germania would not have been as conducive to developing a strong mounted arm. While Thuringian foot warriors may have been a match for the dismounted Franks, they had to use the terrain and obstacles to deal with their mounted opponents – just as the Marcomer and Sunno had done against the Romans in the fourth century.

In 523 all four of Clovis' sons united to attack the Burgundians, apparently supported by the Ostrogothic King Theodoric. At first the Franks were successful. 'They crushed the Burgundians and reduced their country to subjection.' (Gregory of Tours) They also captured and executed the Burgundian King Sigismund (son of Gundobad – see section entitled The Burgundians on page 123).

Despite Gregory's brief description which makes it seem as if the war was won quickly and simply, it took a decade before the Burgundians were finally defeated and absorbed into the Frankish kingdom. Sigismund's son Godomar led a counterattack in 524, defeating the Franks near Veseruntia (Vézeronce-Curtin east of Lyon). Chlodomar was killed in the fighting and it was not until 534 that the Burgundian kingdom was finally subdued and absorbed by the Franks. Childebert, with the support of Theuderic, renewed war against the Visigoths in 531, taking Narbonne from them and killing the Visigothic King Amalaric.

The sons of Clovis were not, however, one big happy family. This passage from Gregory of Tours gives some insight into their natural rivalry:

Theuderic and Childebert made a treaty, and swearing to each other that neither would attack the other, they took hostages from each other, in order that their agreement might be more secure. Many sons of senators were given as hostages on that occasion, but a quarrel arose later between the kings, and they were given over to servitude and those who had taken them to guard now made slaves of them.

Later when Theuderic died,

Childebert and Chlothar rose against Theudibert [Theuderic's son] and wished to take the kingdom from him. Theudibert was defended by his *leudes* [household warriors] after they had received gifts from him, and he [Theudibert] was established in his kingdom. (Gregory of Tours)

Worse was to come. There were plots, brutal murders and perpetual conflict between the sons and grandsons of Clovis. This is not a story of the internecine struggles of the Merovingian dynasty, it is a story of the Franks as the conquerors of Rome – or at least that part of the Roman Empire to which the Franks gave their name. With the fall of the West Roman Empire in 476 and the defeat of Syagrius a decade later we could be forgiven for thinking that, for the Franks, Rome was no more. Yet the Roman Empire endured, not in the city which bore the name but far to the east in New Rome, or Constantinople (now Istanbul) – named after the Emperor Constantine who had made his capital there in the fourth century. With the East Roman Empire still intact, there was one more act to play out between the Franks and Romans.

Chapter 8

The War in Italy

Odoacer

At this point in our story of the Franks as conquerors of Rome we need to return to affairs in Italy and the surviving East Roman Empire.

The Roman Empire in the west came to an end in 476 when Odoacer, leader of the barbarian troops who formed the army of Italy, rose in revolt and overthrew the last Emperor Romulus Augustulus. That a powerful Roman general might rise up against the emperor was nothing new. For centuries many emperors had gained the throne in this way. This time there were differences. Odoacer may have commanded a 'Roman' army but neither he nor his followers were Romans.

Before 476 powerful warlords of non-Roman origin used their position to put puppet emperors on the throne and remain the power behind it. This had been the case from Stilicho to Ricimer and Gundobad. When Odoacer overthrew the last West Roman emperor he and his men decided that they no longer needed a puppet on the throne. Instead Odoacer would rule Italy himself as a king rather than running things in the name of a puppet emperor.

Apart from a few enclaves here and there, when Odoacer sized power, Italy was all that remained of the once mighty Roman Empire in the west and so he became 'King of Italy'. Britain had been abandoned long ago. Spain was contested between the Suebi, Visigoths and Bacaudae while the port cities on the east coast remained under nominal Imperial control. Illyricum had been devastated by repeated invasions, and Africa had been lost to the Vandals. As we saw in Chapter 7, France in the 470s was divided between the Visigoths, Bacaudae, Alamanni, Burgundians and Franks while Aegidius (and later Syagrius) remained divorced from the Imperial court at Ravenna. Only the coast of Provence with its capital at Arles remained under Imperial control.

The Franks in Gaul would have noticed very little change when the last West Roman emperor in Ravenna was deposed by Odoacer other than the fact that it made a future Roman offensive against them highly improbable. The same could perhaps be said for most Romans living in Italy at the time. The senate still met, Roman law still applied and the origin or title of the ruler of Italy probably made very little difference to the vast majority of them. The city of Rome had fallen to the Goths in 410 and was again sacked by the Vandals in 455. These events, especially the first, had a profound psychological impact on the inhabitants of the Roman Empire. They proved that the 'eternal city' was not eternal and exposed the fragility of the Roman state. For many years the bulk of the Roman army had been drawn from German, Sarmatian or Hun recruits, settlers and allies. Barbarian warlords had commanded 'Roman' armies, making or breaking Roman emperors to suit their needs. That there was no longer a titular Roman emperor on the western throne at Ravenna would have changed very little. So the West Roman Empire fell with a whimper, not a bang.

The whole Empire did not fall in 476. Despite enormous pressures from the Goths, Persians and others, the eastern half of the Empire remained more or less intact and a Roman emperor continued to reign in Constantinople. If anyone noticed the dissolution of the western half of the Empire it would have been the court at Constantinople. Without a colleague on the western throne at Ravenna, the East Roman emperor was now the only legitimate authority. Probably most Romans assumed that it would only be a matter of time before the various barbarians would be brought back under control, their rulers having been played off against each other until a suitable candidate could be found to put back on the western throne.

Theodoric and the Ostrogoths

The Visigoths who had settled in Aquitaine were the descendants of those Goths who had defeated the East Roman Emperor Valens at the Battle of Adrianople in 378 and sacked Rome in 410. Along the way, and over the intervening years, they had been joined by many others – including Romans. Other Goths remained beyond the Roman frontier and came to be known as the Ostrogoths – or East Goths. It was these Goths who had followed Attila and fought against their distant Visigothic cousins on the Catalaunian Plains in 451 (see Chapter 5). After the dissolution of Attila's empire, bands of Ostrogoths descended into the western territories of the East Roman Empire, sometimes fighting against the Romans, sometimes fighting for them and at other times fighting each other. In the late 480s Theodoric, son of Thiudimir (Thiudimir had fought with Attila on the Catalaunian Plains), emerged supreme with some 20,000 Ostrogothic warriors at his back roaming through East Roman territory.

The Eastern Empire never recognized Odoacer's control of Italy. Constantinople accepted his rule as a necessary interregnum after which it was assumed that Italy would once more have a Roman emperor. The presence of a powerful Gothic army in his territory presented the East Roman Emperor Zeno with an opportunity to both rid himself of Theodoric's Ostrogoths, and to retake Italy. The plan was to unleash the Ostrogoths as a surrogate Roman army to depose Odoacer.

So it was, in autumn 488, that Zeno gave Theodoric the official position of *Magister Militum*. In the name of Rome he was charged with leading his Goths into Italy to bring it back under Imperial control. Odoacer was not a pushover and it took Theodoric and his Ostrogoths five years to defeat him. Once Theodoric did this he saw no reason to hand Italy back to the Imperial authorities. From 493 to 526, as Clovis and his sons were establishing their hegemony over Gaul, Theodoric ruled Italy. He has come to be known as 'Theodoric the Great' thanks to his relatively benevolent rule, the stability he created, and the way he merged the best of Gothic and Roman societies into a new viable kingdom.

Theodoric created a web of alliances with the other Germanic kingdoms of the former West Roman Empire, including marrying Clovis' sister Audefleda. Good relations with Clovis' Franks were, however, short-lived. When war broke out between the Franks and Visigoths in 507, Theodoric backed his Visigothic cousins. After Clovis' victory over the Visigoths at Vouillé he was stopped from further expansion by an intervention by Theodoric's Ostrogoths. The Ostrogoths then drove the Franks out of the coastal strip between the Lower Rhône and the Pyrenees and took Provence for themselves. The Ostrogoths again intervened in 531 when Clovis' sons, Theuderic and Childebert, took Narbonne from the Visigoths, killing their King Amalaric in the process. The Visigoths elected the Ostrogoth Theudis as their next king and with Ostrogothic support the Visigoths in Spain were able to blunt any further southern expansion by the Franks.

Justinian and the Reconquest

As the Franks in Gaul, Visigoths in Spain and Ostrogoths in Italy were fighting for control of the borderlands between their kingdoms, the political situation in Constantinople changed. In 527 the young, energetic Justinian ascended to the throne of the East Roman Empire. Greek was replacing Latin as the principal language of the Eastern Empire but Justinian was a native Latin speaker who looked to the West and dreamed of re-establishing Rome's ancient glories. By 533 the Roman Empire's frontiers were reasonably secure. Riots in Constantinople had been suppressed and the Roman army was led by the rising star of Belisarius who had won victory against the Persians and put down the riots in the capital city with a brutal efficiency. Then Justinian turned his attention to the West.

In the spring of 533 Justinian sent Belisarius to retake Africa from the Vandals. In a short, brilliant campaign, Belisarius defeated the Vandal armies and took Carthage. The full story of this war is told in the first book in this series – *The Vandals*. The death of Theodoric the Great in 526 was followed by internal squabbles amongst the Ostrogoths of Italy. Once Africa had been taken from the Vandals, Justinian seized the opportunity to extend Roman control over Italy. So it was in 536 that Belisarius invaded Italy from the south while another Roman army moved in to take the Ostrogothic possessions in Dalmatia (modern Croatia).

A detailed account of the war between the Romans and Ostrogoths can be found in the second book in this series – *The Goths*. The initial Roman attack went well and by 540 most of Italy was again under Imperial control. The Emperor Justinian squandered the victory by aggressively taxing the Italians and dividing command of the Roman occupying forces when he sent Belisarius to the East to deal with a new Persian threat. The Ostrogoths rallied and under the leadership of Totila they began to take back what they had lost.

An Opportunity

At this time the Franks, learning that both Goths and Romans had suffered severely by the war, and thinking for this reason that they could with the greatest ease gain the larger part of Italy for themselves, began to think it preposterous that others should carry on a war for such a length of time for the rule of a land which was so near their own, while they themselves remained quiet and stood aside for both. (Procopius)

From the beginning of the War in Italy both the Ostrogoths and Romans sought the aid of the Franks. After Clovis' conversion to Catholic Christianity he had been named consul by the East Roman emperor. Given the hostility between the Goths and Franks in the first decade of the sixth century it would be reasonable to assume that the Franks would have favoured the Romans of Constantinople over the Ostrogoths of Italy. Constantinople, however, was far away while the Ostrogothic Kingdom bordered Frankish lands in Provence. Furthermore, the Ostrogoths were weak and fragmented in the aftermath of Theodoric the Great's death while the East Romans were reasserting themselves. The last thing the Franks needed was a resurgent Roman Empire on their doorstep.

So it was, in 538, that the Franks intervened in Italy, sending a 'vast multitude of Burgundians' (Procopius) to support the Ostrogothic siege of Milan. This was only two years after the Frankish conquest of Burgundy so sending a 'multitude of Burgundians' into Italy must have seemed like a good way of getting their troublesome warriors out of the way.

The following year Clovis' grandson, Theudibert, son of Theuderic, led a Frankish army into Italy to take what they could for themselves.

Thus the Franks crossed the Alps which separate the Gauls from the Italians, and entered Liguria.

Now the Goths had previously been vexed at the thanklessness of the Franks, on the ground that, although they, the Goths, had often promised to give up to them a large territory and great sums of money in return for an alliance, these Franks had been unwilling to fulfil their own promise in any way. When they heard that Theudibert was at hand with a great army, they were filled with rejoicing, lifted up, as they were, by the liveliest hopes and thinking that thereafter they would have the superiority over their enemy [the Romans] without a battle.

As for the Germans [Theudibert's Franks, Alamanni and Burgundians], as long as they were in Liguria, they did no harm to the Goths... When they reached the city of Ticinum [Pavia]... the Franks began to sacrifice the women and children of the Goths whom they found at hand and to throw their bodies into the river as the first-fruits of the war... And the Goths, upon seeing what was being done, fell into a kind of irresistible fear, took to flight and got inside the fortifications.

So the Germans, having crossed the Po, advanced to the Gothic camp, and the Goths were at first pleased to see them coming in small companies toward their camp, thinking that these men had come to fight in alliance with them. But when a great throng of Germans had come up and opened an attack, and by hurling their axes were already slaying many, they turned their backs and rushed off in flight, and passing through the Roman camp ran along on the road to Ravenna. The Romans, seeing them in flight, thought that Belisarius had come to support their own force and had both taken the camp of the enemy and dislodged them from it after defeating them in battle. And wishing to join forces with him, they [the Romans] took up their arms and went forth with all speed. But coming unexpectedly upon a hostile army, they were compelled, much against their will, to engage with them, and being badly worsted in the battle, they all fled, not to their camp (to which it was now impossible to return) but to Tuscany...

The Franks, having defeated both [Gothic and Roman] armies and having captured both camps without a single man in them, for the time being found provisions in the camps. In a short time they had consumed all these on account of their great numbers, and, since the land was destitute of human habitation, they were unable to obtain any other provisions... Indeed they say that at least one-third of the Frankish army perished [from disease and starvation]. Hence it was that, as they were unable to go forward, they remained where they were. (Procopius)

Procopius goes on to say that Belisarius entered into negotiations with Theudibert and convinced him to withdraw.

> Perplexed as he [Theudibert] was already by his present situation, and sharply reproached [by his men who were] for no good reason dying in a deserted land, he broke camp with the survivors of the Franks and retired homeward with great speed. Thus did Theudibert, after marching into Italy, take his departure.

As the war between the Romans and Ostrogoths dragged on, the Franks took the opportunity to expand their influence at the expense of both. Rather than entering into a formal alliance with either side, the Franks found it more profitable to play the one against the other. In the 540s they took over strongholds in Venetia.

> When the arms of the Goths had gained the upper hand in the war, the Franks assumed control of the largest part of Venetia with no right at all. The Romans, for their part, were unable to ward them off any longer. The Goths were unable to carry on the war against the two peoples [Franks and Romans] ... [The Franks] not only enslaved the Romans of that region, but they were also constantly moving forward, plundering and doing violence to the Roman territory. (Procopius)

In 552 Constantinople made a concerted effort to finally overthrow Gothic resistance in Italy. With a powerful army of Romans, Lombards, Heruls, Gepids and Persians, Justinian's General Narses marched from Constantinople, up the Dalmatian coast, with the intent of crossing the alpine passes down into Venetia in north-eastern Italy.

Both the Romans and Ostrogoths made overtures to the Franks who held the fortresses of Venetia. The Ostrogoths were able to secure Frankish neutrality if not active support. The Romans failed to get the Franks to join them or even to allow their army to pass unhindered into Italy. Narses, however, bypassed the Frankish strongholds to break out into northern Italy, decisively defeating the Goths at the Battle of Taginae (modern Gualdo Tadino).

Gothic resistance limped on and repeated attempts to get the Franks to intervene on their behalf fell on deaf ears. The Franks did intervene but did so on their own behalf with the probable intent of picking up the pieces left over from the devastating decades of war between the Ostrogoths and Romans.

The Battle of Casilinum

A large army of Franks, Alamanni and others descended on northern Italy in 553 when Narses was mopping up Gothic resistance near Naples far to the south. The invading army was led by the Alamannic brothers Butilin and Lothar. A Roman delaying force failed to stop the Frankish/Alamannic army which then continued to move south as Narses converged his forces on Rome.

In the spring of 554 Butilin and Lothar split into two columns as each brother pursued his own agenda. Butilin was intent on conquering Italy while Lothar seemed to have second thoughts. Pulling back northwards, Lothar was defeated near Pisaurum (modern Pesaro on the Adriatic coast) and then retreated to the Frankish strongholds in Venetia. Butilin pressed on, bypassing Rome, and moving southwards to pillage the Campanian countryside until heat and disease forced him to also turn back northwards.

Butilin's and Narses' armies clashed when Roman troops attacked Frankish foragers not far from their camp by the Volturnus River near Capua. Both armies probably had close to 20,000 men each. Narses deployed with his infantry in the centre bolstered with dismounted cavalry and archers. His mounted cavalry were formed on both wings with a picked cavalry force hidden off to one flank ready to surprise the enemy there. He also kept a reserve of mounted Heruls ready to intervene when needed. According to Agathias, the Franks formed up in a deep wedge (which he calls a boar's head) with the intent of breaking the Roman line with a fierce charge in the centre.

The pointed part in front [of the Frankish array] being a dense compact mass of shields. From this the two wings stretched back protecting the rear of the boar's head – rows and columns stretching back obliquely, gradually growing further and further apart until it finally reached a very great width. (Agathias)

Butilin's men charged forward with great aggression, piercing the centre of the Roman line 'with a violent impact'. (Agathias) The Franks broke through the Roman centre but Narses' Herul reserve plugged the gap as the mounted Roman cavalry wings closed in on the flanks. Then the hidden force of picked Roman cavalry moved around the rear of Butilin's men. By this time the strength of the Roman army was made up of well-equipped mounted archers and they shot into the densely packed enemy footmen from the flanks and rear. Driven in from all sides, Butilin's men were annihilated.

It is interesting to note that two of the major Frankish interventions in the war were conducted by recently conquered peoples. Although King Theudibert led an army into Italy in 539, the first intervention was conducted by 10,000 Burgundians while at Casilinum it is reasonable to assume that as Butilin and Lothar were Alamanni many, or most, of their followers would also have been Alamanni.

It is impossible to know whether the Burgundians and Alamanni were sent into Italy as a deliberate policy on the part of the Frankish kings or whether they went on their own initiative. It would seem, at least in the case of the Burgundians, early in the war, that they were sent after a series of diplomatic exchanges secured half-hearted Frankish support for the beleaguered Ostrogoths. By unleashing the recently conquered Burgundians into Italy the Frankish monarchs rid themselves of a potential threat to their rule over Gaul while giving ambitious Burgundian warriors an opportunity to acquire new wealth and fame. The Burgundians in 538 did act as allies with the Goths, supporting them in the siege of Milan. When King Theudibert led a Frankish army into Italy the following year he acted like an independent third party, attacking both Goths and Romans.

The motivations of the Alamannic brothers, Butilin and Lothar, are more difficult to ascertain. The Alamanni had been under Frankish sway for longer than the Burgundians. They were probably better absorbed into the Frankish kingdom, although the problem of what to do with ambitious warriors would have remained. Sending them off into Italy either as a matter of policy or simply allowing them to go on their own initiative would have had a number of advantages for the Frankish kings. If things went wrong (as they did) then the Franks would not have lost much and they could always claim to the Romans that the attack was unauthorized and had been conducted by a subject people.

One point worth remembering is that the political and military structures of the Franks in Gaul had long ceased to be tribal, if indeed they ever were. We saw in previous chapters how Childeric and Clovis had absorbed peoples of various origins. Their armies would have contained Gallo-Romans, Alamanni, Burgundians and others as well as Franks. Of the latter, many would have been highly Romanized descendants of the *laeti* (described in Chapter 2), others would have come from the less Romanized Ripuarians from across the Rhine. Any of the various armies which intervened in the War in Italy would have contained a wide mix of warriors from various backgrounds. They were Frankish in that they acknowledged a Frankish king, just as the men of many nationalities who fought for Belisarius and Narses were Roman because they were in the pay of Rome (or more correctly Constantinople). The original ethnicity of any of the individual men would not have mattered.

The End of the War

The defeat at Casilinum did not end Frankish intervention in the war for control of Italy. The conflict continued for another eight years as various bands of Ostrogoths held out against Emperor Justinian's Romans. The last remnants of Gothic resistance were wiped out in 561–2 when Widin, supported by Frankish allies, was crushed by Narses.

It took the Emperor Justinian twenty-eight years to reconquer Italy and destroy the vibrant Romano-Gothic kingdom which Theodoric the Great had created. It was a hollow victory. Whatever blending of Germanic and Roman cultures had begun at the end of the fifth century had been wiped out by the middle of the sixth. The last vestiges of ancient Roman life had been utterly destroyed by three decades of constant warfare. In 568 the Lombards moved into the vacuum and took Italy for themselves. Meanwhile the Franks consolidated their hold over Gaul and any hope of restoring the West Roman Empire was lost until the Frankish King Charlemagne began to carve out the Holy Roman Empire centuries later.

Chapter 9

The Frankish Way of War

On Foot or Horse?

It is generally accepted that (unlike the eastern Germanic tribes such as the Goths and Vandals), the Franks, Alamanni, Burgundians and other western Germans fought primarily on foot rather than on horseback. Although there is some truth to this, it is an oversimplification.

Many of the eastern Germans who lived for a while on the steppes of modern Ukraine would have had the space and pasture needed to raise and maintain good horse herds. These factors remained when some, such as the Ostrogoths, followed the Huns into the Hungarian Plain in the early fifth century. The open spaces where they lived would also have made horse-mounted mobility very important – almost essential. The western tribes who lived in relatively contained spaces in the forested and hilly lands on the east bank of the Rhine would have had less motivation or ability to develop cavalry armies.

That some Franks, Alamanni and Burgundians fought on horseback when they had suitable opportunities is indisputable. Various Frankish graves contain horse furniture and spurs while in some cases horses were interred nearby. Gregory of Tours' account of Clovis' son Theuderic fighting the Thuringians (see Chapter 7) includes the detail that the Thuringians dug pits to disrupt the Frankish horsemen. The Franks of the sixth century – with the wealth of their conquests and the varied terrain of most of France at their disposal – would have had the opportunity to raise and maintain a substantial number of good cavalry mounts.

If an increasing number of Frankish, Alamanni and Burgundian warriors may have had the means to mount up in the first decades of the sixth century, they were still perfectly happy to fight on foot just as their ancestors had done. It may still have been their preferred way of fighting. Against the Thuringians a significant mounted force may have given the Franks an edge. Against the Ostrogoths and Romans in Italy – where every good solider was primarily a cavalryman – this would not have been the case.

In the centuries that followed, the Frankish warriors evolved into the finest cavalry of Western Europe – becoming the chivalry of medieval France. Most evidence suggests that this transition did not really start to take hold until the eighth century – well beyond the scope of this book. The evolution from tribal warriors on the Rhine to the rulers of France did, however, naturally transform the way the Franks fought. As they absorbed the last elements of the Roman army in northern Gaul along with the Alan and Sarmatian *laeti*, they would have found recruits who were more familiar with mounted warfare than their tribal ancestors. With all of Gaul at their disposal, along with the captured treasures of the Alamanni, Burgundians and Visigoths, the Franks of the sixth century would have had the wealth and land to equip their warriors with good weapons, armour and horses.

The Evolution of the Roman Army

The most detailed descriptions we have of Frankish warfare come from Procopius and Agathias. Writing in the sixth century they both give fairly consistent accounts of how the Franks fought. From their point of view the Franks were still a mass of warriors who tended to fight aggressively on foot. Their descriptions of the way the Franks used throwing axes and heavy javelins is also consistent with the archaeological evidence.

At this point it is worth considering how the East Roman army of the sixth century – the one which fought Butilin at Casilinum – had evolved from that which had defeated their Alamanni ancestors at Strasbourg in the late fourth century (see Chapter 3).

The Roman legions and auxiliaries that had formed the core of Julian's army at Strasbourg were now relegated to a supporting role. The main strength of the sixth century East Roman army lay in its cavalry. Most of these were mounted archers but they were not lightly equipped skirmishers. Wearing body armour of mail or scale, and equipped with good swords, they were perfectly happy closing into hand-to-hand combat as well as shooting arrows from a distance. Some also carried spears in addition to their bows and swords but probably not all of them.

This transformation of the regular Roman cavalry into horse archers probably occurred gradually during the fifth century. Most likely it came about due to the success of Hun and Persian horse archers against earlier Roman armies along with the availability of Hun and Persian recruits.

Procopius describes the Roman cavalry of his day:

> The bowmen of the present time go into battle wearing corselets and fitted out with *greaves* [leg protectors] which extend up to the knee. From the right-hand side hang their arrows, from the other a sword. And there are those who have a spear also attached to them, and at the shoulders a sort of small shield without a grip, such as to cover the region of the face and neck. They are expert horsemen and are able without difficulty to direct their bows to either side while riding at full speed, and to shoot at an opponent whether in pursuit or flight. They draw the bowstring along by the forehead about opposite the right ear, thereby discharging the arrow with such an impetus as to kill whoever stands in the way, shield and corselet alike having no power to check its force.

The later sixth century military manual, the *Strategikon*, describes the training exercises carried out by the Roman cavalryman of the time to enable him to use both missile and shock tactics:

> On horseback at a run, he should fire one or two arrows rapidly and put the strung bow in its case. Then he should grab the spear which he has been carrying on his back. With the strung bow in its case, he should hold the spear in his hand, then quickly replace it on his back and grab the bow.

This made the Roman cavalryman of the mid sixth century someone who could either fight from a distance or close into combat. He could ride up to his opponents, shower them with arrows, retreat out of harm's way and then suddenly turn back to attack with spear or sword. These regular Roman troopers were augmented by a number of foreign auxiliaries. These included fast-moving, more lightly equipped Hun horse archers. Other auxiliaries included Gepids, Lombards and Heruls. These eastern

Germanic warriors usually fought as cavalry armed with spears and shields but on several occasions they dismounted to fight on foot as some of them did at Casilinum.

Amongst the regular Roman cavalry were the *foederati*. Initially this term described barbarians in Roman service but by the mid-500s it had come to mean something else. 'Now at an earlier time the only barbarians had been enlisted amongst the *foederati*... but at the present time there is nothing to prevent anyone from assuming the name, since time will by no means consent to keep names attached to the things to which they were formerly applied.' (Procopius) It may be that the *foederati* of the sixth century army were equipped in Germanic style with spears and shields for close combat rather than with bows but there is no hard evidence to support this supposition.

The role of the regular Roman infantry was to hold ground, provide a secure rallying point for the cavalry, guard the baggage and garrison towns. They were typically a mix of spearmen and archers with the former deployed in the front ranks forming a phalanx and protected by large oval shields, with the latter shooting overhead from behind. Typically the archers accounted for about a quarter of the infantry. At Casilinum it was these troops who held the centre, blunting Butilin's attack, reinforced by dismounted cavalry.

All the best troops of the sixth century Roman army, whether mercenaries or regulars, were mounted even if they occasionally dismounted to fight on foot. The same was true for the Ostrogoths. From the perspective of a contemporary Roman writer like Procopius or Agathias, the tactics of the Frankish, Burgundian and Alamannic armies that descended into Italy in the 530s–50s must have astounded them. Amongst the East Romans and almost all their other enemies – Persians, Vandals, Lombards and Ostrogoths – infantry played a subordinate role. The offensive use of infantry was a thing of the long-distant past.

Frankish Weapons and Tactics

The Romans had no equivalent to the aggressive infantry tactics of the Franks. Sixth century Roman infantry were second-rate troops, more suitable for garrison duties rather than standing firm in line of battle.

When they were deployed in battle, the Roman infantry usually had to be stiffened by dismounted cavalry as they were at Casilinum and in several other battles against the Goths. In such circumstances it would have made sense for the Franks, Alamanni and Burgundians to fight on foot to capitalize on the one advantage they had over the Romans rather than meeting them on terms in which the Romans had come to excel.

The modern historian Bernard Bachrach has postulated that the descriptions of Frankish tactics by Roman historians were distorted by the lenses through which they observed the events of their day. The offensive use of infantry would have been so surprising to them that they ignored everything else and concentrated their descriptions on the Frankish foot warriors. He has a point but probably overstates it.

This is what the contemporary writers Procopius and Agathias have to say of the Frankish fighting methods:

> Under the leadership of Theudibert [the Franks] marched into Italy. They had a small body of cavalry about their leader, and these were the only ones armed with spears, while all the rest were foot-soldiers having neither bows nor spears. Each man carried a sword, a shield and an axe. Now the iron head of this weapon [the axe] was thick and exceedingly sharp on both sides, while the wooden handle was very short. And they are accustomed always to throw these axes at one signal in the first charge and thus to shatter the shields of the enemy and kill the men. (Procopius)
>
> A great throng of Germans came up and opened an attack [against the Goths]. By hurling their axes they slew many. (Procopius)
>
> The military equipment of this people [the Franks] is very simple... They do not serve on horseback except in very rare cases. Fighting on foot is both habitual and a national custom and they are proficient in this. At the hip they wear a sword and on the left side their shield is attached. They have neither bows nor slings, no missile weapon except the double-edged axe and the angon which they use most often. The angons are spears which are neither very short nor very long. They can be used, if necessary, for throwing like a javelin and also in hand to hand combat, the greater part of the angon is covered with iron and very little wood is exposed. Above,

at the socket of the spear... some points are turned back, bent like hooks and turned toward the handle. (Agathias)

In battle the Frank throws the angon. If it hits an enemy the spear is caught in the man and neither can the wounded man nor anyone else draw it out. The barbs hold inside the flesh causing great pain and in this way a man whose wound may not be in a vital spot dies. If the angon hits a shield it is fixed there, hanging down with the butt on the ground. The angon cannot be pulled out because the barbs have penetrated the shield. Nor can it be cut off by a sword because the wood of the shaft is covered with iron. When the Frank sees this situation he quickly puts his foot on the butt of the spear, pulling down so [his enemy] falls, his head and chest left unprotected. The unprotected warrior is then killed either by a stroke of the axe or a thrust with another spear. (Agathias)

Although Procopius says that the Franks did not carry spears, Agathias says that angons (javelins with long iron heads) were their primary weapons. The accounts are not entirely inconsistent. A charge by men on foot was proceeded with a volley of heavy throwing weapons – axes and/or javelins. This disrupted the enemy formation and the ability of the individual enemy warrior to defend himself. Then the Franks closed in for the kill. Such weapons and tactics would have been familiar to the ancient Romans if not their sixth century descendants.

These descriptions are perfectly consistent with the weapons and equipment found by archaeologists in Frankish graves. Many examples of relatively small, curved axe heads have been found, as have a number of long javelin shafts with conical armour-piercing heads which have small barbs at the base. The prominent iron shield bosses found in many Frankish graves would have been perfect for the warrior to punch into his opponent as he followed up the missile volley to finish his enemy off with a handheld weapon such as a short sword or a conventional spear.

A number of relatively conventional spearheads have also been found in Frankish graves which support Agathias' statement that the Frank might finish off his opponent with a spear, contradicting Procopius who said that the Franks did not carry them. Archaeological evidence shows that a throwing axe (francisca) along with a short sword with a single edge (scramasax), were almost universal amongst Frankish warriors. Graves containing angon heads and long double-edged swords are almost always high-status warriors. A reasonable conclusion is that the best warriors, fighting in the front ranks, carried angons, franciscae and good swords, while lesser men may only have been armed with franciscae and short swords. This assumption helps to reconcile the apparently contradictory descriptions of Procopius and Agathias.

The sixth century descriptions of Frankish fighting methods are consistent with what Sidonius Apollinaris' had to say of them in the previous century (quoted in Chapter 5). Volleys of axes and spears preceded a charge into close combat with fast-running young men whirling their shields, anxious to be the first to reach the enemy.

Both Procopius and Agathias say that the Franks did not use bows, slings, or other longer-range missile weapons. When seen through the eyes of sixth century Romans whose mounted troopers were bow-armed and a substantial proportion of their infantry were too, this may well have seemed the case. Arrowheads and light javelin heads have been found in Frankish graves and an analysis of Alamannic graves shows that poorer men may have been archers while richer men tended to fight hand-to-hand. It may be that such men would have fought to defend their home territory but were left behind on a major external expedition. We saw in Chapter 3 how in previous times the Franks and Alamanni were not averse to using missile weapons when it suited the terrain or their situation. At any time a number of men may have used bows in battle. Against the masses of bow-armed Romans in sixth century Italy it would have been even more pointless to bother with light missile weapons than attempting to meet the well-trained Roman cavalry on horseback.

So, what can we conclude from this?

The likelihood is that, after their conquest of Gaul, the Franks had a high proportion of good warriors who owned horses and could fight on horseback if the situation demanded it. Most, or all of them, could also fight effectively on foot in hand-to-hand combat and may even have preferred to do so – especially against enemies who had better cavalry. The Goths and Romans often dismounted to form a defensive line but the Franks also took the offensive when on foot. Indeed they seemed to prefer offensive tactics. Their throwing weapons and shields with prominent bosses seem most suited to a relatively loose attack formation which left enough room for each man to throw his axe or spear and punch forward with his shield as he charged into combat. When needed they could also call on men with bows to support them.

At the Battle of Vouillé Gregory of Tours characterized the Visigoths 'fighting at a distance', while the Franks 'tried to come to close combat'. This may be nothing more than a disparaging comment to contrast Visigothic cowardice with Frankish bravery. On the other hand, 'fighting at a distance' could describe hit-and-run tactics appropriate for men on horseback armed with javelins as well as spears. The Franks, armed and equipped with hand-to-hand weapons and very short-range missiles, would naturally have preferred 'to come to close combat' without bothering with preliminaries which would place them at a disadvantage. At Casilinum the Alamanni and Franks decided that their best option was to make a headlong charge on foot. They succeeded in piercing the Roman line but against an enemy with combined arms – foot, horse and archers – they were surrounded and cut to pieces. At Vouillé this tactic worked although we do not know how or why.

The headlong charge of the Franks came to be seen by the Romans as a characteristic of their way of warfare for centuries. A later sixth century Roman military manual (the *Strategikon*) has this to say of them:

> The fair-haired races place great value on freedom. They are bold and undaunted in battle. Daring and impetuous as they are, they consider any timidity and even a short retreat as a disgrace. They calmly despise death as they fight violently in hand to hand combat... They are undisciplined in charging, as if they were the only people in the world who are not cowards.

Describing how Roman troopers were trained to use lances in a charge, learning from the Germans but maintaining better discipline, the *Strategikon* has this to say:

> They (the front ranks) lean forward, cover their heads with their shields, hold their lances high as their shoulders in the manner of the fair-haired races. Protected by their shields they ride in good

order, not too fast but at a trot, to avoid having the impetus of the charge breaking up their ranks before coming to blows with the enemy, which is a real risk.

Of course, these are generic descriptions of Germanic tactics and are not specific to the Franks. The Germanic Vandals, for example, fought exclusively on horseback by the sixth century and apparently had no tactic other than to charge into close combat. By the time the *Strategikon* was written, the Vandals were no more and the Ostrogoths had been defeated. The most important Germanic peoples, with whom the East Romans still had to deal with, were the Lombards and, of course, the Franks. The Lombards certainly had a sizeable force of mounted lancers. Many of them had fought for the Romans against the Ostrogoths and Franks. As the *Strategikon* was written at about the same time the Lombards were moving into Italy, it is more than possible that the description of the 'fair-haired race's' tactical methods would have been influenced more by the Lombards than by the Franks.

In the years that followed, the East Romans came to call all Germans 'Franks', regardless of their origin. They were still renowned for their ferocious charge and increasingly it was on horseback. In the later medieval period, French armies were noted for the prowess of their mounted men at arms which often swept all before them.

Agathias wrote that the Franks did not wear armour and went into battle half-naked. This can be nothing more than a Greco-Roman stereotype of savage barbarians. From the time of Childeric in the mid fifth century, the Franks had access to Roman armouries and they also had talented smiths. Even if every man might not have been fully kitted out with helmet and body armour, the majority of a war leader's *comitatus* of full-time retainers surely would have been. Graves of many high-status warriors contain helmets and some also have body armour. That lesser men were not buried with them does not necessarily mean they did not have access to armour. For a relatively poorer man such valuable items of equipment would likely have been passed on to his sons rather than being interred with him.

Chapter 10

The Legacy of the Franks

The title of this series of books is *The Conquerers of Rome.* Each volume has attempted to tell the story of three of the most important Germanic tribes who took much of the Western Empire for themselves – the Vandals, the Goths and the Franks. Many other Germanic peoples also played a part, such as the Angles and Saxons in Britain and the Lombards in Italy. The non-Germanic Sarmatians, Alans and Huns had a pivotal role even if the latter never succeeded in settling within the Roman Empire.

We will leave the story of the Franks in the sixth century after their last failed attempt to take another part of the Empire from the Romans. The intervention of the Franks in Italy may have been against 'Romans' whose capital was then Constantinople rather than Rome, but it was a continuation of the attempt by the emerging Germanic kingdoms to carve out bits of the West Roman Empire for themselves. The last of these was the Lombard invasion of Italy in 568 which picked up the pieces after the long war between Romans, Ostrogoths and Franks.

Unlike the Vandals and Goths, the Franks did not take the city of Rome but they did conquer Roman Gaul. The Vandal kingdom in Africa was destroyed by the Romans in the mid sixth century and later the Arabs moved in. The Ostrogothic kingdom of Italy was also destroyed by the Romans in the sixth century but the Visigothic Kingdom in Spain continued until the Arab conquest of 711. While the kingdoms of the Vandals and Goths were relatively short-lived, that of the Franks endured.

What was the key to their success? How had the Franks managed to hold on to their conquests while the initially more powerful Vandals and Goths failed? It was down to timing, geography and no small amount of luck.

The Frankish takeover of Roman Gaul was more of an absorption rather than an outright conquest. They expanded gradually from the

Rhine. Although they were as aggressive as other Germanic peoples in their dealings with Rome in the third and fourth centuries, the Franks soon learned that they got more if they served as Roman allies, making themselves indispensable to the Romans as defenders of the Rhine frontier. In exchange they became wealthier and better equipped. As their leaders served in senior positions in the Roman army they learned how to conduct strategic campaigns and command large armies of mixed forces. Their reward was increasing grants of land inside the Empire, first as *laeti* and then with tracts of frontier which they ruled themselves.

The Vandals and Goths also attempted to make similar accommodations with Rome but having been driven from their original homelands by the Huns they did not have a secure base to fall back on. Both these peoples had to migrate thousands of miles, ever seeking a place to call their own inside Roman territory. For brief periods they managed it. Various bands of Goths experienced times when they were accepted as pseudo-Roman armies but these periods were fleeting. For much of their history the Vandals and Goths were seen by the Romans as enemies and they had to constantly struggle to maintain what they had won.

Once the Franks had taken control of much of northern and eastern France, the lands they held were far from the remaining Roman power centres of Italy and Asia Minor. The Visigoths in southern France and Spain, and the Vandals in Africa could be reached by Roman fleets while the Frankish holdings were far from the Mediterranean coast. It is not surprising that the one bit of France the Franks had difficulty holding on to, was Provence. Easily reachable from the Mediterranean, or overland from Italy, the Romans and later the Ostrogoths of Italy were able hold Provence against Frankish expansion.

The Franks benefited from the fact that they really only began their conquest of Gaul when the Roman Empire in the West had ceased to be a significant power. Rather than having to fight Imperial armies, the Franks were able to pick up the pieces of a province which had been ravaged by the Vandals and Huns, fought over by rival Roman factions, and occupied by Visigoths, Burgundians, Britons, Saxons and Alamanni. When Clovis began his conquest of Gaul he picked off the various factions one by one – making temporary alliances and drawing support from other Franks east of the Rhine. By the time Clovis had established his hegemony over

Gaul, and probably earlier, his followers were no longer a Germanic tribe. They were an amalgam of Franks, Alamanni, Burgundians and Gallo-Romans. They were primarily Christian and their society probably owed more to the Romans than the ancient Germanic tribes from which their leaders' ancestors had come from.

Clovis benefited from the fact that he was still a pagan in his early years while the Vandals and Goths had converted to the Arian form of Christianity. When he did convert he had the good sense, or good luck, to convert to Catholic Christianity. This enabled him to win over the support of the Gallo-Roman authorities at a time when bishops, rather than secular authorities, were the leaders of the local populace. This allowed the Romans to see him as a defender of their faith against the heretical Arian Visigoths. So as the Franks took on the other barbarian kingdoms in Gaul they had some degree of popular support from the locals for whom allegiance to the Roman Church had replaced allegiance to the Roman Empire.

The Frankish attempt to take advantage of the War in Italy between the Romans and Ostrogoths did not end well but neither did it cost them much. Two of their major interventions were conducted by recently conquered Burgundians and Alamanni. The losses sustained by these warriors would not have greatly troubled the Frankish kings. When King Theudibert led an army into Italy he was probably testing the water. After a few successful engagements against both the Ostrogoths and Romans, and taking a few key fortresses in Venetia, he sensibly withdrew. By not becoming decisively embroiled in Italy the Franks were able to consolidate their hold on France, free of the sort of external threat which might have destroyed their recently won kingdom.

In the years that followed, the Franks continued to fight against raiders and enemies on their borders. None of these really threatened to overthrow their hold on France. In typically aggressive fashion the Franks took offensive actions to weaken bordering kingdoms such as those of the Visigoths in Spain and Thuringians beyond the Rhine.

At other times the Franks fought amongst themselves. Theirs was not a unitary kingdom. After Clovis' realm was divided amongst his four sons, rivalries and territorial ambitions led to conflict amongst his successors once external threats had been dealt with. The result of Clovis' division of his kingdom amongst his sons after his death was that while his descendants retained and expanded their hegemony over Roman Gaul they never held it as a united kingdom under a single monarch.

So, what was the legacy of the Franks? In a nutshell it was France. The Franks took it, gave it their name and held it. When the Arabs took Spain from the Visigoths in the eighth century they crossed the Pyrenees into France only to be stopped by the Franks at the Battle of Tours in 732. As a result, France remained western and Christian with an unbroken lineage which could be traced back to the embers of Roman Gaul.

Appendix I

The Fifth Century Roman Army of Gaul

The following is a list of the units assigned to the *Magister Equitum per Gallias* – commander of the Roman field army of Gaul. It comes from the *Notitia Dignitatum*, a list of offices and military commands at the start of the fifth century. Technically the listed units would have provided a substantial force of around 25,000 men able to intervene to deal with any barbarian incursions. That the Gallic army failed to do this so spectacularly in 407, when the Vandals, Alans and Suebi crossed the Rhine, or in 451 when the Huns did the same, calls into question whether it existed at all, except on paper.

Many units were frequently drawn off to Italy to defend the Roman heartland from various barbarian threats or to fight usurpers (see Appendix II). There was probably no time in which any Roman commander was able to call on the full force. That Julian only commanded 13,000 men at the Battle of Strasbourg, at a time when the West Roman Empire was still fully intact, is an indication of the reality over theoretical paper strengths.

We do not know for certain the exact sizes of any of the individual units. It is generally accepted that a vexillation of cavalry had a paper strength of around 300 men, an auxilia 500 men and a legion 1,000–1,500 men. The 5,000-man legions of the early Empire had long been broken up into smaller detachments. These are theoretical numbers. In reality, many units would have had far less men available for action at any time. Some may have been so run-down to have been little more than a rump from which more men could theoretically be recruited around. Records from previous years show that many units might only be able to deploy little more than half their theoretical strength.

There were three grades of units: *palatini* (palatine units initially commanded by the emperor); *comitatenses* (regional troops recruited to defend their province); and *pseudocomitatenses* (units drawn from the frontier forces). Some of the *pseudocomitatenses*, such as the *Prima Flavia*

Gallicana, were descended from the legions of old, others were auxiliaries or newly raised units of barbarians.

Some units of the same name are distinguished as *seniores* or *juniories* – seniors or juniors. The likely explanation is that at some time in their history a number of soldiers were drawn off from the original unit to form a new one which then acted independently, presumably brought back up to strength by new recruits as a better alternative to recruiting a new unit from scratch.

Unlike the frontier forces the field army units had no fixed bases. They would tend to be located in towns away from the frontier ready to intervene when called on. After the Vandal invasion many went over to Constantine III while others may have remained in the vicinity of Arles under Ravenna's control. In the fourth century Ammianus mentions concentrations of troops at Sens and Reims in central Gaul while the frontier forces were in action around Trier and Cologne on the Rhine.

Cavalry Vexillations
Equites Batavi Seniores (*palatini*)
Equites Cornuti Seniores (*palatini*)
Equites Batavi Juniores (*palatini*)
Equites Brachiati Juniores (*palatini*)
Equites Honoriani Seniores (*comitatenses*)
Equites Honoriani Taifali Juniores(*comitatenses*)
Equites Armigeri Seniores (*comitatenses*)
Equites Octavo Dalmatae (*comitatenses*)
Equites Dalmatae Passerentiacenses (*comitatenses*)
Equites Prima Gallia (*comitatenses*)
Equites Mauri Alites (*comitatenses*)
Equites Constantiaci Feroces (*comitatenses*)

Auxiliary Infantry (all *palatini*)
Mattiaci Juniores
Leones Seniores
Brachiati Juniores
Salii Seniores (possibly Salian Franks)
Gratianenses

Bructerii
Ampsivarii
Valentinianenses
Batavi Seniores
Batavi Juniores
Britones
Atecotti Honoriani Seniores
Sagittarii Nervi Gallicani (archers)
Jovii Juniores Gallicani
Mattiaci Juniores Gallicani
Atecotti Juniores Gallicani
Ascarii Honoriani Seniores

Legionary infantry
Lanciarii Sabarienses (*palatini*)
Armigeri Defensores Seniores (*comitatenses*)
Lanciarii Honoriani Gallicani (*comitatenses*)
Menapi Seniores (*comitatenses*)
Secundani Britones (*comitatenses*)
Ursarienses (*comitatenses*)
Praesidienses (*comitatenses*)
Geminiacenses (*comitatenses*)
Cortoriacenses (*comitatenses*)
Honoriani Felices Gallicani (*comitatenses*)

Pseudocomitatenses (all infantry, some drawn from frontier legions, others from auxiliaries)
Prima Flavia Gallicana
Marienses
Abrincateni
Defensores Seniores
Mauri Osismiaci
Prima Flavia
Superventores Juniores
Balistarii (possibly crossbowmen)
Defensores Juniores
Garronenses

Anderetiani
Acincenses
Cornacenses
Septimani
Cursarienses
Musmagenses
Romanenses
Insidatores
Truncensimani
Abulci
Exploratores

In addition to the field army the *Notitia* lists a number of prefects and tribunes stationed in Gaul who were neither under the *Magister Equitum's* direct command nor those of the *Duces* who commanded the frontier forces. These were:

Praefectus Classis Fluminis Rhodani - naval forces on the Rhône based between Arles and Vienne

Praefectus Classis Barcariorum - naval forces on Lake Neuchâtel

Praefectus Classis Araricae - naval forces on Lake Constance

Praefectus Classis Anderetianorum - naval forces on the Seine based at Paris

Praefectus Militum Musculariorum - soldiers based at Marseilles

Tribunus Cohortis Primae Flaviae Sapaudicae - soldiers based at Grenoble

Tribunus Cohortis Noevempopulanae - soldiers based at Lapurdo in Aquitaine

In addition to these units, prefects of Sarmatian and Taifal settlers had command of *laeti* at Poitiers, Paris, Reims, Amiens, Rennes, Langres and on the Armorican borders. Other prefects commanded German *laeti* at Chartres, Bayeux, Coutances, Le Mans, Rennes, Tongres, Auvergne and throughout Flanders. Many of these, especially in the north, would have been Franks.

Appendix II

The Fifth Century Roman Army of Italy

M any of the units which Julian commanded in Gaul in the fourth century (see Chapter 3) are not listed under the command of the *Magister Equitum per Gallias*. In the fifth century almost all of these units are listed in the *Notitia Dignitatum* under the *Intra Italiam cum viri illustris magistri peditum* (the illustrious commanders of foot in Italy). This demonstrates how the deployment of individual units was not fixed. The units which fought the Franks and Alamanni in Gaul in the mid fourth century were in Italy at the start of the fifth. Quite possibly they had been drawn off from Gaul to defend Italy against Radagasius (see Chapter 4) and never returned. Several units are listed under more than one command which further calls into question the accuracy of these lists.

Many units seem to have been brigaded together in some sort of permanent or semi-permanent arrangement. On several occasions Ammianus mentions the *Comites* and *Promoti* working together (see Chapter 3). It may well be that these two units operated together as a single tactical grouping and the same is true for many of the infantry units such as the Cornuti and Brachiati, and Petulantes and Celtae.

Cavalry Vexillations
Comites Seniores (*palatini*)
Equites Promoti Seniores (*palatini*)
Equites Brachiati Seniores (*palatini*)
Equites Cornuti Seniores (*palatini*)
Comites Alani (*palatini*)
Equites Mauri feroces (*comitatenses*)
Equites Constantes Valentinianenses Juniores (*comitatenses*)

Auxiliary Infantry (all *palatini*)
Cornuti Seniores
Brachiati Seniores
Petulantes Seniores
Celtae Seniores
Heruli Seniores
Batavi Seniores
Mattiaci Seniores
Jovii Seniores
Victores Seniores
Cornuti Juniores
Leones Juniores
Exculcatores Seniores
Grati
Savini
Felices Juniores
Atecotti Honoriani Juniores
Brisigavi Juniores
Mauri Honoriani Juniores
Galli Victores
Marcomanni

Legionary infantry
Joviani Seniores (*palatini*)
Herculiani Seniores (*palatini*)
Divitenses Seniores (*palatini*)
Tungrecani Seniores (*palatini*)
Pannoniciani Seniores (*palatini*)
Moesiaci Seniores (*palatini*)
Octavani (*palatini*)
Thebei (*palatini*)
Mattiarii Juniores (*comitatenses*)
Septimani Juniores (*comitatenses*)
Regii (*comitatenses*)
Germaniciani (*comitatenses*)

Pseudocomitatenses (all infantry)
Prima Julia
Tertia Julia
Placidi Valentinianici Felices
Gratianenses Juniores
Pontinenses

Five prefects and their forces are also listed as being under the command of the *Magister Peditum* in Italy. These were:

Praefectus Classis Venetum – naval forces based at Aquiliea

Praefectus Classis Ravennatium cum curis eiusdem civitatis – naval forces based at Ravenna

Praefectus Classis Comensis cum curis eiusdem civitatis – naval forces based at Como

Praefectus Classis Misenatium – naval forces based at Miseno

Praefectus Militum Juniorum Italicorum – soldiers based at Ravenna

The *Magister Officiorum* (Master of Offices) commanded the *Scholae* or guards' cavalry. These elite troops had replaced the Praetorian Guard after Constantine the Great disbanded the Praetorians in the early fourth century. They would normally be expected to accompany the emperor or a similarly important member of the Imperial family on campaign. In his descriptions of Julian's campaigns against the Franks and Alamanni (see Chapter 3), Ammianus Marcellinus frequently refers to the *Scutarii* (shield men), Gentiles (foreigners) and armoured troops. The former would probably have been one or more of the units of the *Schola Scutariorum*, the second the *Schola Gentilium* and the third the *Schola Armaturarum*.

The Master of Offices in the west had the following units under his command:

Schola Scutariorum Prima

Schola Scutariorum Secunda

Schola Armaturarum Seniorum

Schola Gentilium Seniorum

Schola Scutatorium Tertia

In addition to these regular military units, the *Notitia* lists seventeen prefects of Sarmatian *laeti* who had been settled throughout Italy. Unlike in Gaul, there appears to have been no German equivalent.

Chronology

Note: Some fifth century dates are far from certain. Gregory of Tours is the main near-original source for some of them and he may have been more poetic than scientific in his dating system, especially for the reign of Clovis. Where there is some doubt or the exact date is not precisely known I have marked it as circa (*c.*,).

In Chronological Order

166–180:	The Marcomannic Wars.
186:	Maternus leads an uprising of army deserters and disaffected Gallo-Romans.
235–284:	Upheaval and endemic civil war in the Roman Empire.
235–260:	First Alamannic and Frankish raids into Gaul.
251:	The Goths destroy the Roman army at Arbutus, killing the Emperor Decius.
253:	Renewed Gothic raids across the Danube.
260:	Sassanid Persians defeat and capture the Emperor Valerian. Alamanni raid across the Rhine, some moving into Italy and reaching the outskirts of Rome.
260:	Postumus takes control of Gaul, creating the 'Gallic Empire'.
267–8:	Goths and Heruls launch amphibious attacks across the Black Sea. Athens sacked.
269:	Claudius II defeats the Goths at the Battle of Naissus.
274:	Aurelian restores order in the West after the collapse of the 'Gallic Empire'.
286:	Aelianus and Amandus lead a revolt of the Bacaudae in Armorica.

280s:	Maximian clears the English Channel, campaigns against the Bacaudae and restores the Rhine frontier.
324:	Constantine defeats his rival Licinius aided by the Romano-Frankish General Bonitus.
325:	The Council of Nicaea establishes the Catholic version of Christianity.
354:	Constantius leads an army against the Alamanni. Arbetio is defeated at Lake Constance.
355:	Julian appointed Caesar and sent to Gaul to campaign against the Franks and Alamanni.
355:	Silvanus, of Frankish descent, appointed to lead the Roman army against the Alamanni.
356:	Julian withstands a siege of Sens and retakes Cologne from the Franks. Many of the Franks sue for peace.
357:	Julian defeats the Alamanni at the Battle of Strasbourg.
363:	Julian's invasion of Persia ends in disaster and the death of the emperor.
c., 370–374:	The Huns defeat the Alans and Goths, pushing them westward.
373–375:	Renewed war between Rome and Persia.
c., 373:	German tribes cross the Rhine defeat the Romans under Valentinian I but are later defeated in turn. Many of the survivors are recruited into the Roman army.
375–6:	Huns move into Gothic territory sending refugees south and westward.
376:	Gothic refugees seek asylum inside Roman territory.
376:	The Gothic refugees rise up against the Romans.
378:	The Alamannic Lentienses cross the Rhine preventing Gratian from sending reinforcements to the East against the Goths. The Lentienses are defeated at Colmar by the Frank Mallobaudes commanding a West Roman army.
378, 9 August:	The Goths destroy the East Roman army at the Battle of Adrianople.

382:	Goths settled in the Balkans under treaty with the Eastern Emperor Theodosius.
382:	Magnus Maximus proclaimed emperor in Britain. Moving to Gaul, he establishes his capital at Trier.
388:	Magnus Maximus, supported by Alamanni, is defeated by Theodosius' East Roman forces.
380s:	Genobaud, Marcomer, and Sunno lead a Frankish incursion into Gaul, destroying a Roman army. They are later defeated by Arbogast, a Frank leading Roman troops.
381:	The Arian version of Christianity is declared heretical.
392:	Death of Valentinian II. Arbogast puts Eugenius on the throne.
394:	Eugenius and Arbogast defeated by Theodosius at the Battle of Frigidus.
395:	Death of Theodosius. The Roman Empire divided with the West under Honorius and the East under Arcadius. Stilicho holds supreme power. Alaric leads a rebellion of Goths in the Balkans.
396:	Alaric's Goths plunder Greece and Thrace.
c., 400:	The Huns move further west, settling on the Hungarian Plain and triggering off another wave of Germanic migrations.
401:	Alaric invades Italy for the first time but is driven back.
405:	Radagasius invades Italy. Stilicho withdraws troops from Rhine frontier to deal with him.
406:	Radagasius defeated by Stilicho near Florence.
406:	British army revolts proclaiming Constantine III as emperor.
406, 31 December:	Vandals, Suebi and Alans cross the Rhine.
407:	Constantine III crosses from Britain to Gaul. Constantine's forces keep the Vandals and their allies bottled up in northern Gaul.
407:	Major revolt of the Bacaudae in Armorica.
408:	Stilicho executed. Alaric again invades Italy.

408–409:	Alaric blockades Rome.
409:	The Vandals, Alans and Suebi cross the Pyrenees into Spain.
410, 20 August:	Alaric's Goths sack Rome.
411 or late 410:	Alaric dies and is succeeded by Athaulf.
411:	Honorius' General Constantius defeats Constantine III in Gaul.
412:	Athaulf's Goths move into southern Gaul.
414:	The Goths move against the Vandals, Alans and Suebi in Spain.
418:	The Goths are settled in Aquitaine by the Romans.
422:	Renewed Visigothic campaign against the Vandals on behalf of the Romans.
423:	Honorius dies.
425:	The 6-year-old Valentinian III becomes Western emperor with his mother Galla Placidia the power behind the throne.
427:	Power struggle between Boniface, Felix and Aeitus for control of the Western Empire.
429:	The Vandals cross over to Africa.
430:	The Visigoths fail in an attempt to take Arles.
433:	Rua, king of the Huns dies and is succeeded by Attila and Bleda. Aetius is given supreme military power in the West.
435–37:	Rebellion of the Bacaudae in north-western Gaul led by Tibatto.
436:	Defeat of the Burgundians by Aeitus' Hun allies.
436–9:	Conflict between the Visigoths and Romans in Gaul.
439:	The Vandals capture Carthage.
441–2:	Huns raid throughout the Balkans.
443:	Burgundians resettled in Burgundy.
445:	Bleda murdered. Attila becomes sole king of the Huns.
447:	Attila's Huns again ravage the Balkans and threaten Constantinople.
449:	Basilius leads a revolt of the Bacaudae of northern Spain.

c., 450:	Majorian destroys a band of Franks led by Chlogio near Arras.
451:	Attila invades Gaul and is defeated by Aetius at the Battle of the Catalaunian Fields near Troyes in France. Franks fight on both sides.
452:	Attila invades Italy.
453:	Death of Attila.
454:	The Huns are defeated at the the Battle of Nedao by a coalition of Germanic tribes. Aeitus is murdered by Valentinian III.
454–70:	The Ostrogoths settle in Pannonia, expand their territory at the expense of their Germanic neighbours.
455:	Valentinian murdered.
455:	The Vandals sack Rome.
455:	Avitus proclaimed Western emperor with the support of the Visigoths.
457:	Avitus abdicates and is replaced by Majorian with Ricimer the power behind the throne.
458:	The Roman Aegidius takes Lyons from the Burgundians. The Frank Childeric goes into exile.
c.,460:	Aegidius is proclaimed king of the Franks. He campaigns against the Visigoths and Saxons.
461:	The Emperor Majorian executed by Ricimer and replaced by Libius Severus. Aegidius does not recognize Severus.
463:	Euric's Visigoths defeated at Orléans by Romans and Franks.
464:	Death of Aegidius. Syagrius inherits his lands and army. Childeric returns from exile, defeats Count Paul and consolidates his hold over the Salian Franks.
468:	The Battle of Mercurium. The Vandals destroy a huge Roman invasion fleet off the coast of Tunisia, ending Roman hopes of reconquering Africa.
473:	Ostrogoths under Thiudimir and Theodoric cross the Balkans to invade Thrace and Greece. Others follow Vidimir to join up with the Visigoths in Gaul.

473:	Gundobad leaves Roman service to become king of the Burgundians.
474:	Theodoric becomes king of the Ostrogoths.
475:	Orestes, Attila's former secretary, proclaims his son Romulus Augustulus West Roman emperor.
476:	Odoacer leads a mutiny of the barbarian troops in the Roman army of Italy. He overthrows Romulus and becomes king of Italy.
c., 481:	Childeric dies and is succeeded by Clovis.
c., 486:	Clovis defeats Syagrius.
489:	Ostrogoths under Theodoric invade Italy.
c., 490:	Clovis campaigns against the Thuringians.
493:	Theodoric overthrows Odoacer and becomes king of Italy.
c., 494:	Visigoths start expanding into Spain.
c., 496:	The Franks defeat the Alamanni at the Battle of Tolbiac.
c., 500:	Clovis is baptized.
c., 500:	Clovis supports the Burgundian Godegisel against his brother Gundobad.
502–5:	War between Persia and the East Roman Empire.
507:	The Visigoths in Gaul defeated by the Franks at the Battle of Vouillé. King Alaric II killed. The victory leaves Clovis' Franks the most powerful force in Gaul.
508:	Clovis given the title of Consul by the East Roman Emperor.
c., 510:	Clovis brings the Ripuarian Franks under his control.
511:	Clovis convenes the Council of Orléans.
511:	Traditional date of Clovis' death.
c., 520:	Theuderic and Chlothar attack and defeat the Thuringians.
523:	Clovis' sons successfully attack the Burgundians and kill their kings.
524:	Chlodomar killed in a Burgundian counterattack.
526:	Death of Theodoric the Great, king of the Ostrogoths.
527–565:	Reign of Justinian in the Eastern Empire.

531:	The Franks defeat the Visigoths near Barcelona, kill their king and take Narbonne.
533:	Belisarius' East Romans invade Africa and capture Carthage.
534:	The Franks defeat the Burgundians and absorb their kingdom.
535:	The East Romans attack Ostrogothic possessions in Sicily and Dalmatia.
536:	Belisarius invades Italy, takes Naples and Rome.
538:	Burgundians, sent by the Franks to aid the Ostrogoths, move into northern Italy.
539:	Theudibert leads a Frankish army into Italy against both Ostrogoths and Romans.
540:	The Franks take over Venetia in north-eastern Italy.
542:	Under Totila the Ostrogoths rally and begin to retake Italian cities previously lost to the Romans.
546:	The Ostrogoths retake Rome.
552:	The Roman General Narses invades Italy from the North. He defeats Totila at the Battle of Taginae.
553:	The Alamannic brothers Butilin and Lothar invade Italy.
554:	Lothar defeated at Pisaurum, Butilin defeated at Casilinum.
568:	Successful Lombard invasion of Italy.
635:	Arabs defeat the East Roman Emperor Heraclius at Yarmuk.
640:	Arabs conquer Egypt.
647:	Arabs invade and conquer Roman North Africa.
711:	Arabs and Berbers invade and conquer Spain.
732:	The Franks defeat the Arabs at the Battle of Tours.
751:	The Merovingian dynasty replaced by the Carolingians.

Notable Frankish, Alamannic and Burgundian Leaders

In Chronological Order

Chrocus. A third century Alamannic leader who overran Gaul in the 250s.

Gennobaudes. The earliest known Frankish leader who pledged allegiance to Rome in the 280s.

Bonitus. A Frank who became *Magister Militum* under Constantine, he played a key role in helping Constantine defeat his rival Licinius in 324.

Silvanus. Bonitus' son who was *Magister Peditum* under Constantius and was proclaimed emperor by the Gallic army in 355. He reigned for twenty-eight days.

Chnodomar and Vestralp. Alamannic 'kings' who were defeated at the Battle of Strasbourg in 357. They were supported by Urius, Ursicinus, Serapio, Suomar and Hortar.

Mallobaudes. A Frank who served under the Emperor Gratian, defeated the Lentienses in 378 and was given the title of *Alamannicus Maximus*.

Priarius: Leader of the Alamannic Lentienses who was defeated by Mallobaudes.

Genobaud, Marcomer, and Sunno. Ripuarian Frankish war leaders who led an invasion of Roman Germania near Cologne. They were eventually defeated by Arbogast (see below) in the late 380s.

Richomer (or Richomeres). A high-ranking Roman general of Frankish origin who campaigned against the Goths in the late fourth century and eventually became consul. He was killed at the Battle of Frigidus in 394.

Arbogast (died 394). Richomer's nephew who rose to supreme power in the West. He put Eugenius on the West Roman throne after doing away with the Emperor Valentinian II. He was defeated by the East

Roman Emperor Theodosius at the Battle of Frigidus, fighting against his Uncle Richomer. He committed suicide after the battle.

Gundicharius. King of the Burgundians killed by Huns serving the Roman Aeitus in 436.

Chlogio. A Salian Frankish war leader who rose to prominence in the 440s. He may have been either the father or grandfather of Childeric. His two sons took different sides when Attila invaded Gaul, the eldest siding with the Huns and the youngest with the Romans.

Merovech. The legendary founder of the Merovingian dynasty. If he existed at all he may have been one of Chlogio's sons and the father of Childeric.

Aegidius (died 464). A Roman warlord who had served under Aetius and supported Majorian. He was recognized by the Franks as their king.

Childeric (died *c.*,481). A Salian Frankish war leader possibly descended from Chlogio who rose to become their king after the death of Aegidius.

Arbogast II. A Frankish leader who held the west bank of the Rhine around Trier and Cologne in the 460s. He may have been descended from the first Arbogast.

Clovis (died *c.*,511). Son of Childeric who united the Franks, defeated the Gallo-Roman Syagrius, the Thuringians, Alamanni and Visigoths to create what would become the Kingdom of France.

Ragnachar. A Salian Frankish leader who held Cambrai in the 480s and supported Clovis against Syagrius. He was later killed by Clovis.

Chararic. A Salian Frankish leader who failed to support Clovis against Syagrius and was later killed by Clovis.

Clotilda. Clovis' Christian Burgundian wife whose parents were murdered by Gundobad, sparking off a blood feud between the Franks and Burgundians. She is credited with turning Clovis towards Christianity.

Gundobad. A Burgundian who rose to high rank in the West Roman Empire in the early 470s. He became king of the Burgundians in 473 killing one brother (Clotilda's father) and driving his other brother (Godegisel) to seek an alliance with Clovis.

Sigibert the Lame. Leader of the Ripuarian Franks who defeated the Alamanni at the Battle of Tolbiac in 496 with Clovis' support.

Chloderic. Son of Sigibert the Lame who had his father assassinated. He supported Clovis against the Visigoths in 507 and was later killed by Clovis.

Theuderic (died 511). Clovis' eldest son by a concubine.

Chlodomar (died 524). Clovis' eldest son with Clotilda. Died in battle against the Burgundians.

Childebert (died 558) Clovis' second son with Clotilda.

Chlothar (died 561) Clovis' youngest son with Clotilda.

Sigismund. Burgundian king, son of Gundobad, captured and executed by the Franks in 523.

Godomar. Sigismund's son who defeated the Franks in 524.

Theudibert (died 548). Theuderic's son who led a Frankish army to intervene in the War in Italy between the Ostrogoths and Romans in 539.

Butilin and Lothar. Alamannic brothers who led an invasion of Italy in 554 and were defeated by the Romans.

The Later Roman Emperors

In Chronological Order

Marcus Aurelius (121–180)

Commodus (180–192)

Pertinax (193)

Didius Julianus (193) Notoriously bought the throne from the Praetorian Guard who had put it up for auction.

Pescennius Niger (193–4) Campaigned against the Bacaudae in Gaul.

Clodius Albinus (193–7)

Septimius Severus (193–211)

Geta (211)

Caracalla (211–217) Campaigned against the Alamanni

Macrinus (217–18)

Diadumenianus (218)

Elegabalus (218–22)

Severus Alexander (222–35)

Maximinus (235–38)

Gordian I (238)

Gordian II (238)

Balbinus (238)

Pupienus (238)

Gordian III (238–44)

Philip the Arab (244–49)

Decius (249–5) Killed by the Goths at the Battle of Abritus.

Gallus (251–3)

Valerian (253–60) Captured by the Persians at the Battle of Edessa.

Gallienus (253–68) Initially co-ruler with Valerian. He campaigned against the Rhine tribes and is credited with reforming the Roman cavalry to make it more effective.

Claudius Gothicus (268–70)

Aurelian (270–5) Restored order in Gaul after the collapse of the 'Gallic Empire'.

Tacitus (275–6)

Probus (276–82)

Carus (282–3)

Carinus (283–5) Western emperor.

Numerian (283–4) Eastern emperor, died on campaign against the Persians.

Diocletian (284–305) Restored order to the Roman Empire and reorganized the government.

Maximian (286–305) Co-ruler with Diocletian. He campaigned against the Bacaudae and Alamanni.

Constantine the Great (306–337) Made Christianity the official religion.

Constantine II (337–40)

Constans (337–50)

Constantius II (337–61) Campaigned against the Alamanni.

Julian (261–4) Waged successful campaigns against the Franks and Alamanni, defeating the Alamanni at the Battle of Strasbourg. He died on campaign against the Persians.

Jovian (363–4)

Valentinian I (364–75) West Roman emperor.

Valens (364–78) East Roman emperor who lost his life at the Battle of Adrianople.

Gratian (375–83) West Roman emperor who campaigned against the Lentienses.

Theodosius I (379–395) The last emperor to rule the whole Empire.

Magnus Maximus (383–8) British usurper, defeated by Theodosius.

Valentinian II (383–92) West Roman emperor deposed by Arbogast.

Eugenius (392–4) Western usurper put on the throne by Arbogast and defeated by Theodosius at the Battle of Frigidus.

Arcadius (383–408) Initially co-emperor with his father Theodosius and then sole emperor of the East from 395.

Honorius (393–423) Initially co-emperor with his father Theodosius and then sole emperor of the West from 395.

Constantine III (407–411) Proclaimed emperor by the British army, he moved into Gaul to establish control over Britain, Gaul and Spain, leaving Honorius controlling only Italy and Africa. He was defeated by Honorius' General Constantius.

Priscus Attalus (409 and also 414–415) A usurper who was twice proclaimed emperor by the Visigoths and deposed by Honorius' armies.

Jovinus (411–413) A usurper who briefly filled the vacuum after Constantine III's overthrow in Gaul.

Theodosius II (408–450) East Roman emperor.

Constantius III (421). Honorius' general who defeated Constantine III and was briefly recognised as co-emperor by Honorius.

Joannes (423–425) West Roman emperor supported by Aetius and deposed by Theodosius II's army.

Valentinian III (425–455) Son of Constantius III and Galla Placidia who was Honorius' sister. He became West Roman emperor when he was only 6-years-old. Galla Placidia ruled as the power behind the throne before he came of age.

Marcian (450–457) East Roman emperor.

Petronius Maximus (455) West Roman emperor killed by the Roman mob when the Vandals sailed from Africa to sack Rome.

Avitus (455–456) A Gallo-Roman aristocrat proclaimed Western emperor with the backing of the Visigoths and deposed by Ricimer.

Majorian (457–461) Made Western emperor by Ricimer and then deposed after the failure of his attempt to reconquer Africa from the Vandals.

Leo I (457–474) A soldier who was made East Roman emperor with the support of the Ostrogoths.

Libius Severus (461–465). Made Western emperor by Ricimer but not recognized by Constantinople, nor by Aegidius.

Anthemius (467–472) An Eastern senator who became Western emperor as a result of a deal between Ricimer and Leo. He was deposed by Ricimer.

Olybrius (472) Western emperor.

Glycerius (473–474) Proclaimed Western emperor by the Burgundian Gundobad and deposed by the armies of the Eastern Empire.

Julius Nepos (474–475) Put on the Western throne by the Eastern emperor, Leo.

Leo II (474) Eastern emperor.

Zeno (474–491) Leo I's son-in-law. He was deposed by Basilicus in 475 but regained the throne in 476. He sent Theodoric and the Ostrogoths into Italy against Odoacer.

Basilicus (475–476) A general and another brother-in-law of Leo I who briefly seized the Eastern throne from Zeno.

Romulus Augustulus (475–467) The last West Roman emperor, placed on the throne by his father Orestes who had been Attila the Hun's secretary. He was deposed by the Italian army under Odoacer.

Anastasius I (491–518) Eastern emperor who gave Clovis the title of Consul.

Justin (518–527) Eastern emperor.

Justinian (527–565) Justin's nephew who reconquered Africa from the Vandals and Italy from the Ostrogoths.

Glossary

Agri Decumates: The triangle of land bound by the Upper Rhine and Upper Danube in what is now Baden in modern Germany. When it was abandoned by Rome in the third century the Alamanni moved in and made it their homeland.

Alamanni (also Alemanni and Alemannen): A confederacy of Germanic tribes living on the Upper Rhine from the third century.

Alans: A nomadic Sarmatian people who originated to the north of the Black Sea. Some of them fought with the Goths at Adrianople. Others later merged with the Vandals.

Angon: A javelin used by the Franks which had a long iron head not dissimilar to the ancient Roman pilum.

Arians: Followers of a version of Christianity initially proposed by the Bishop Arius, which was widely adopted by many German tribes. It held that Jesus was from God but not the same as God the Father.

Armorica: Roughly equating to modern Brittany this became a semi-autonomous region controlled by the Bacaudae in the fifth century and was later settled by Britons resulting in the modern name of Brittany.

Augustus: The official title of the Roman emperors derived from the name taken by Octavian – the first Roman emperor.

Auxilia Palatina: Elite auxiliaries capable of fighting skirmish actions as well as in the main line of battle.

Auxilia: Auxiliary units of the later Roman army.

Bacaudae: A name given to native Romans who had broken from Imperial control to run their own affairs. There were endemic Bacaudae uprisings throughout the fifth century in Gaul and Spain.

Barritus: A war cry used by the Romans, quite possibly adopted from Germanic tribesmen.

Batavians: An ancient Germanic tribe from the modern Netherlands which was probably absorbed into the Frankish confederacy. Many units in the later Roman army were named as Batavi and were possibly initially recruited from the Franks.

Bucellarii: Soldiers forming the personal bodyguards and private armies of late Roman generals. The name comes from *bucellatum* which was a hard tack biscuit forming part of a soldier's rations. Such troops were maintained by the commander himself rather than by the state.

Burgundians: A Germanic people living on the Middle Rhine in the early fifth century who were later settled into that part of France which now bears their name – Burgundy.

Caesar: The title given to junior rulers in the late Roman Empire who were subordinate to the Augustus.

Catafractarii (cataphracts): Heavily armoured cavalry lancers of the later Roman army who may also have ridden armoured horses. Such troops fought against the Alamanni at the Battle of Strasbourg. They were probably recruited from Sarmatian *laeti*.

Comes (Count): A senior Roman officer who commanded troops of the regional field armies.

Comitatenses: Units of the late Roman regional field armies.

Comitatus: A retinue of skilled warriors serving as full-time retainers to a powerful leader.

Cuneus: A wedge-like formation favoured by the Franks and Alamanni. More like an attack column than a true wedge. It was also described as the 'boar's head' formation.

Draco: A dragon standard which was carried by many later Roman and Germanic units.

Dux (Duke): A senior Roman officer who commanded frontier forces.

Fabricae: Roman arms factories under central Imperial control.

foederati (federates): Initially barbarian troops serving in the Roman army under their own leaders. By the sixth century they were regular units possibly recruited from barbarians, usually Germans.

Francisca: A throwing axe which was the typical weapon of the Frankish warrior.

Franks: A confederacy of Germanic tribes living on the Lower and Middle Rhine from the third century.

Frisii (Frisians): A Germanic people living on the coast of the modern Netherlands. They were associated with the Franks but retained a separate identity into modern times.

Gaul: The Roman name for an area including modern France, Belgium and parts of Germany west of the Rhine.

Gepids: An east Germanic tribe related to the Goths who remained beyond the Roman frontier.

Goths: The most powerful Germanic people in the third to fifth centuries who established two kingdoms inside the Roman Empire. The Visigoths, descended from the clans who crossed the Danube in 376, settled first in Western France and later moved into Spain. The Ostrogoths, who remained beyond the Roman frontiers until the late fifth century, established a kingdom in Italy.

Heruls: An east Germanic people. They were noted for their light equipment and lack of armour.

Huns: A nomadic people from central Asia whose westward movements sparked off the Germanic migrations. Their warriors fought on horseback with bows.

Illyricum (Illyria): The Roman name for the area including modern Croatia and parts of the former Yugoslavia.

Juthungi: A Germanic tribe which invaded Italy in the 260s. They may have been descended from the earlier Semnones and were loosely associated with the Alamanni.

Laeti: Settlements of German and Sarmatian prisoners of war inside Roman territory. They provided recruits for the army in exchange for their land.

Legio (Legion): By the fourth century a Roman legion was a unit of around 1,000 men who fought on foot with spears, javelins and swords.

Lentienses: An Alamannic tribe.

Leudes: Household warriors of a Frankish king.

Lex Salica: Frankish laws first drawn up towards the end of Clovis' reign.

Limes: The Roman frontier.

Limitanei: Roman troops who manned the frontier garrisons of the Limes.

Lombards: A Germanic people who remained outside Roman territory until the sixth century. Many Lombards fought for the East Romans in Italy. In 568 they moved into Italy to take the north for themselves.

Magister Equitum (Master of Horse): One rank below the *Magister Militum* who theoretically commanded the cavalry but in reality led a mixed force. Therefore the *Magister Equitum intra Gallias* commanded the Gallic field army including both horse and foot.

Magister Militum (Master of Soldiers): The most senior Roman military commander below the emperor.

Magister Officiorum (Master of Offices): The high-ranking Roman official who controlled the *fabricae* and commanded the *scholae*.

Magister Peditum (Master of Foot): As above but theoretically commanding the foot. The *Magister Peditum Intra Italiam* commanded both horse and foot of the Italian field army.

Merovingian: The name given to the dynasty of Frankish kings founded by Clovis. They took their name from Merovech, Clovis' legendary grandfather.

Nibelungenlied: A medieval retelling of a fifth century legend in which Siegfried, a Frankish warrior, sought service with the Burgundians.

Notitia Dignitatum: A list of offices and army units of the later Roman Empire.

Ostrogoths: The branch of Goths descended from those who remained outside Roman territory in the fourth century and who followed Theodoric the Great into Italy at the end of the fifth century.

Palatini (Palatine): The most senior non-guards units of the late Roman field army.

Pannonia: The Roman name for the region of the Middle Danube, before the bend, that includes parts of modern Austria, Hungary and Slovenia.

Riparenses: Roman troops who manned the river frontiers.

Ripuarians: A branch of the Franks who remained east of the Middle Rhine.

Rugians: An east Germanic tribe related to the Goths. Many of them were absorbed by the Ostrogoths.

Salians: A branch of the Franks from the Lower Rhine who took over Flanders and parts of northern France.

Sarmatians: A nomadic Iranian people who moved into the area beyond the Roman Middle Danube frontier in the second century AD. They were famous for their heavy cavalry lancers.

Schola (plural Scholae): Mounted guards units of the later Roman army.

Scirii (Scirians): An east Germanic people who were absorbed by the Huns in the fifth century. After the collapse of the Hun empire some were absorbed by the Goths. Odoacer was probably a Scirian.

Scramasax: A short single edged sword which was carried by most Frankish warriors.

Securis: A hand axe which was a sidearm for some late Roman soldiers.

Spangenhelm: A style of conical helmet formed of several pieces held together with reinforcing bands. It usually had a nasal guard, cheek pieces, and neck guard. The style probably originated amongst the Sarmatians along the Danube in the second century AD.

Suebi (also Suevi): A group of Germanic tribes, some of whom probably helped to form the Alamannic confederacy. They were noted for a particular hairstyle in which warriors knotted their hair in what became known as the Suebian knot. Some of them joined in the Vandal migration and settled in Spain. Others remained in Germany giving their name to modern Swabia.

Taifali (also Taifals): A barbarian tribe living in close proximity to the Goths in the third to fourth centuries. They may have been Germanic or possibly Sarmatian. They joined in the Gothic third century raids and a band of them linked up with some of the Goths who had crossed the Danube in 376/7.

Vexilationes (Vexillations): Detachments of troops drawn from a Legion and also the name of cavalry units of the later Roman army.

Visigoths: The branch of Goths descended from the followers of Alaric who ended up settling first in south-western France and then in Spain.

Select Bibliography

Primary Sources
Agathias, *Histories*.
Ammianus Marcellinus, *Res Gestate*.
Anonymous, *The Gallic Chronicle of 452*.
Cassius Dio, *Roman History*.
Cassiodorus, *Variae*.
Claudian, *On the Consulship of Stilicho*.
Gregory of Tours, *History of the Franks*.
Herodian, *The Roman Histories*.
Hydatius, *Chronicle*.
Isidore of Seville, *History of the Kings of the Goths, Vandals and Suebi*.
Jerome, *Chronicle*.
Jordanes, *Getica*.
Libanius, *Orations*.
Maurice, *Strategikon*.
Notitia Dignitatum.
Priscus of Panium, *Fragments*.
Procopius, *History of the Wars*.
Prosper of Aquitaine, *Chronicle*.
Sidonius Apollinaris, *Poems and Letters*.
Tacitus, *Germania*.
Zosimus, *New History*.

Secondary Sources
Rather than an exhaustive list of every single work I have ever read, the following sources are those I have found most useful in writing this book. I recommend all of them to those readers who wish to learn more about the Franks and Alamanni and their impact on the late Roman Empire. As this book has necessarily skimmed over the later Merovingian period, readers may wish to consult some of the listed books for more detail.

Bachrach, Bernard S, *Merovingian Military Organization* (1972) pp. 481–751.

Bishop, Michael C, and Coulston, Jon CN, *Roman Military Equipment from the Punic Wars to the Fall of Rome* (London, 2006).

Boss, Roy, *Justinian's Wars* (Stockport, 1993).

Bury, JB, *The Invasion of Europe by the Barbarians* (London, 1928).

Christlein, Rainer, *Die Alemannen* (Stuttgart, 1978).

Coombs-Hoar, Adrian, *Eagles in the Dust* (Barnsley, 2015).

Delbrück, Hans, *The Barbarian Invasions* Translated by Walter J Renfroe (Nebraska, 1990).

Dixon, K, and Southern, P, *The Roman Cavalry* (London, 1992).

Drinkwater, JF, and Elton, H, *Fifth-century Gaul: A Crisis of Identity* (Cambridge, 1992).

Elton, Hugh, *Warfare in Roman Europe, AD 350–425* (Oxford, 1996).

Gibbon, Edward, *The Decline and Fall of the Roman Empire* (London, 1777–88).

Goffart, Walter, *Barbarians and Romans* (Princeton, 1980).

Goldsworthy, Adrian, *The Fall of the West* (London, 2009).

Gordon, Colin Douglas, *The Age of Attila* (Toronto, 1966).

Halsall, Guy, *Barbarian Migrations and the Roman West* (Cambridge, 2007).

Halsall, Guy, *Warfare and Society in the Barbarian West 450–900* (2003).

Hatt, JJ and Schwartz J, *Das Schlachtfeld von Oberhausbergen* (Darmstadt, 1978).

Heather, Peter, *Empires and Barbarians* (London, 2009).

Heather, Peter, *Goths and Romans* (Oxford, 1991).

Heather, Peter, *The Fall of the Roman Empire: A New History of Rome* (Oxford, 2006).

Heather, Peter, *The Goths* (Oxford, 1996).

Hoffmann, Deitrich, *Das Spaetroemische Bewegungsheer und die Notitia Dignitatum* (Düsseldorf, 1970).

James, Edward, *The Franks* (Oxford, 1998).

Jones, AHM, *The Late Roman Empire 284–602: Social, Economic and Administrative Survey* (Oxford, 1964).

Junkelmann, M, *Die Reiter Roms* (Mainz, 1993).

Lot, Ferdinand, *The End of the Ancient World and the Beginning of the Middle Ages* (Paris, 1939).

Luttwark, EN, *The Grand Strategy of the Roman Empire* (London, 1976).

MacDowall, Simon, *Catalaunian Fields* (Oxford, 2015).

MacDowall, Simon, *Germanic Warrior* (Oxford, 1996).

MacDowall, Simon, *Late Roman Cavalryman* (Oxford, 1995).

MacDowall, Simon, *Late Roman Infantryman* (Oxford, 1994).

MacDowall, Simon, *The Battle of Adrianople* (Oxford, 2000).

MacDowall, Simon, *The Goths* (Barnsley, 2017).

MacDowall, Simon, *The Vandals* (Barnsley, 2016).

Mathisen, Ralph W, and Shanzer, Danuta, *The Battle of Vouillé, 507 CE: Where France Began* (Berlin, 2012).

Muhlberger, Stephen, *The Fifth-Century Chroniclers: Prosper, Hydatius, and the Gallic Chronicler of 452*, (Cambridge 1981).

Oman, Charles, *The Art of War in the Middle Ages* (Oxford, 1885).

Pestano, Dane, *Clovis, King of the Franks - Towards a New Chronology* (Sussex 2016).

Thompson, Edward A, 'Peasant Revolts in Late Roman Gaul and Spain', *Past and Present* Series No. 2 (Oxford, 1952).

Thompson, Edward A, *Romans and Barbarians: The Decline of the Western Empire* (Madison, 1982).

Ueda-Sarson, Luke, *Notitia Dignitatum* http://www.ne.jp/asahi/luke/ueda-sarson/

Wallace-Hadrill, John M, *The Barbarian West 400–1000* (Oxford, 1967).

Wolfram, Herwig, *History of the Goths* Translated by Thomas J Dunlap, (University of California Press, 1990).

Wood, Ian, *The Merovingian Kingdoms 450–751* (Harlow, 1994).

Index

Basina, 104–105

Basinus, 104–106

Batavians,

Germanic tribe, 30–1, 180

Roman auxiliaries, (*Batavii*) 31, 45–8, 50, 159–60, 163

Belisarius, 3, 138, 140–1, 144, 172

Belgium, 2, 31, 85, 113, 123, 182

Black Forest, 4, 8, 15, 52

Boniface, 78, 82, 169

Bonitus, 33, 37–8, 167, 173

Bourges, 101, 106

Britain, 18–19, 25–6, 28–9, 45, 48, 53, 60, 63, 65, 67, 71, 73–5, 77, 80, 81, 94, 101, 103, 110, 135, 154, 168

Britons, 2, 29, 74, 101–102, 106, 108, 110, 113, 155, 180

Brittany, 2, 24, 75, 77, 80, 94, 102, 113, 129, 180

Bucellarii, 95, 181

Burgundians, 1–2, 10, 68–70, 72, 75–6, 78, 80, 84, 87–9, 93–5, 98–9, 108, 113, 120, 123, 125–9, 133, 135, 139–40, 143–9, 155–6, 170–5, 178, 181

Butilin, 142–3, 146, 148, 172, 175

Cambrai, 85, 107, 113, 174

Carthage, 82, 103, 138, 169, 172

Casilinum, battle of, 142–6, 148–9, 152, 172

Cassiodorus, 126, 185

Catalaunian plains, battle of, 95–6, 98, 100–101, 105, 110

Cataphracts (*catafractarii*), 41, 45, 47–8, 181

Catholic Christianity, 115–17, 122, 129–30, 139, 156, 167

Cavalry, 5, 11–12, 21–2, 30, 36–8, 41–8, 62, 65, 93–4, 142–3, 147–9, 158–9, 162, 164, 176, 181–4

use by the Franks, 98, 133, 145–6, 149, 151,

Celtic peoples, 26, 50, 74–5, 93, 102

Chamavi (also Hamavi), 4, 6, 32, 58

Chararic, 113, 122, 174

Chatti, 4–5, 58

Childebert, son of Clovis, 132–4, 137, 175

Childeric, Frankish king, 86, 91, 104–14, 126, 131, 144, 153, 171, 174

Chlodomar, son of Clovis, 120, 132–3, 171, 175

Chlogio (also Chlodio and Clodio), 19, 103–104, 108–10, 122–3, 188, 192

Chlothar, son of Clovis, 132, 134, 171, 175

Chnodomar, Alamannic king, 44, 46–9, 53–6, 98, 173

Clotilda (also Clothilde, Chrodechildis, Clothild), wife of Clovis, 117–20, 124, 132, 174–5

Clovis, Frankish king, 58, 105, 108, 111–34, 137, 139, 144–5, 155–6, 166, 171, 174–5, 179, 182–3

conversion to Christianity, 110, 117–21

Colmar, 51–3, 62, 167

Comitatenses, 21, 93, 158–64, 181

Comitatus (retinue), 10, 23, 88, 153, 181

Constance, Lake, 36, 161, 167

Constans, Roman emperor, 33, 71, 73, 177

Constantine I, Roman emperor, 19–23, 29, 33, 37, 119, 121, 134, 164, 167–9, 173, 177

Constantine III, Roman usurper, 63, 65, 67, 72–6, 79, 102, 159, 168–9, 178

Constantinople, 4, 60, 63, 79, 89–90, 103, 119, 134, 136–9, 141, 144, 154, 169, 178

Constantius II, Roman emperor, 36–42, 48, 167, 177

Constantius III, Roman emperor, 76, 169

Consul, 33, 111, 119, 129, 131, 139, 171, 173, 179, 185

Cornuti, Roman auxiliaries 43–8, 159, 162–3

Cuneus (wedge formation), 11, 46, 99, 142, 181

Dalmatia, 138, 141, 172

Danube, 4, 7, 14–15, 23, 25, 30, 35, 48–50, 61, 71, 88, 166, 180, 182–4